THE
HISTORY OF
INDIA

ADVISORY BOARD

THE
HISTORY OF
INDIA

John McLeod

The Greenwood Histories of the Modern Nations
Frank W. Thackeray and John E. Findling, Series Editors

Greenwood Press
Westport, Connecticut • London

Library of Congress Cataloging-in-Publication Data

McLeod, John, 1963–
     The history of India / John McLeod.
        p. ; cm.—(Greenwood histories of the modern nations, ISSN 1096–2905)
     Includes bibliographical references and index.
     ISBN 0–313–31459–4 (alk. paper)
        1. India—History.   2. India—History—1947–   I. Title.   II. Series.
DS463.M224   2002
     954—dc21   2002276829

British Library Cataloguing in Publication Data is available.

Library of Congress Catalog Card Number: 2002276829
ISBN: 0–313–31459–4
ISSN: 1096–2905

First published in 2002

Greenwood Press, 88 Post Road West, Westport, CT 06881
An imprint of Greenwood Publishing Group, Inc.
www.greenwood.com

Printed in the United States of America

∞

The paper used in this book complies with the
Permanent Paper Standard issued by the National
Information Standards Organization (Z39.48–1984).

10 9 8 7 6 5 4 3 2 1

Contents

Series Foreword *by Frank W. Thackeray and John E. Findling*   vii

Preface   xi

Timeline of Historical Events   xv

1   The Settings   1

2   The Birth of India   11

3   Religion, Trade, and Conquest   29

4   The Rise and Fall of the Mughal Dynasty   49

5   A Century of Realignment   65

6   Indians and British Rule   81

7   The Struggle for Independence   101

8   Building the New India   129

9   The Rise of the Nehru-Gandhi Dynasty   145

10   The Fall of the Nehru-Gandhi Dynasty   161

11   India Today   177

Notable People in the History of India   195

Appendix: Mughal Emperors, British Viceroys, Prime Ministers
    of India   199

Glossary   203

Bibliographic Essay   213

Index   217

Series Foreword

The Greenwood Histories of the Modern Nations series is intended to provide students and interested laypeople with up-to-date, concise, and analytical histories of many of the nations of the contemporary world. Not since the 1960s has there been a systematic attempt to publish a series of national histories, and, as series editors, we believe that this series will prove to be a valuable contribution to our understanding of other countries in our increasingly interdependent world.

Over thirty years ago, at the end of the 1960s, the Cold War was an accepted reality of global politics, the process of decolonization was still in progress, the idea of a unified Europe with a single currency was unheard of, the United States was mired in a war in Vietnam, and the economic boom of Asia was still years in the future. Richard Nixon was president of the United States, Mao Tse-tung (not yet Mao Zedong) ruled China, Leonid Brezhnev guided the Soviet Union, and Harold Wilson was prime minister of the United Kingdom. Authoritarian dictators still ruled most of Latin America, the Middle East was reeling in the wake of the Six-Day War, and Shah Reza Pahlavi was at the height of his power in Iran. Clearly, the past thirty years have been witness to a great deal of historical change, and it is to this change that this series is primarily addressed.

With the help of a distinguished advisory board, we have selected nations whose political, economic, and social affairs mark them as among the most important in the waning years of the twentieth century, and for each nation we have found an author who is recognized as a specialist in the history of that nation. These authors have worked most cooperatively with us and with Greenwood Press to produce volumes that reflect current research on their nation and that are interesting and informative to their prospective readers.

The importance of a series such as this cannot be underestimated. As a superpower whose influence is felt all over the world, the United States can claim a "special" relationship with almost every other nation. Yet many Americans know very little about the histories of the nations with which the United States relates. How did they get to be the way they are? What kind of political systems have evolved there? What kind of influence do they have in their own region? What are the dominant political, religious, and cultural forces that move their leaders? These and many other questions are answered in the volumes of this series.

The authors who have contributed to this series have written comprehensive histories of their nations, dating back to prehistoric time in some cases. Each of them, however, has devoted a significant portion of the book to events of the past thirty years, because the modern era has contributed the most to contemporary issues that have an impact on U.S. policy. Authors have made an effort to be as up-to-date as possible so that readers can benefit from the most recent scholarship and a narrative that includes very recent events.

In addition to the historical narrative, each volume in this series contains an introductory overview of the country's geography, political institutions, economic structure, and cultural attributes. This is designed to give readers a picture of the nation as it exists in the contemporary world. Each volume also contains additional chapters that add interesting and useful detail to the historical narrative. One chapter is a thorough chronology of important historical events, making it easy for readers to follow the flow of a particular nation's history. Another chapter features biographical sketches of the nation's most important figures in order to humanize some of the individuals who have contributed to the historical development of their nation. Each volume also contains a comprehensive bibliography, so that those readers whose interest has been sparked may find out more about the nation and its history. Finally, there is a carefully prepared topic and person index.

Readers of these volumes will find them fascinating to read and useful in understanding the contemporary world and the nations that comprise it. As series editors, it is our hope that this series will contribute to a heightened sense of global understanding as we enter a new century.

Frank W. Thackeray and John E. Findling
Indiana University Southeast

Preface

More than many other countries, India is often described in clichés. Foreigners may preserve old ideas of the exotic East and regard India as a land of spirituality or of poverty; or they may reflect the preoccupations of the Western media and see in it a place of violence and disasters, both natural and man-made. Indians may think of their homeland as a modern industrial and military power, as the world's largest democracy, or as a country where an ancient civilization thrives alongside the latest computer technology.

Like most clichés, all these images contain some truth and much exaggeration, but none represents more than a small part of reality. Clichés and reality alike are rooted in India's long history, and this book is intended to introduce that history. I hope it will tell general readers and students something about India and its people, about what the country has been in the past, and what it is today. If it helps them understand where conventional representations of India come from, and then move beyond them, it will have attained its goal. Given its length, the book can offer no more than a taste of the history of India, but I hope that this taste inspires readers to learn more about the subject.

The book begins with an introduction to the settings on which the history of India has been played out—geographical, political, human, and cultural. This is followed by ten chapters recounting that history, from the earliest permanent village settlements to the opening of the twenty-first century. In accordance with the goals of *The Greenwood Histories of the Modern Nations* series, about half the book concerns the last 100 years. The title of each chapter suggests its theme. Most of the time, political history is used as a framework for presenting economic, social, cultural, and religious developments.

The book includes several features that are intended to help the reader make sense of what can be a complicated story. The time line lists some of the principal events in the history of India, and the maps show major rivers, regions, and cities, as well as the twenty-eight states of modern India. In addition, there are short biographical notes on forty leading people who appear in the book, and an appendix that lists the Mughal emperors, British viceroys, and prime ministers of India. The glossary explains Indian terms, and the bibliographic essay points interested readers toward other works on the history of India.

Historians do not simply collect facts, they also organize and analyze them. As they grasp for convincing interpretations, they inevitably argue with one another. The history of India seems to be particularly liable to provoke scholarly arguments. At the moment, the hottest questions concern two matters that lie 4,000 years apart: the identity of the ancient Aryans, and the reasons why many Indian Muslims demanded a state of their own during the 1940s. In such controversies, I have adopted the position that seems to me to accord best with the evidence. I know that one day some of my interpretations will be proved wrong, and new debates will arise over issues that now seem settled.

Indians write in the nine related Indic scripts and in the Perso-Arabic and Roman alphabets. Each of these operates on different principles, which makes transliteration complicated. Moreover, all Indian languages use sounds that are absent in English. For example, most have two forms of each of *a, i, u, t,* and *d,* which are quite different to an Indian's ear but can seem almost identical to foreigners. Scholarly transliterations use diacritical marks to keep them all straight—for example, Mahātmā Gāndhī. Because this book is aimed at nonspecialists, I have dispensed with diacritics, while writing words and names in such a way that they are recognizable to readers who know Indian languages.

To add to the confusion, the pronunciation of the same letter may vary in different parts of India, and the Indian forms of Arabic words and names often diverge from the original. I have normally written Perso-Arabic words in accordance with Indian pronunciation, but Arabic words directly connected with the Muslim religion are given in their

Arabic forms. An example is *dhimmi*: Arabs pronounce *dh* as the English *th* in "this," whereas Indians make it *z* or *j*. As this word is used in connection with Islam, I have written it as *dhimmi* rather than *zimmi* or *jimmi*.

Since the nineteenth century, many Indians have adopted English spellings for their names. I have followed their lead, even though they do not always follow the system of transliteration used in this book. Thus, Rammohun Roy, Sir Syed Ahmed Khan, and Atal Bihari Vajpayee, the forms preferred by the bearers of those names, rather than the "scientific" Rammohan Ray, Sayyid Ahmad, and Vajpeyi. Along the same lines, I have kept the traditional nonscholarly English spellings of some place-names—Bengal, Deccan, and Punjab, which (if I were being consistent) would appear as Bangal, Dakhan, and Panjab. I have written the highest-ranking caste in Hinduism as "Brahmin," as the more correct "Brahman" would be indistinguishable from the name of the substance from which (according to Hindu philosophy) all things in the universe emerged.

Unfortunately, all this makes it impossible for the layman to know how to pronounce Indian words correctly. It is probably safest (though wrong as often as not) to treat all vowels as long, which means pronouncing them as if they were Italian or Spanish. Most consonants may be pronounced as in English, with *th* and *ph* having their sounds in "pothole" and "uphill"; in *gh*, *dh*, and *bh*, the *g*, *d*, or *b* is followed so closely by an *h* that the two consonants almost become one sound. (This points to yet another complication: scholars use *dh* to represent completely different sounds in Arabic and in Indian languages. The same is true of *gh*, which in Perso-Arabic words is pronounced rather like a French *r*.)

Without diacritics, it is also impossible to know where the stress lies in Indian words, why in "Upanishads" it is on the first syllable, whereas in "Debendranath" it is on the last. The reader is therefore advised to give a more or less equal stress to each syllable.

In place of the more familiar Before Christ (BC) and Anno Domini (AD), I have employed Before the Common Era (BCE) and Common Era (CE). This is only right in a book about a country where the great majority of the people do not regard Jesus of Nazareth as either their Messiah (Christ) or their Lord (Dominus).

I have accumulated many debts in writing this book. The bibliographic essay names some of the authors whose work has been particularly influential in molding my thought. Over the years, my teachers, colleagues, and students have stimulated my studies of India. I am particularly grateful to Professor N.K. Wagle, who introduced me to Indian history, and to "Shastriji" J.C. Sharda, a superb teacher of Hindi to a less-than-superb student. Naren and Jagdish will not agree with everything that I have written; but I must thank them for sparking and maintaining my interest in the land of their birth, and for their continuing friendship and encouragement through the many years since I sat in their classrooms. Any errors of fact or interpretation in this book are entirely my own, however.

It has been a pleasure working with the series editors of *The Greenwood Histories of the Modern Nations*, Professors Frank W. Thackeray and John E. Findling, and my editors at Greenwood, Dr. Barbara A. Rader, Kevin Ohe, and Betty C. Pessagno. My colleague Professor Justin McCarthy produced the two fine maps. Finally, Dr. Mary Hora remains (in the words of the author's dedication in the first book that she ever gave me) "the most severe of critics, but—a perfect Wife!"

Timeline of Historical Events

BCE

c. 7000	First permanent village settlements in Balochistan
c. 4300	First use of copper
c. 3200	First village settlements in Indus and Sarasvati valleys
c. 2600–2500	First use of bronze
c. 2500–2000	Harappan urban civilization
c. 2000–1600	Collapse of Harappan urban civilization
c. 2000–1000	Spread of Aryan ways eastwards to Ganges (including Brahminical religion, Vedic language); composition of Rig Veda
c. 1300	Disappearance of the Sarasvati
c. 1000	First use of iron
c. 1000–550	Spread of Aryan world across North India; formation of oligarchies and kingdoms; composition of Brahmanas

c. 700–500	First wave of religious speculation; composition of Aranyakas and Upanishads
c. 550	Emergence of Gangetic urban civilization
c. 550–350	Second wave of religious speculation; emergence of Buddhism and Jainism; rise of Magadha
c. 325–185	Mauryan dynasty (Magadha)
c. 272–235	Reign of Ashoka Maurya
3rd century BCE– 3rd century CE	Foreign kings in Northwest (including Kanishka)
1st century BCE– 3rd century CE	Satavahana or Andhra dynasty (Deccan)

CE

1st–3rd centuries	Probable composition of Shangam literature
1st millennium	Completion of *Mahabharata* and *Ramayana*; consolidation of Hinduism
c. 320–550	Gupta dynasty (North India)
c. 375–415	Reign of Chandra Gupta II
6th–11th centuries	Pallava dynasty (Tamil country)
6th century–1310	Pandya dynasty (Tamil country)
606–647	Reign of Harshavardhana (North India)
636 or 644	Muslim Arab attack on pirates near Bombay
644	Arab conquest of Balochistan
711–713	Arab conquest of Sindh
743–974	Rashtrakuta dynasty (Deccan)
c. 750–1161	Pala dynasty (Bengal)
9th century–1019	Gurjara-Pratihara dynasty (North India)
9th century–1310	Chola dynasty (Tamil country)
962–1186	Ghaznawid dynasty (Afghanistan)
997–1030	Reign of Mahmud the Ghaznawid; raids into India
11th century– 1194	Gaharwar dynasty (North India)

c. 1097–1223	Sena dynasty (Bengal)
12th century– 1215/16	Ghauri dynasty (Afghanistan)
1192–1206	Ghauri conquest of North India
1206–1526	Sultanate of Delhi
1223–1224	First Mongol invasion of South Asia
1296–1324	Ala ud-Din Khalji and Ghiyas ud-Din Tughluq of Delhi subjugate most of India
1330s–1340s	Sultanate of Delhi loses Bengal and south India (Vijayanagara, Bahmani sultanate)
1398	Sack of Delhi by Temür; collapse of sultanate of Delhi
1451–1526	Reunification of North India by Lodi sultans of Delhi
1469–1539	Lifetime of Nanak
1526–1857	Mughal dynasty
1565	Defeat and collapse of Vijayanagara
1556–1605	Reign of Akbar
1600	Foundation of English East India Company
1628–1658	Reign of Shah Jahan; conquest of Ahmadnagar; construction of Taj Mahal and Shahjahanabad (Old Delhi)
1658–1707	Reign of Aurangzeb; war with Marathas; conquest of South India
1699	Foundation of Khalsa
1719–1748	Reign of Muhammad Shah; disintegration of Mughal empire; Marathas become dominant power in South Asia
1739	Sack of Delhi by Nadir Shah
1750s	Rise of Mysore
1757	Siraj ud-Daula of Bengal defeated by East India Company at Battle of Plassey
1761	Marathas defeated by Afghans at Battle of Panipat

1765	East India Company appointed diwan of Bengal and Bihar
1798–1846	East India Company establishes supremacy over almost all of India
1799–1839	Ranjit Singh ruler of Sikh empire
1856	First steam-powered cotton mill in India
1857	Great revolt against British rule
1858	Transfer of control from East India Company to British Crown
1885	Foundation of Indian National Congress
1905	Partition of Bengal
1906	Foundation of All-India Muslim League
1909–1910	Morley-Minto Reforms
1912	Capital moved from Calcutta to New Delhi
1914–1918	World War I
1916	Lucknow Pact
1919	Montagu-Chelmsford Reforms; Rowlatt Acts; Amritsar Massacre; beginning of Khilafat movement
1920	Mahatma Gandhi enters politics; starts noncooperation satyagraha; becomes leader of Indian National Congress
1922	End of noncooperation satyagraha
1927–1928	Simon Commission
1929–1931	Collapse of Indian agricultural prices
1930–1933	Salt Tax satyagraha
1930–1932	Round Table Conferences
1935	Government of India Act passed
1937	First elections under the 1935 Act
1939–1945	World War II
1940	Muslim League endorses creation of Muslim states
1942–1943	Quit India rebellion

1947	Partition and independence; Jawaharlal Nehru prime minister
1947–1948	First Indo-Pakistani war
1948–1949	Merger of kingdoms of "Indian India"
1948	Assassination of Mahatma Gandhi
1950	Constitution in effect; beginning of creation of Nehruvian economy
1952	First Lok Sabha election; Congress wins majority
1957	Second Lok Sabha election; Congress wins majority
1962	Third Lok Sabha election; Congress wins majority; war with China
1964	Death of Jawaharlal Nehru; Lal Bahadur Shastri becomes prime minister
1965	Second Indo-Pakistani war; beginning of Green Revolution
1966	Death of Lal Bahadur Shastri; Indira Gandhi becomes prime minister
1967	Fourth Lok Sabha election; Congress wins majority
1969	Split of Indian National Congress
1971	Fifth Lok Sabha election; Congress (R) wins majority; third Indo-Pakistani war
1974	Successful tests of nuclear explosives
1975–1977	The Emergency
1977	Sixth Lok Sabha election; Janata Party wins majority
1980	Seventh Lok Sabha election; Congress (I) wins majority; Indira Gandhi returns as prime minister
1983–1993	Militants' campaign in Punjab
1984	Army attacks Golden Temple complex; assassination of Indira Gandhi; Rajiv Gandhi becomes prime minister; eighth Lok Sabha election; Congress (I) wins majority

1987–1991	Indian intervention in Sri Lanka
1989	Ninth Lok Sabha election; Congress (I) wins plurality, but National Front forms government; beginning of militants' campaign in Kashmir
1990–1992	Militants' campaign in Assam
1991	Assassination of Rajiv Gandhi; tenth Lok Sabha election; Congress (I) wins plurality; P.V. Narasimha Rao becomes prime minister; beginning of economic liberalization
1992	Destruction of Babri Masjid
1996	Eleventh Lok Sabha election; BJP wins plurality, but United Front forms government
1998	Twelfth Lok Sabha election; BJP wins plurality; Atal Bihari Vajpayee becomes prime minister; successful tests of nuclear weapons
1999	Expulsion of infiltrators in Kashmir; thirteenth Lok Sabha election; BJP wins plurality
2001	Census confirms that India's population exceeds 1 billion

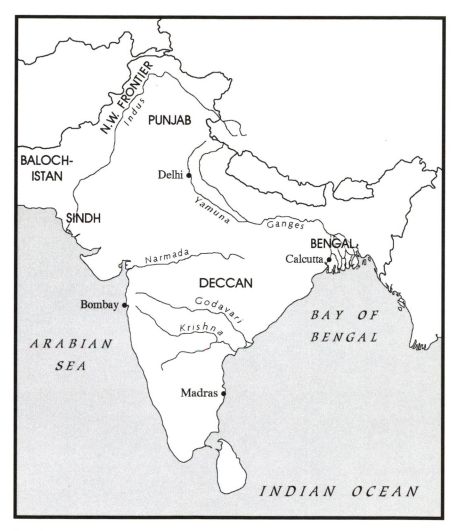

South Asia

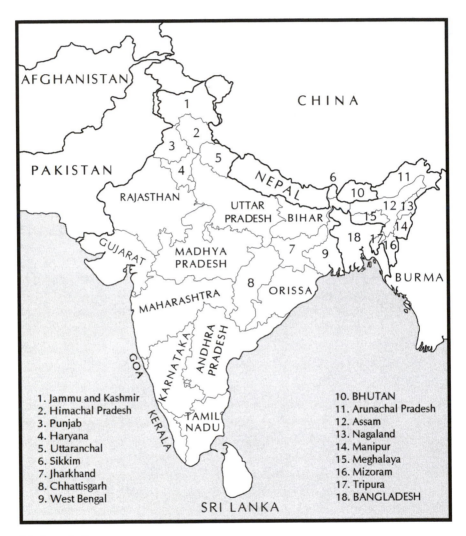

AFGHANISTAN

CHINA

PAKISTAN

NEPAL

1

2

3

5

4

RAJASTHAN

UTTAR
PRADESH

BIHAR

6

11

10

12 13

15

14

18

17

16

GUJARAT

MADHYA
PRADESH

7

9

8

ORISSA

BURMA

MAHARASHTRA

GOA

KARNATAKA

ANDHRA
PRADESH

KERALA

TAMIL
NADU

1. Jammu and Kashmir
2. Himachal Pradesh
3. Punjab
4. Haryana
5. Uttaranchal
6. Sikkim
7. Jharkhand
8. Chhattisgarh
9. West Bengal

10. BHUTAN
11. Arunachal Pradesh
12. Assam
13. Nagaland
14. Manipur
15. Meghalaya
16. Mizoram
17. Tripura
18. BANGLADESH

SRI LANKA

Modern India

1

The Settings

THE GEOGRAPHICAL SETTING

South Asia. The Indian subcontinent. India. Like many geographical terms, these are imprecise. South Asia logically refers to Malaysia, the southernmost country of mainland Asia. By convention, however, Malaysia is placed in Southeast Asia, and "South Asia" is applied to an area that lies considerably to the west. In its widest sense, it embraces India, Pakistan, Bangladesh, Nepal, Bhutan, Sri Lanka, and Maldives, which form the South Asian Association for Regional Co-operation.

The "Indian subcontinent," so called to suggest that—although a part of the Asian continent—it is in many ways self-contained, may cover the same seven countries, or exclude the two island states, Sri Lanka and Maldives. "India" is the name of the Republic of India, the subcontinent's largest country; historically, it also covers Pakistan and Bangladesh, which before 1947 were parts of India.

This book is a history of the Republic of India, including Pakistan and Bangladesh until they became separate states. When referring to events that occurred before the middle of the twentieth century, it applies the designations South Asia, Indian subcontinent, and India interchangeably to the area now occupied by all three countries.

Geologists say that the subcontinent was once an island, and that it has been driven into the rest of Asia by plate tectonics. As a result, it is shaped rather like a diamond, bounded on two sides by arms of the Indian Ocean (the Arabian Sea on the west, and the Bay of Bengal on the east), and on the other two by mountain ranges that were thrown up by the collision with Asia. The diamond measures roughly 2,000 miles from both north to south and east to west. The Republic of India has an area of 1,222,243 square miles, which makes it the seventh-largest country in world. It is in the same league as Argentina or Kazakhstan, and considerably under half the size of Brazil or Australia. Pakistan and Bangladesh add another 364,351 square miles. Even then, however, the subcontinent would easily fit twice over into the United States.

Nevertheless, this area is large enough to allow for great diversity in terrain. South Asia is separated from its neighbors to the north by the Himalayas and their offshoots the Karakoram and the Hindu Kush, which include some of the highest mountains in the world. Lower but still impressive ranges of mountains mark much of the boundary with Afghanistan and Iran in the west; in the east, India extends toward the hills of Burma. Inside of these highlands come the basins of two great rivers, the Indus and the Ganges, huge flat expanses of land separated from each other by the Thar or Great Indian Desert and a range of low hills. This crescent-shaped region is often called the Indo-Gangetic plain.

Many of the great rivers of north India deposit silt in mountain valleys, on the plains, and at their mouths. As a result, much of the Indo-Gangetic plain is quite fertile. The Indus rises in Tibet. It flows through India and Pakistan, where it is joined by many tributaries that give Punjab ("five waters") its name, and empties into the Arabian Sea. (Since 1947, Punjab has been divided between India and Pakistan.) The Ganges and its tributary the Yamuna originate in Himalayan glaciers and, after running through north India, flow into the Bay of Bengal through a huge delta, two thirds of which now lies in Bangladesh.

South of the Gangetic plain the land rises slowly into the Vindhya mountains, the traditional boundary between northern and southern India. Then comes peninsular India or the Deccan, most of which is a dry, hilly plateau. To the west, the plateau ends in a range of mountains called the Western Ghats, below which a narrow strip of land runs along the Arabian Sea. The rather lower Eastern Ghats separate the plateau from the coastal plain on the Bay of Bengal. The Narmada, immediately south of the Vindhyas, is the main west-flowing river of the Deccan. Most of the peninsula's other rivers (which include the Godavari and the Krishna) begin in the Western Ghats and run eastward into the Bay of Bengal. The Deccan rivers are fed by rain. This means that they become torrents if the rains are heavy and virtually dry up if the rains fail. They leave little silt in inland valleys, although several of them break into large fertile deltas in the coastal plains. Finally, most of the Tamil country, the southern tip of India, is a dry plain.

India includes tropical rain forests and deserts, rocky hills and savannas, dry forests and farmland; in 1994, 23 percent of its land area was forested, just under 4 percent was meadowland or pasture, and 57 percent was used for agriculture. There is great regional variation in climate. The Tamil country is hot for twelve months of the year, the Deccan plateau similar but with somewhat lower temperatures. The Indo-Gangetic plain has the hottest weather in all India in June, and warm days with cool nights in January. The mountainous areas of the north see harsh, snowy winters, and pleasant summers.

Nevertheless, most of the subcontinent shares a climate of three seasons. During the hot weather, which typically runs from March to June, the temperature rises steadily, reaching 110°F in the northern plains. This makes it difficult to work during the day, and people try to confine their activities to night and early morning. Then comes the southwest monsoon, moisture-bearing winds that blow off the Indian Ocean in two branches; one heads eastward from the Arabian Sea, the other northward from the Bay of Bengal, until they merge over the Gangetic Plain. The monsoon reaches south India in June, Gujarat on the west coast in early or mid-July, and Punjab in the north a week or two later. Its winds bring rainstorms that may last a few minutes or several hours each day. The rain reduces temperatures and waters the fields. It also ruins roads and may cause flooding; though if it fails, India faces disaster. The final season of the year is the cold weather, from November to March, when cool dry air from central Asia blows across the subcontinent.

Terrain and climate make India home to a great range of wildlife. The national bird is the peacock. Even in big cities, the visitor will see monkeys, vultures, and parrots, and the country is known around the world for elephants and snakes (including the King cobra, which can be up to twelve feet long). Over half of the world's 5,000 to 7,000 tigers live in India. Their number is steadily declining, thanks to poaching and the destruction of their habitat; and Project Tiger, a program established to rebuild India's tiger population, seems to be enjoying considerably less success than it did during the 1970s and 1980s. (This is only one symptom of the effects on wildlife of the spread of human settlement over the last century, despite the efforts of a long-established conservation movement.) Other fauna include cats and dogs, foxes and jackals, rhinoceroses, mongooses, deer, birds ranging from flamingos to pheasants, and freshwater and sea fish. Among domesticated animals are humpbacked oxen, water buffaloes, horses, and camels, as well as sheep, goats, and pigs.

THE POLITICAL SETTING

Indians pride themselves on the fact that their country is the "world's largest democracy." Almost alone in the developing world, India has been a democracy since its independence from colonial rule. The only break occurred between 1975 and 1977, when prime minister Indira Gandhi established a temporary dictatorship after declaring a state of emergency. It is unlikely that any future leader will repeat Mrs. Gandhi's experiment: Over the last twenty-five years, democratic practices have become so firmly entrenched in India that no dictatorial regime could find the public support it would need to survive. A military coup is also highly unlikely, which sets India apart from most of its neighbors (Pakistan, Bangladesh, and Burma have all been under military rule). Control over the Indian armed forces has always remained in civilian hands. Despite the use of troops in political situations—for example, against antigovernment demonstrations—the armed forces have not been politicized, in the sense that they do not take sides in politics.

Like the United States, India has a federal political system. The central government is led by the prime minister, whose equivalent in each of the country's twenty-eight states is a chief minister. Elections to the lower house of the federal parliament and the state legislatures are held regularly. They are generally free and fair, although often accompanied by violence. Though voter turnout in India is lower than in most developed countries, it is higher than in the United States. Parliament and state legislatures meet regularly, and use their power to decide who will or will not be prime minister or chief minister. Political leaders who lose elections or legislative majorities peacefully hand over power to successors from opposition parties. The judiciary is often called a pillar of democracy, and the Supreme Court of India has generally remained free of political interference. The same is true of some (though not all) of the state supreme courts, which are called high courts. Admittedly, the effectiveness of the judicial system is reduced by the fact that India has far too few judges. This has produced a backlog of 27 million cases, including over 20,000 pending before the Supreme Court.

A further sign of Indian democracy is the existence of numerous political parties to serve different ideological, social, or regional constituencies. Indians, unlike Americans, face no real difficulties if they want to start viable new parties. Nevertheless, it looks as if (for the time being) federal politics in India have settled down to a two-party system, based on the Bharatiya Janata Party or BJP, and the Indian National Congress (Indira) or Congress (I). With smaller affiliated parties, the BJP and Congress (I) both have support across much of the country, and they may alternate in power for some time to come. The current leader of the BJP is the prime minister of India, Atal Bihari Vajpayee; Congress (I) is headed by Sonia Gandhi, the Italian-born widow of the former prime minister Rajiv Gandhi.

THE HUMAN SETTING

With just over 1 billion people, India is the second-most populous country on earth. (If Pakistan and Bangladesh were still part of India, it would supersede China in first place.) The population is young: in 1995, 62 percent of Indians were under age 30. Another 15 to 20 million Indian expatriates and people of Indian ancestry live in other countries—businessmen and workers in the Arab states of the Middle East; the descendants of Indian plantation laborers in the former British colonies of Fiji, Mauritius, Trinidad and Tobago, and Guyana; and emigrants who since the nineteenth century have settled in the United Kingdom, the United States, Canada, and Australia. Between 1990 and 2000, Indians formed the fastest-growing community in the United States, where their numbers more than doubled (reaching 1,678,765). Many of the new arrivals are employed in the computer field.

To many Westerners, India is first and foremost a land of religion. Whether Indians really are more religious than other people is open to debate, but their country is the home of several major faiths. Hinduism and Islam together account for 93 percent of the population, and India's other religions include Christianity, Sikhism, Buddhism, and Jainism. There are also small (and declining) numbers of Jews and Zoroastrians.

Over thousands of years, the mixture of different peoples, indigenous and foreign, has created what can only be described as an Indian ethnicity. But even though many Indians share such biological traits as blood group, they vary greatly in physical appearance. In the northwest, people are often relatively fair in color; northeasterners and the inhabitants of the Himalayan regions may resemble the Burmese and the Tibetans; many south Indians are quite dark. Since the nineteenth century, this has led some Indians and foreigners to conclude that north Indians have some European blood, whereas southerners are either the aboriginal inhabitants of the country or immigrants from Africa. There is, however, no real evidence to support such views.

Most of the principal languages of India belong to two families, the Indo-European and the Dravidian; only one language from outside these groups has official status in the country (this is Manipuri, which is spoken in eastern India and belongs to the Sino-Tibetan family). English, Italian, Russian, and Persian are also Indo-European tongues, although there is not necessarily any blood relationship among their speakers. The Dravidian languages are unique to the Indian subcontinent. Most of them are found in the south, but the existence of scattered pockets in central India and western Pakistan suggests that they were once spoken over a much larger area than at present.

Hindi, an Indo-European tongue, is the most widely spoken language in South Asia. It is the first language of 400 million Indians, and is spoken by another 260 million. These figures are somewhat misleading, however, as the name "Hindi" is used in two senses. On the one hand, it is applied to numerous dialects spoken across north India, some of them mutually unintelligible. On the other, it refers to a literary language created in the nineteenth century from the Delhi dialect. The same dialect gave rise to Urdu, typically associated with Muslims, which is the official language of the Muslim country of Pakistan and is also spoken by 51 million Indians. Colloquial standard Hindi and Urdu are identical, or nearly so. The forms taught in schools and used in government may be quite different, however, for Hindi draws new vocabulary from the ancient Sanskrit language, which also supplies its script, whereas Urdu uses Persian and Arabic for both new words and its alphabet.

Among the other major languages of India are Bengali (82 million speakers in India) and Marathi (74 million), both from the Indo-European family; and the Dravidian languages Telugu (78 million) and Tamil (63 million). Gujarati, Kannada, Malayalam, Oriya, Punjabi, and Assamese are each the mother tongue of millions of people. Furthermore, at least 190 million Indians, perhaps many more, speak English as a second language. For much of the upper middle class in large cities, English is the usual language of daily communication. Rohinton Mistry, Arundhati Roy, and Salman Rushdie, who were all born in India, rank among the most highly acclaimed novelists writing in English at the beginning of the twenty-first century. (The British author Sir V.S. Naipaul, winner of the 2001 Nobel Prize in Literature, is of Indian descent, but he was born in Trinidad.)

Farming is by far the largest single occupation in India, and in 1995, 73 percent of the population was rural. India's country people live in villages, which may have thousands of inhabitants and to a Westerner look more like small towns; they are defined as villages because their people—petty landowners or rich farmers, poorer peasants, laborers, craftsmen—are either agriculturalists or in some way connected with agriculture.

Beginning in the mid-nineteenth century, and gaining speed in the 1950s, a large modern industrial sector has grown up in India. The country now meets many of its own industrial needs, and exports such diverse products as gemstones, trucks and cars, iron and steel, and clothes. Industrialization has contributed to urbanization, and over a quarter of all Indians live in cities. These include Delhi, of which the capital New Delhi is a part, with 7.2 million people in 1991; the ports of Greater Bombay (9.9 million), Calcutta (4.39 million), and Madras (3.84 million) (these are now officially called Mumbai, Kolkata, and Chennai, respectively, but the older English names are retained in this book); the high technology centers of Bangalore (3.3 million) and Hyderabad (3.1 million); and the industrial city of Ahmedabad (2.9 million). The urban population includes many poor people from the countryside. They often live in the slums that contain a third of India's city dwellers, and work as laborers or in services (10 million people make *biris*, cheap cigarettes). But India also has a huge urban middle class—businessmen, professionals, senior bureaucrats, and the like. Many of its members come from families that formed the rural elite two or three generations ago.

When they travel long distances to see friends, go on vacation, or visit ancestral villages, most Indians do so by train. India has 40,000 miles of railroad, as well as more than 2 million miles of roads. Just under half of this length is paved, and the roads are used heavily by trucks, cars, motorcycles, scooters, not to mention oxcarts and camel carts.

Many say that the persistence of poverty represents modern India's greatest failure: In 1999, 26 percent of the country's population was unable to afford basic necessities, and over half of its children were malnourished. In rural areas, the poor are typically landless laborers, or peasants without enough land to support themselves. Many of the urban poor are unskilled or semiskilled workers, who in so populous a country may have little hope of receiving sufficient wages to live on. Predictions that recent economic changes would give them jobs in, for example, computer data entry have proved only partly correct.

Poverty is greater for some regions and people than for others. It is worst in the states of Orissa on the east coast and Bihar and Uttar Pradesh in north; all three have high populations that are growing fast, and inadequate resources for development and social welfare. From the 1950s until the 1990s, the government might have helped poor states by building factories in places of high unemployment. Now India has adopted a free market economy, however, and industrialists look for access to markets, skilled and literate workforces, and good infrastructure. The poor states are weak in all these areas, and are therefore falling even further behind the richer ones.

Over half the population of India belongs to three disadvantaged groups. There are 160 million members of "Scheduled Castes," commonly called Untouchables in the West, who historically formed the lowest division of Hindu society. Then come 140 million Indians belonging to "Scheduled Tribes"—until recently these people, known as Tribals, lived in forests and remote areas, as hunters and gatherers or shifting cultivators. Finally, 230 million Hindus are included in the "Other Backward Classes," which traditionally ranked immediately above Untouchables. By and large, social and economic conditions for SCs, STs, and OBCs (as they are called) lag behind those of the communities that make up the bulk of the rural elite and urban middle class. In villages, SCs often live in a segregated neighborhood, with houses of poor quality. Although the law bans discrimination against them, their children may be excluded from schools, or ignored by teachers. This leaves most SCs without the skills required to take up the places that the Indian constitution reserves for them in legislatures, government employment, and universities.

Although India has a vigorous women's movement, and it is almost forty years since the country's first female prime minister took office, women form another disadvantaged group. Many Indians—even educated women—prefer sons to daughters, as a son will carry on the family and care for elderly parents (whereas on marriage, a daughter becomes part of someone else's family). Technology that determines the sex of a fetus has led to increasing abortion of female fetuses by parents determined to have a son. The poor concentrate food, health care, and whatever other resources they have on sons. They may also be more reluctant to send their daughters to school than their sons. This is often because they do not want them to be taught by men, and women teachers are scarce. This in turn becomes self-perpetuating: Because they lack education, few women can become teachers; poor girls therefore continue to stay away from school and are unable to advance when they reach adulthood.

Deadly adult diseases such as cholera and tuberculosis are rampant among the poor, and India now has the world's largest number of people with the human immunodeficiency virus. Nevertheless, rich or poor,

Indians are living longer than they were fifty years ago. A baby born in 1947 had a life expectancy of thirty-two years; a boy born in 1998 could look forward to living sixty-two years, and a girl sixty-four. The main reason is a great reduction in death rates among infants and children, thanks to free immunization against major childhood diseases, and government-funded health care centers across the country. (These programs are being dismantled with the shift to a free market, which may worsen medical conditions for the poor.)

THE CULTURAL SETTING

India spends less on education than many other countries in Asia and Africa. One out of every ten villages has no school. Besides their worries about male teachers, many rural parents do not send their children to school because they believe that education brings no financial returns. Low levels of education have certainly held back the country's economic growth. This may be changing, however. In 1961, the literacy rate for adult males in India was 34 percent, and for females 13 percent. By 1995, the figures stood at 66 percent for males and 38 percent for females. This was followed by a big increase in female literacy, which is now close to the rate for males. In 2001, the Indian Parliament debated a constitutional amendment declaring primary education to be a fundamental right, although it remains to be seen whether measures will be implemented to ensure that all children can avail themselves of this right.

Literate or not, for millennia Indians have enjoyed poetry, drama, architecture, sculpture, painting, music, and dance; and the development of Indian culture is one of the themes of this book. Today, the arts are diffused through many media. India is one of the world's greatest centers of book publishing. Its daily newspapers have a circulation of 20 million, and it has 2 million personal computers (up from under 10,000 in 1989). Television broadcasting started in India in 1959, and from the beginning was a government monopoly. (Radio had been taken over by the government in 1930, three years after the first broadcasts.) In the 1980s, more and more Indians began to buy television sets, first in the middle class and then across society. In the 1990s, private television was legalized. Satellite and cable channels proliferated, and in 1997 the federal government transferred control of the state-owned radio and television to an autonomous organization. All this greatly increased the quantity, and many said the quality, of the programming available to Indians. At the end of the 1990s, there were 66 million televisions in India (one for every four households), and TV had become as central to popular entertainment as film.

The history of Indian film goes back to the beginning of the twentieth century. The country has produced several great filmmakers, of whom the director Satyajit Ray (winner of an Academy Award for lifetime achievement in 1992) was the most celebrated. On a more popular level, there is the Bombay-based "Bollywood" film industry, which helps make India the largest producer of movies in the world. The country turns out 800 pictures every year. Besides watching television and films, the people of India play many sports. *Kabaddi*, a sort of tag, is popular among children. Indians may be the world's best field hockey players, and their men's field hockey team has won eight gold medals at the Olympics. If India has a national sport, however, it is cricket. All Indians seem to follow international cricket matches, and emigrants play the game wherever they go.

In 2001, Bollywood released a blockbuster movie called *Lagaan*. The lagaan is the land revenue, a tax on agricultural production that for centuries financed Indian governments. The film contains the typical Bollywood mixture of fights (including martial arts battles inspired by Hong Kong movies), love scenes, interludes of song and dance, and a melodramatic plot. It is set in rural India in 1893, with a team of villagers playing cricket against their British colonial rulers to win exemption from the lagaan. The movie reminds us that Indians combine a love of Bollywood and cricket with an awareness of their past. This suggests that understanding India today requires some knowledge of its history. That history goes back many millennia.

2

The Birth of India

THE HARAPPANS

For thousands of years, the only humans in India lived in small bands that wandered about in quest of food. Then, around 7000 BCE, some of these hunters and gatherers learned to domesticate animals and grow crops, and settled down in permanent villages in what is now the province of Balochistan in Pakistan. The herdsmen and peasants were gradually joined by craftsmen, including potters, weavers, and jewelers. The most important craftsmen of all were toolmakers, who after 4300 BCE began to make tools out of copper, alongside the stone that had been used since the arrival of humans in the subcontinent. As villagers exchanged their goods with one another and with the people who lived around them, a barter economy developed.

The inhabitants of some remote tracts (called Tribals in modern India) continued to live as hunters and gatherers until the twentieth century, supplementing their diet through shifting cultivation. Village settlements gradually spread across South Asia, however. Sometimes, hunters and gatherers adopted agriculture or herding. Other times, people from existing village communities colonized forested or uninhabited regions. About 3200 BCE, village settlements began to appear in the valleys of the

Indus and the Sarasvati, two great rivers that flowed through western South Asia from the Himalayas to the Arabian Sea.

Between 2600 and 2500 BCE, craftsmen in the Indus and Sarasvati valleys began to work bronze, which is a harder metal than copper. People learned how to write, although it is unknown whether they invented writing on their own or acquired it from elsewhere. And cities—large settlements where most people were neither peasants nor herdsmen—came into being. It is not clear whether these developments were connected, or why they happened. However, they mark the birth of the first urban civilization of South Asia. We do not know what the people of this civilization called themselves. Today, they are often called the Harappans, from Harappa, the modern name of one of their principal cities.

The Harappan urban civilization lasted from about 2500 to 2000 BCE. It centered on the Indus and the Sarasvati, in the modern Pakistani provinces of Sindh and Punjab, but it covered most of what is now Pakistan and much of northwestern India. We know less about it than about any other great civilization of the ancient world. This is mainly because no one has been able to decipher the Harappan writing. Our knowledge of the Harappans therefore depends almost entirely on archeological finds. Unfortunately, many of the theories that have been based on these finds are mere guesses, and they sometimes contradict each other. For example, some scholars say that the Harappans lived under a centralized government of priests who lived at the cities of Harappa in the north and Mohenjo Daro in the south; others believe that each of the half dozen major Harappan cities was independent and run by merchants.

However, archeology does tell us that the Harappans' houses were built of bricks (in standard sizes) and connected to underground sewers that carried away waste. Though they varied in size, the houses followed an identical floor plan. Unlike other ancient peoples, the Harappans did not construct ornate palaces or temples, although large buildings that were presumably used for governmental or religious purposes stood on a walled platform beside each city. Nor do they seem to have had large statues, though they did make small human and animal figurines and models of objects such as wagons. The figurines provide a clue about Harappan religion, as the discovery of numerous female figures and phallic symbols may mean that the Harappans worshipped fertility deities.

We also know that trade and manufacturing were central to the lives of the Harappans. They mass-produced tools and jewelry at factory towns, each specializing in a particular line of goods. In fact, it has been suggested that the Harappan economy was based on the distribution of these tools and jewelry. This theory may explain how three of the features that mark Harappan urbanization are connected: the introduction of bronze made it possible to manufacture better tools than before; by letting them send orders and invoices, writing allowed merchants to ship goods over a wide area; and perhaps the cities were located for access to raw materials, because all of them were either near mines or at the end of trade routes.

The best-known Harappan relics are small square seals made of a stone called steatite, which depict animals, religious scenes, and inscriptions. The seals were apparently used by merchants to identify their goods. Harappan objects, including seals, have been found in the countries of the Persian Gulf. This shows that the Harappans traded with the Near East, although it is unknown how significant this commerce was to their economy. Of course, not all Harappans were merchants or craftsmen. Outside of the cities, peasants and herdsmen continued to live much as they always had, except that they could now acquire the new manufactured goods.

Then, about 2000 BCE, the urban features of the Harappan civilization began to disappear. Within four centuries they were gone. Buildings and sewers fell into disrepair; cities were abandoned; trade collapsed; the mass production of metal tools and jewelry ended; and people apparently stopped using inscribed seals and writing. The Harappans thereafter lived in small communities. There was little contact among these settlements, and cultural practices increasingly diverged within what had been a unified civilization.

The Harappans must have been hit by a disaster, but scholars cannot agree on what happened. Proposed explanations include a buildup of salt in the soil, foreign invasion, and epidemics. Whatever the nature of the crisis, it was apparently compounded by environmental changes in the Harappan heartland. It has been suggested that the land along the lower Indus became waterlogged; and shifts in the earth's crust, and perhaps also sedimentation, diverted the headwaters of the Sarasvati to other rivers between 2500 and 1700 BCE. The once-mighty Sarasvati shrank, shifted its course, and dried up altogether about 1300 BCE. This meant that the Indus and Sarasvati regions could no longer support large populations. As a result, after abandoning their cities, the Harappans also more or less deserted their heartland. Between about 1700 and 1600 BCE they resettled in the east, in the modern Indian states of Punjab and Haryana, and western Uttar Pradesh.

THE ARYANS

The collapse of urban civilization must have been traumatic for the Harappans, whose way of doing things no longer worked. This seems to explain why, over the next few centuries, more and more of them adopted new social and religious practices. If they did not already speak it, they also learned the language of the people who had evolved those practices. Indians who followed these practices and spoke this language called themselves Aryans, or "ones to be respected." It is often said that the Aryans were immigrants to South Asia. Their language, which we sometimes call Vedic, belongs to the same Indo-European linguistic family as English, and we know that the Indo-European languages originated on the steppes of modern Ukraine, Russia, and Kazakhstan. Yet there is no evidence that the Aryans ever lived anywhere except India. It seems paradoxical to have people who were native to India but spoke a language that came from elsewhere. One explanation is that before or during the days of the Harappan urban civilization, speakers of what became the Vedic language made their way to South Asia. Because we do not know what the language of the Harappans was, it is possible that some or all of them spoke Vedic during the urban phase of their civilization. However, it is more likely that these Vedic-speakers remained on the fringes of the Harappan world until urban civilization broke down, when they made themselves rulers of some Harappan villages. The Vedic-speakers and their Harappan subjects became the first Aryans. Something made Aryan culture attractive to Harappans, and it spread rapidly among them.

Our knowledge of this culture comes from the Rig Veda, a collection of 1,028 hymns, ballads, and songs that were apparently composed over many centuries between 2000 and 1000 BCE. Three other works are grouped with the Rig Veda to form the Samhitas, or collections: the Sama Veda, poems from the Rig Veda in a different order; the Yajur Veda, instructions for priests; and the Atharva Veda, magic spells. The Samhitas were very holy to the Aryans. Priests had to memorize them perfectly, and passed them on by word of mouth (writing apparently vanished from South Asia with the end of urban civilization).

The Rig Veda tells us that the Aryans were grouped into independent tribes. Some tribes were ruled by councils, which may have consisted of elders. Others were headed by a chief, who was chosen by the tribe or its elders for his prowess in war and his generosity in distributing plunder. Cattle herding was the most prestigious occupation among the Aryans, and cows formed the basis of their wealth. Within each tribe, the

Rajanyas (later called Kshatriyas), or warriors and herdsmen, dominated the more numerous Vaishyas (peasants) and craftsmen; the latter included bronzesmiths who made tools and weapons, and the makers of the warriors' chariots.

The Aryan tribes lived in villages, but frequently abandoned them to find new pastures. They often battled with each other, mainly to acquire cattle. They also fought people who did not follow their social and religious practices, whom they called Dasas, Dasyus, and Panis. The Rig Veda describes the Dasas as black, which some scholars believe means they were darker in complexion than the Aryans. Others point out that the difference between the Dasas and Aryans seems to have been cultural rather than racial, and that the Vedic word for "black" often merely suggests that something is bad. Captured Dasas were incorporated into Aryan tribes under the name of Shudras and were compelled to do menial work.

The main gods of the Aryans were male. They included Indra, god of war and weather, who led the Aryans in battle. Like an ideal Aryan chief, he was brave and fun loving. Agni was god of fire, and Varuna an all-knowing father who oversaw Rita, the law that keeps order in the universe. To ensure that the gods remained well disposed, the Aryan tribes held sacrifices. As tribesmen watched and prayed, the Brahmins or priests made elaborate preparations and then slaughtered animals. The priests were so central to the ritual life of the tribes that we often use the word Brahminical to describe the Aryan religion.

By 1000 BCE, the eastward migration of Aryan tribes, and the adoption of Aryan ways by the inhabitants of north India, had brought the Aryan world to the Ganges River. It then spread eastward, across the Gangetic plain; southward into Madhya Pradesh; and probably northward into the upper Indus Valley and Nepal. Nevertheless, not everyone in north India became an Aryan. Especially in hills and forests, many people continued to live as hunters and gatherers or as nomads.

By about 550 BCE, the central Gangetic plain had become the center of the Aryan world. The plain could not sustain large cattle herds, but it was agriculturally productive. Land therefore replaced cattle as the basis of wealth among the Aryans. Meanwhile, about 1000 BCE, Indian smiths learned to work iron. Some scholars believe that iron tools were crucial to the Aryan movement across the Gangetic plain, arguing that such tools made it possible to clear the plain's forests and to cultivate its heavy black soil.

Meanwhile, for reasons that are unclear, the Aryan tribes gave way to oligarchies and kingdoms, which were often associated with a particular territory rather than with a mobile group of people. In oligarchies, the dominant men elected a ruler. In kingdoms, the chief became a king; he inherited his position and was consecrated by Brahmins in a ritual that had not existed at the time of the Rig Veda. The consecration signified that the king had the approval of the gods, which made it hard to challenge his position. During this period, Brahmins developed many new sacrifices, often to reinforce the king's power. Some Brahmins specialized in particular sacrifices. The ancestors of the current prime minister of India, Atal Bihari Vajpayee, were Brahmins who performed the Vajapeya, a sacrifice that rejuvenated an old king. In the sixth century BCE, the Aryan world was divided into sixteen states. The kings of Magadha, in what is now the Indian state of Bihar, were particularly powerful thanks to their control of trade on the Ganges and of iron deposits. By the fourth century BCE, they had conquered most of the other Aryan oligarchies and kingdoms.

THE SECOND URBANIZATION

About 550 BCE, urban civilization returned to South Asia with the re-emergence of cities and the revival of long-distance trade. The reasons for this second urbanization are just as disputed as those for the disappearance of the Harappan urban civilization a thousand years earlier. The new cities were concentrated in the central Gangetic plain.

Trade was made easier when coins were introduced in South Asia around 400 BCE. By this time, merchants had acquired another useful tool with the revival of writing, which was well established by the middle of the fifth century BCE. The most widely used script, Brahmi, may have been borrowed from the Near East, or it may have developed in India (there are doubtful suggestions that it is derived from the Harappan script). The Vedic language had changed greatly, both with the passage of time and as it was learned by people who spoke other tongues. The changes took different forms in different places and eventually produced several distinct new languages, called Prakrits (natural).

The Vedic language remained in use in the Brahminical religion and was learned by Brahmins. It was now called Sanskrit (refined). Sanskrit was apparently never written at this stage, and the new scripts were used exclusively to write Prakrits. However, the Brahmins continued to compose sacred literature in Sanskrit, which they passed on orally. The principal Brahmin work of this period is the Brahmanas, textbooks explaining sacrifices.

But the Brahminical religion was not static. In the Rig Veda, souls of good people spend eternity in the World of the Fathers, and souls of bad people in the House of Clay. After 1000 BCE, the belief spread that souls only stay temporarily in heaven before being reborn on earth. Our deeds (*karma*) in life determine the nature of the rebirth. Those who were good may return as fortunate humans, whereas those who were bad will become birds or insects. When these beings die, the whole process is repeated. The notions of karma and reincarnation have been central to many Indian religions ever since.

However, many people found the prospect of endless rebirth to be boring. There was a consensus that with special understanding, one might escape the cycle. This understanding is explained in two Sanskrit works, the Aranyakas and the Upanishads, completed between 700 and 500 BCE. The Upanishads say that everything—space, gods, living beings—emerged from a substance called Brahman (not to be confused with the Brahmins), which continues to exist in all of them. He who wishes to escape rebirth must meditate on this concept until he understands that both the universe and his own soul are Brahman and therefore identical. He will then lose consciousness of everything except Brahman and reach a new level of existence where he is free.

Some scholars have suggested that these doctrines were popular because they relieved anxiety caused by the end of Aryan tribal society. Another theory connects the new teachings with economic change: Newly wealthy merchants resented the wastefulness of Brahminical sacrifices and sought alternative means of salvation. In any case, the belief in rebirth and escape became so widespread that the Brahmins accepted the Aranyakas and the Upanishads alongside the Samhitas and the Brahmanas as part of their scriptures, which are collectively called the Vedas. (The term Vedas is sometimes more specifically applied to the Samhitas.)

The authors of the Aranyakas and Upanishads represent a first wave of religious speculation in the Aryan world. They were followed by a second wave between the sixth and fourth centuries BCE, with teachings so different from those of the Brahmins that they developed into separate religions entirely. The best known teacher of this second wave was Siddhartha Gautama, called Buddha (the Enlightened One), who founded Buddhism. The Buddhist scriptures contain stories about the life and teachings of Buddha, but in most cases their authenticity is doubtful. It is not even certain when Buddha lived; Buddhist sources place his death around 483 BCE, but many scholars now believe that a date between 378 and 358 BCE is nearer the truth.

Similarly, it is unclear what Buddha actually taught. It may have been quite different from what appears in the Buddhist scriptures. In any case, the scriptures assert that the heart of Buddhism is the teaching that there are four Noble Truths: Life is full of unpleasantnesses; the unpleasantness is caused by our thirst to satisfy ourselves; we can end the unpleasantness by stopping the thirst; and we can stop the thirst with the Noble Eightfold Path, or a life of moderation. This thirst arises because we think that we are individuals. Actually, according to Buddhism, the universe and everything in it are ever-changing compounds of elements. The only stable thing is Nirvana, which is similar to the state that followers of the Upanishads reach when they realize that everything is Brahman. Nirvana is attained by ethical conduct, such as performing good works and abstaining from killing. Buddha's most dedicated followers formed an order of monks and nuns, who gave all or part of their lives to preaching and to monastic devotion. By the third century BCE, India was covered with Buddhist monasteries.

Another great religious teacher was Vardhamana, called Mahavira (Great Hero), the founder of the Jain religion. The life and teachings of Mahavira are as uncertain as those of Buddha. According to the Jain scriptures, Mahavira was a contemporary of Buddha. He is said to have taught that the universe contains an infinite number of living entities or souls. These are found in everything, including plants and stones. For this reason, nonviolence or *ahimsa* is central to Jain notions of righteousness, and Jain monks must refrain from killing even insects.

THE MAURYAS

In 330 BCE, Alexander the Great, king of Macedon, defeated and killed Darius III of Iran. Alexander and his army then headed east through Iran to northwestern India, which had been conquered by the Iranians almost 200 years earlier. Alexander reached Indian Punjab, but when his army threatened to mutiny, he withdrew. A man named Chandragupta Maurya, and his Brahmin adviser who is called Kautilya, Chanakya, or Vishnugupta, apparently took advantage of the disorder that followed the Macedonian withdrawal to seize territory in Punjab. From this base, they moved eastward, and, about 325 or 321 BCE, defeated the king of Magadha. Chandragupta founded the Mauryan dynasty of Magadha. He must have ruled all, or almost all, of the Aryan world. In 305 BCE, he seems to have defeated Seleucus Nicator, a Greek general who had made himself king of Syria and Iran after Alexander's death, and added parts of Afghanistan to his dominions.

Chandragupta ruled Magadha until about 297 BCE, when his son Bindusara became king. Bindusara probably conquered territory in the vast

Deccan plateau of peninsular India (the modern states of Maharashtra, Karnataka, and Andhra Pradesh). He died about 272 BCE. The next king was his son Ashoka, one of greatest monarchs in the history of India. Thanks to the conquests of previous kings of Magadha, Ashoka ruled a huge empire, extending from Afghanistan to Karnataka, and from Gujarat to Kalinga on the Bay of Bengal, even if he did not (as is sometimes said) rule the whole subcontinent. Kalinga played a pivotal role in Ashoka's life, as eight years after he became king, he subjugated the region in a bloody war. Ashoka claimed to have been transformed by remorse over the loss of life in Kalinga. Whether he really was or not, he apparently became a Buddhist and adopted a new ethical system in his administration.

Ashoka was the first known ruler in South Asia to set up inscriptions, texts carved in stone and publicly displayed. His inscriptions, which are found all over India, include a pillar at Sarnath, where Buddha is said to have preached his first sermon. Its capital bears sculpted lions, which have been adopted as a symbol of modern India. Thanks to his inscriptions, we know more about Ashoka than any previous Indian king. The inscriptions suggest that Ashoka was a devout Buddhist. But despite what has sometimes been said, Ashoka's personal Buddhist beliefs seem to have been distinct from the ethical policy that he adopted after the Kalinga war. He used the Prakrit word *dhamma* for this policy, which called on his people to make kindness to other living things the guiding principle of their lives. He led the way by providing medical care for humans and animals, planting fruit trees along the sides of roads to give shade and food, and becoming a partial vegetarian. It is likely that the policy of dhamma agreed with Ashoka's own beliefs, but it was also politically useful: the king probably hoped it would bridge the many divisions (religious, linguistic, economic, cultural) among his subjects with an ideology that almost everyone could accept, all under his leadership.

Besides Ashoka's inscriptions, we have two major sources of information about Mauryan India. One is the fragments of a book by Megasthenes, a Greek ambassador to Chandragupta's court. The other source is a Sanskrit book called *Arthashastra*, which is said to have been written by Chandragupta's adviser Kautilya. The existing version of *Arthashastra* was edited 500 years after Kautilya's time, but many scholars believe it contains passages by Kautilya, along with later additions. Kautilya supposedly wrote *Arthashastra* to show Chandragupta how to rule Magadha. The book contains information on Mauryan government, although it is unclear how much of it is what Kautilya (or later authors) wanted and how far it reflects the way things really were. In any case, *Arthashastra* describes a centralized administration, under the personal control of the king. It recommends that the king have secret agents all over the country, both to detect dissent and to keep in touch with the people. Whether this was actually done or not, we know that Ashoka ruled through a large body of paid bureaucrats.

The majority of the population of Mauryan India was rural. As they do today, peasants lived in villages near their fields. Their main food crops were wheat and barley in the north, rice in the Gangetic plain, and millet in dryer areas (such as the Deccan). From before the time of the Mauryas, the principal tax in India was the land revenue, later called the *lagaan*, which was collected at a rate of between one sixth and one third the value of the crop.

By the time of Chandragupta, cities existed in the old Aryan world of north India, and probably also in the Deccan. Elsewhere, the Mauryas may have established new cities, for by the end of the dynasty, urban settlements existed in all parts of India except the extreme south. Nevertheless, outside of the Gangetic plain, Mauryan cities fall into distinct clusters. These were apparently separated from one another by regions inhabited by Tribals, where the Mauryas may have only controlled the roads linking the urbanized areas.

Cities were centers for administration, manufacturing, and commerce. Mauryan India had an extensive trade with the Mediterranean world. Its significance is shown by the fact that Indians called all foreign merchants *Yavanas*, Greeks. Merchants had used writing for several centuries before the accession of Ashoka, and it was now employed by the government as well. The language of administration was Magadhi, the Prakrit spoken in Magadha. There is little evidence that Sanskrit was written before Mauryan times, but *Arthashastra* is in Sanskrit, and it is difficult to believe that it was handed down orally. This suggests that Brahmins like Kautilya now wrote in Sanskrit, most likely in the Brahmi script that was already used for Prakrits.

The greatest Mauryan city was the capital, Pataliputra, in the modern state of Bihar. In Pataliputra, archeologists have found a pillared hall, apparently built by Chandragupta, which is the oldest known stone building in India. In keeping with his Buddhist leanings, Ashoka built at Buddhist holy places. The Mauryan period seems to mark the beginning of Buddhist construction in permanent materials.

Ashoka died about 235 BCE. The Mauryan empire began to disintegrate almost immediately, showing that dhamma was insufficient to hold together so vast a territory. The decline has been connected with economic decay, poor communications, problems in managing the bureaucracy, or war. About 185 BCE, the last Mauryan king of Magadha was overthrown, but the Mauryas had played a key role in the development of South Asia. By bringing Gangetic civilization to more of India than ever before, they created lasting cultural and economic ties over much of the country, particularly among the urban areas. India was politically divided after the death of Ashoka, but cities and the Gangetic civilization (which now becomes Classical Indian civilization) continued to spread, and trade grew steadily.

INDIA AFTER THE MAURYAS

After the Mauryas, the social and economic center of India shifted from the Gangetic plain to the northwest and the south. The northwest was repeatedly conquered by foreigners who adopted Indian culture and religious beliefs—Greeks from Afghanistan, Parthians from Iran, and Shakas and Kushanas from Central Asia. The greatest Kushana king, Kanishka, ruled much of Central Asia, and northern India at least to the eastern frontiers of Uttar Pradesh, if not beyond. The wealth of the Kushanas was based on trade. By this time, there was a flourishing commerce between India and China, mainly in luxury goods. Thanks to their control of Central Asia, the Kushanas were able to tax traders on the Silk Road, the overland trade route from China to the Roman Empire, which was then at the peak of its importance. Kanishka was a patron of Buddhism, which about this time spread along the trade routes from India into Central Asia.

North Indian sculptors and architects played a major part in the development of Indian artistic traditions. Their work was almost always religious in nature—Buddhist, Jain, or Brahminical. The sculptures and buildings of the Gandhara school in the northwest showed the influence of the Greeks and the Romans and molded later Buddhist art. At the end of the first century BCE, sculptors at Mathura in the upper Gangetic plain borrowed Greco-Roman and other elements from the northwest and apparently produced the first statues of Buddha (until then, depicting him had been regarded as sacrilege). The Mathura school developed into Classical North Indian sculpture and then into Hindu sculpture.

Gangetic civilization spread in the Deccan during and particularly after the Mauryan period. The process was encouraged by local kings, who sought power and legitimation by associating themselves with the prestigious culture of the north. To this day, the Deccan marks the southern limit of languages derived from Sanskrit: The inhabitants of Maharashtra adopted Prakrit languages (which became modern Marathi), whereas those of Andhra Pradesh and Karnataka did not. Although culturally part of the Gangetic world, they retained their own languages, which belong to the Dravidian family.

The greatest post-Mauryan dynasty of the Deccan was that of the Satavahanas or Andhras, from the first century BCE to the mid-third century CE or later. The Satavahanas were apparently of Tribal origin, but they adopted Gangetic culture. They fostered the Brahminical religion and the Prakrit and Sanskrit languages. After the Satavahanas, the Deccan was divided into smaller kingdoms. These were centers of rock-cut architecture, sacred buildings carved into the living rock. The best-known of these creations are the Buddhist and Jain remains at Ajanta and Ellora in Maharashtra.

Like the northwest, the Deccan was part of a network of internal and international trade, which may have been the source of the wealth of the builders of Ajanta and Ellora. It is possible that Indian sailors were already visiting Southeast Asia and China, but most of the Deccan's seaborne trade between the first and third centuries CE was with the Roman Empire, which bought Indian luxury goods (such as spices and fine textiles) in return for gold.

Meanwhile, by the mid-first millennium BCE, pottery and iron were used in the land of the Tamils, the extreme south of India (modern Tamil Nadu and Kerala; the people of Kerala were not regarded as separate from Tamils until the eleventh century CE). The Tamil country was not ruled by Ashoka, but it had friendly relations with him, and by Mauryan times Buddhist and Jain ascetics traveled in the area. The main source of our knowledge of early Tamil history is the Shangam literature, a collection of heroic poems that were probably composed orally between the first and third centuries CE. The poems suggest a region in different stages of development, with hunters and gatherers in some places and peasant villagers in others. The clan-based political structure seems to have been giving way to kingdoms, which may reflect the spread of ideas and institutions from the north. At this point, the only cities in the Tamil country were apparently ports that traded with the Roman Empire and were dominated by foreign merchants.

THE END OF ANCIENT INDIA

After the Kushanas, north India seems to have broken into small kingdoms and oligarchies. In the fourth century CE, it was reunited by the Gupta kings, the greatest of whom, Chandra Gupta II (c. 375–415), also dominated much of the Deccan. In the fifth century, however, north India again fragmented following attacks by a people called the Hunas, who were presumably identical with the Huns of European history. It was temporarily reunited by a king named Harshavardhana (606–647), whose death in 647 is often regarded as marking the end of ancient India.

Meanwhile, the Tamil world of the Shangam age gave way to a society that resembled that of the rest of India, with an economy based on peasant agriculture, a religion dominated by Brahmins, and governments headed by divinely sanctioned kings. By the sixth century, there were two major Tamil dynasties, the Pallavas and the Pandyas. The Deccan and the Tamil country were wealthy thanks to a flourishing trade with Southeast Asia and China, which replaced the now defunct Roman Empire as India's main overseas markets.

By Gupta times, the Prakrits were evolving into the modern languages of northern and central India, while the Dravidian tongues of the south were becoming modern Telugu, Kannada, Tamil, and Malayalam. However, the most striking linguistic development in India after the Mauryas was the revival of Sanskrit. It had always been learned by Brahminical priests, no matter what their first language, but was now also used for nonreligious purposes. By Gupta times, educated men learned Sanskrit as a matter of course, and the ancient language had replaced Prakrits on inscriptions. Several reasons have been suggested for the increasing use of Sanskrit. Perhaps the foreign kings of the northwest fostered the most prestigious Indian language to show that, despite their ancestry, they *were* Indian. Or perhaps the languages spoken in different parts of India had become so diverse that communication was impossible, and Sanskrit (already known by priests) provided a solution.

In any case, the widespread use of Sanskrit made possible the development of a rich Sanskrit literature. Its most famous examples are two poems, the *Mahabharata* and the *Ramayana*, which were revised and added to over many centuries until they reached their present forms in the first millennium CE. The *Mahabharata* is the longest single poem in the world, and tells the story of a war between two sets of cousins, the Kauravas and the Pandavas. The *Ramayana* is the story of Rama, king of Kosala, and his faithful wife Sita.

Literature was not the only interest of the educated classes of ancient India. They made advances in the sciences, and the world is indebted to the Indian mathematicians who invented the decimal system, with a symbol for zero. This notation was later borrowed by the Arabs, who passed it on to Europe, where the Indian numerals were called Arabic numerals.

BUDDHISM AND HINDUISM

Probably thanks to Ashoka, Buddhism spread across India after the Mauryas. This was accompanied by a change in Buddhist theology. A belief arose that rather than reach Nirvana, someone who lived an exemplary life would be reborn as a Bodhisattva ("one whose essence is perfect knowledge") with the power to answer the prayers of ordinary mortals for salvation. It has been suggested that this doctrine was borrowed from Christianity.

Buddhists who believed this teaching called it the Mahayana, or Great Vehicle to Nirvana, and they referred to traditional Buddhism as the Hinayana, or Lesser Vehicle. Indian monks carried Mahayana Buddhism to China, from where it reached Japan. By the time of the Guptas, Mahayana had replaced Hinayana as the dominant form of Buddhism in India. Hinayana survived in Sri Lanka, and from there it was taken to Southeast Asia. In the eighth century CE, a third form of Buddhism appeared, Vajrayana, the Vehicle of the Thunderbolt. Vajrayana Buddhists used magic, called the thunderbolt, to maintain the goodwill of a pantheon of goddesses. In the eleventh century, Vajrayana Buddhism was adopted in Tibet, where it developed into modern Tibetan Buddhism.

It is sometimes said that during the first millennium CE, the old Brahminical religion won back the allegiance of Indians whose ancestors had lapsed into other faiths. It would be more correct to say that in this period the Brahminical religion merged with folk beliefs, regional traditions, and elements of Buddhism, Jainism, and other religions to form a new faith. The term Hindu was not used in India until long after this period, but it is convenient to refer to this new faith as Hinduism. Hinduism is now the religion of 81 percent of the population of India, or 814 million people, and 16 million in Pakistan and Bangladesh.

Hinduism has no religious leadership with authority over all believers, and no single set of beliefs. Nevertheless, most of the many varieties of Hinduism share certain tenets. Chief among them is the notion of karma, which entered the Brahminical religion at the time of the Upanishads: Every deed that we perform determines what sort of body our souls will be reborn in after our current life ends. Most modern Hindus adhere to the Upanishadic doctrine that one may escape rebirth by recognizing the identity of the human soul with the universal essence of Brahman. This, however, is difficult to achieve, and Hindus therefore usually try to live their lives as best they can, so as to be born in a better situation in their next incarnation. One of the main elements of a good life is devotion to God. Devotional practices existed among some north Indian followers of the Brahminical religion by 100 BCE. Modern Hindu devotionalism, however, owes more to teachings that developed in the Tamil country, and gradually spread across India—God loves us and will save us if we repent our sins. We too can love God and show it through worship and hymns rather than with Aryan-style sacrifices.

As the use of the term *God* suggests, there was a tendency toward monotheism among Hindus. Most educated Hindus came to regard one of two deities as the basic form of God, with the other divine beings as manifestations that He assumes for special circumstances. These two deities are Vishnu, a minor god in the Rig Veda, and Shiva, a fertility god whom Hindus identify with the Rig Vedic god Rudra. Since Gupta times, there have been efforts to bring together the worshippers of Vishnu and Shiva with the concept of the Trinity. This presents their deities as aspects of the same divinity: God has three forms, Brahma who created everything, Vishnu who preserves, and Shiva who destroys. Most Hindus continue to concentrate on either Vishnu or Shiva, however, and there are only two temples dedicated to Brahma in India today. Devotees of Vishnu often worship him in one of the forms that he is said to have taken to come down to earth, notably Krishna (a character in the *Mahabharata*) and Rama (the hero of the *Ramayana*). Some Hindus do not believe in any God, and look instead to Rita, the Rig Vedic law of the universe. The worship of the Mother Goddess is strong in some parts of India, particularly the state of West Bengal. Other Hindus venerate holy men, such as Sai Baba of Shirdi, who died in 1917. The many sacred rivers and places of Hinduism include the Ganges river, and holy places that were destinations for pilgrims by Gupta times. These include the shrines of Vishnu (in his form of a deity called Jagannath) at Puri in Orissa; of Meenakshi the Mother Goddess at Madurai in Tamil Nadu; and of Shiva at Amarnath in Kashmir. Certain animals and plants are also holy, especially the cow. By the first century CE, even nonvegetarians agreed that the cow was so sacred it should not be killed. The reasons for this are debated; Hindus say it is because the cow represents the Mother. And every village in India has its own guardian deity.

Hindus worship both at home and at a temple. Brahmins, the descendants of the old Aryan priests, may perform or lead the worship, which involves veneration of the deity's statue, picture, or symbol. The Brahminical religion does not seem to have used temples before the second century BCE, but by Gupta times, India was covered with Hindu temples, each usually dedicated to a particular deity. The basic structure of temples has been unchanged since the sixth century CE, although there are differences between north and south Indian styles of architecture.

A good Hindu may not escape rebirth, but his or her soul will spend many years in heaven and then be reborn in a happy new life. Righteous conduct is outlined in the Hindu Scriptures. These include the ancient Vedas, from the Rig Veda to the Upanishads, but most Hindus believe that the main message of the Scriptures is that outlined by Vishnu in his guise as Krishna in the Bhagavad Gita, a section of the *Mahabharata*. This is that we should each fill our assigned role in this world, not because it will benefit us but because it is what God wants us to do; and we should love God, who loves us.

Implicit in this is the belief that God has given different functions to different people. The main factor in determining one's function is caste. A caste is a group of people who marry each other, eat with each other, and follow specific occupations. Castes are ranked, and the higher the caste, the purer it is in religious terms. This means that lower castes may pollute higher ones. Each caste has its own rules, so that one must act in the way appropriate for a member of one's caste. Many Hindus believe that a person's caste in this life is determined by his or her conduct in a preceding one.

It is often said that the caste system came into being to maintain the supremacy of the Aryans over other Indians with the Aryans assigning themselves to the higher castes and everyone else to the lower. This assumes that the Aryans were a separate ethnic group, and it has been seen that this assumption is questionable.[1] It also confuses caste with *varna*. The varnas were the four categories of ancient Aryan society—Brahmins, or priests; Kshatriyas, or warriors; Vaishyas, or peasants; and Shudras, or people who had not willingly become Aryans. If a community decided to adopt the Aryan ways and language, its people fitted themselves into these categories. It is not known exactly how varna functioned among the Aryans. It involved some sort of ranking and some connection to occupation, but it may have been used only at religious ceremonies. Moreover, at least for Brahmins, Kshatriyas, and Vaishyas, people's varnas could change if they took up new occupations.

Between 1000 and 550 BCE, the varna system was apparently modified: As trade increased, Vaishyas came to be associated with merchants, and peasants and craftsmen (even if originally Vaishyas) were regarded as Shudras. By this time, the Aryans were divided into both varnas (perhaps only on religious occasions) and *jatis* or groups of people who were related by blood. Gradually, varna and jati merged to form the caste system, and in modern India caste is called jati. Perhaps sometimes, occupational groups became more and more exclusive until they were castes; and as Aryan culture spread across India, Tribals and others were incorporated as new castes. The formation of the caste system was a very gradual process. It began in the north and slowly spread. For many centuries the system remained flexible: One could change caste, marry outside of caste, and eat with people from other castes. The caste system apparently did not reach its classic form until the thirteenth century CE or later, and it has continuously evolved since then. There are now over 3,000 Hindu castes. The highest-ranking castes are Brahmins. They trace their ancestry to the Aryan priesthood, although the majority of them pursue nonreligious jobs. By several centuries BCE, there was a new group of castes at the bottom of society, the Untouchables, who were considered so polluting that they could not draw water from communal wells, enter temples, and so forth. Often, Untouchables were originally people whose work was regarded as very degrading.

For a Hindu, breaking caste rules is a sin against *dharma*, the same word as Ashoka's policy dhamma. In Hinduism, it refers both to the Hindu religion itself and to the laws that tell humans how to act. Brahmin theologians said every man should live by his own *varnashramadharma* (law of caste and stage of life). The idea of Stages of Life (*ashramas*) teaches that a man's life should be divided into four parts, with different responsibilities at each: After initiation into the Hindu community, he is a student (studying the Vedas, and perhaps other subjects too); after marriage, he is a householder; when his grandchildren are born, he retires to the forest to meditate and perform penance; and when he no longer wants any material things, he gives up all and wanders till he dies. The householder stage is the most important part of life (few men go through the hermit or wanderer stages). Marriage is expected of a Hindu man, and the householder should enjoy sexual relations during this part of his life, and father children. Until 1955, Hindu men in India were permitted to marry more than one wife, although few ever did.

The typical Hindu family is a joint family: The household is headed by a senior male; he administers the property, but it is owned in common by the other adult males (his brothers, sons, and so forth), who often all live in the same house with their wives and children. Aryan women of the three higher varnas originally studied the Vedas, which made them full participants in religious life. By about the beginning of the common era, this was no longer the case. A woman's function was held to be marriage and caring for her family. Daughters were regarded as less desirable than sons: They cannot help their parents or perpetuate the family, as on marriage they become part of the husband's family; they need a dowry; they cannot perform their father's funeral rites. Still, women in traditional Hindu society did have some rights: They could own some personal property, and women from the higher classes were educated.

Devotional Hinduism spread through India during the first millennium CE, probably because it offered a spiritual comfort missing from Jainism and Buddhism. Jainism began to decline in the fourth century CE, and today there are a mere 4 million Jains in India. It will be seen in the next chapter that Buddhism eventually disappeared altogether from its homeland. Meanwhile, foreign merchants brought other religions to India. Whatever the truth of a legend that the Apostle Thomas preached in India, we know that by the sixth century there were Christians in Kerala on the southwest coast. A thousand years later, the Portuguese converted many Hindus on the west coast (especially in Goa) to Roman Catholicism, and in the nineteenth and twentieth centuries Protestant missionaries made further converts, especially in northeastern India. Today, there are 23 million Christians in India, forming 2.3 percent of the population.

Merchants were probably also responsible for introducing Judaism and Zoroastrianism to the west coast of India, which in the seventh century had its first encounters with a faith that had a profound impact on the subsequent history of the subcontinent. This was Islam.

NOTE

1. This being said, Indian and American geneticists recently released a study asserting that the paternal ancestors of modern upper-caste Hindus have genetic patterns characteristic of Europeans, whereas those of the lower castes do not. If this is true, it means that the higher castes are descended from European men, which seems to support theories that the Aryans were immigrants to South Asia and that the upper castes are their descendants. The methodology and the conclusions of the study are currently being debated.

3

Religion, Trade, and Conquest

ISLAM

In the last chapter, it was suggested that the death of King Harshavardhana in 647 may be taken as the end of the ancient period of Indian history. Any classification of history as "ancient," "medieval," and "modern" is arbitrary. Nevertheless, during the first half of the seventh century, a chain of events began that had momentous effects on India— so momentous that, in retrospect, Harshavardhana's reign does seem to constitute a turning point.

Harshavardhana may not even have been aware of these events, which began at Mecca in western Arabia, 2,500 miles from his kingdom. In 610, four years after Harshavardhana came to the throne, a Meccan trader named Muhammad began to receive what his followers believe were visits from the archangel Gabriel. According to Gabriel, God had sent a succession of prophets to reveal His message to humanity, but mortals had always lost or distorted that message. Muhammad had been chosen as the last prophet, and he was to ensure that the word of God was preserved correctly. The heart of the divine message, which Muhammad's followers recorded in the book called the Quran, is that humans must worship God alone and surrender themselves to Him. The religion that was revealed to Muhammad was therefore called Islam, "submission," and those who followed it Muslims, "those who submit."

Muhammad preached God's message and acquired a growing number of followers. He instructed Muslims to carry out a constant struggle (jihad) to please God and spread His word, promising them the rewards of heaven if they did so. In 622, Muhammad moved from Mecca to the town of Medina, where he built the first mosque, or Muslim place of worship. He also organized a government and an army, and in 630 he returned to Mecca and captured it from its non-Muslim rulers. Two years later, he died. Most Muslims accepted a man named Abu Bakr as their new religious leader and secular ruler, and Abu Bakr became the first khalifa, or successor, of Muhammad.

Half a century later, the khalifa Muawiya named his own son as his heir. This transformed the khalifa into the hereditary ruler of what had become an immense Muslim empire. Islam first spread rapidly among the polytheistic, Jewish, and Christian Arabs. Then, between 632 and 732, the now Muslim Arabs destroyed the Sasanian empire of Iran, conquered the Near Eastern possessions of the Byzantine empire, and expanded westward as far as Spain and Portugal and eastward into Central Asia.

EARLY MEDIEVAL INDIA

By this time, there were four broad political and cultural regions in South Asia: the East, comprising Bengal, Bihar, Jharkhand, and Orissa; the North, the upper and central Gangetic plain; the peninsular Deccan; and the Tamil country of the far south. Each of these regions was subdivided into several kingdoms, whose rulers normally recognized the overlordship of the most powerful of their number. This structure created stability within each region. There was, however, frequent warfare between the overlords of different regions, who wanted one another's territory, wealth, and markets. Occasionally, an overlord such as Harshavardhana extended his power outside of his own region, but such supremacy was never more than temporary.

The kings of early medieval India derived much of their authority from the fact that they were regarded as earthly representatives of the patron deities of their families. Religious rituals that emphasized this aspect of kingship—whether Hindu, Jain, or Buddhist—played a prominent role in most kingdoms. Kings distributed gifts to nobles, Brahmin priests, and temples in return for their participation in these rituals and their loyalty. The gifts included land, apparently usually meaning the right to collect and keep the land revenue (the tax on agricultural production) from a given area. All this created a decentralized political hierarchy in most of the subcontinent, although the precise structures differed from place to place. At the top, there was a great king, often a regional overlord. Then came lesser kings who accepted his supremacy, the recipients of land grants from both great and lesser kings, and the local chieftains, rulers of miniature kingdoms comprising groups of neighboring villages, who kept order in their territories and passed on the land revenue to their superiors. At the very bottom were the headmen of each village.

Indian notions of kingship, social organization, and religious practice continued to spread into Tribal areas, and Tribals were absorbed into Indian society. Sometimes, Hindu settlements were founded in Tribal areas. Other times, Tribal leaders refashioned themselves as Hindu kings, as chieftains in the south had done during and after the time of the Mauryas.

Of the four regions of South Asia, Bengal had been the easternmost province of the Mauryas and the Guptas. It had a large Tribal population. Like other Indian monarchs, kings in Bengal granted land to Brahmins. Much of this land was in Tribal areas, where the Brahmins introduced labor-intensive rice cultivation to people who until then had practiced hunting, fishing, and gathering or shifting cultivation. As they became rice-growing peasants, the Tribals adopted the language that became modern Bengali, and their beliefs were assimiliated to Hinduism or Buddhism. The Pala kings of Bengal (c. 750–1161) were generous patrons of Buddhism, and the greatest of them, Dharmapala (c. 770–810), dominated East and North India.

Dharmapala's principal rivals were the Gurjara-Pratiharas, the leading dynasty of the early medieval North, who originated in Rajasthan and were the strongest kings in India in the early and mid-ninth century. Perhaps as early as the days of the Gurjara-Pratiharas, or perhaps not until the fifteenth century, the incorporation of Tribal areas into the greater Indian world led to the formation of a new caste in North India. Its members, the Rajputs, were apparently descended from the founders of Hindu colonies in Tribal areas. Over several centuries, Rajputs of disparate origins came to regard themselves as a caste. They ranged from true kings, especially in Rajasthan and Gujarat, through local chieftains, down to village headmen. Till the twentieth century, the Rajputs dominated much of Rajasthan, Gujarat, and the central and upper Gangetic plain.

The Deccan and the Tamil country were henceforth as important as the North in Indian history. To strengthen their authority, kings in the south granted land in Tribal areas to Brahmins and temples, with much the same effects as in Bengal. The Rashtrakuta kings of the Deccan (743–974) campaigned in the Tamil country and the North, and in the ninth century succeeded the Gurjara-Pratiharas as the principal Indian dynasts. They were patrons of sculpture and rock-cut architecture. In the Tamil country, a dynasty called the Cholas subjugated the Pallava and Pandya kings in the late ninth century. A hundred years later, the Cholas became the leading monarchs of the subcontinent. The Cholas presided over the flowering of classical Tamil culture. Perhaps their greatest monument is the temple of Shiva at Thanjuvur. They declined in the late eleventh century and ended in the thirteenth.

Trade was a major source of wealth for all the great kingdoms of India. To produce exports such as spices and textiles, many kings fostered agriculture by encouraging cultivation in Tribal areas, and, particularly in the arid parts of the south, by building irrigation works. After falling off with the decline of the Roman Empire, trade to the west picked up as the Sasanian and Byzantine empires were consolidated (before these fell to the rising power of Islam). Meanwhile, India's trade with Southeast Asia and China grew steadily. Indian cultural and religious practices spread in Southeast Asia, probably as indigenous kings adopted Indian culture. One result of this was the construction of the great Hindu temples at Angkor in Cambodia.

Trade brought colonies of foreign merchants to all the ports of India. In some areas, Hindus increasingly left sea travel to foreigners, and by the twelfth century there was a widespread belief among many Hindus that foreign travel brought religious impurity. This idea lasted till the twentieth century.

India's trade to the east and west traveled by both caravan and ship. By the seventh century, a great network of seaborne commerce linked the economies of countries all along the shores of the Indian Ocean. The Arab conquests of the seventh century united this Indian Ocean trading world with that of the Mediterranean, making India's overseas trade part of a huge new economy under Muslim Arab domination.

It has been suggested that the inflow of wealth from trade determined the strongest dynasty in India. Thus, for several centuries, the largest share of India's foreign trade traveled westward, up the Persian Gulf and into the Arab empire. The Rashtrakutas controlled the west coast of India, and their participation in the Gulf trade made them wealthy and powerful. Then, in the tenth and eleventh centuries, India's trade with the west shrank, thanks to Turkish incursions in the Arab world. At the same time, trade with Southeast Asia grew, and preeminence passed from the Rashtrakutas to the Cholas of southeastern India.

THE COMING OF ISLAM

It was trade that gave India its first contact with Islam. This came in either 636 or 644, when an Arab force attacked a nest of pirates near Bombay. In 644, during their conquest of Sasanian Iran, the Arabs took over Balochistan, now the westernmost province of Pakistan. During the seventh century, Arab merchants in the Indian ports joined their compatriots in converting to Islam. The Mappila Muslims of south India claim descent from these Arab traders and their Indian wives. Some Indians converted to Islam, and Hindu kings in south India from the Cholas onward often hired Muslim mercenaries.

In 711–713, the Arabs moved eastward from Balochistan to conquer Sindh. Sindh was on the sea route from the Indian west coast to the Persian Gulf. It was ruled by a Brahmin king, and its people included both Hindus and Buddhists. The Arabs justified the conquest on the grounds that Sindhi pirates had captured Muslim women, but the real reasons may have been to safeguard sea trade, or to round out the frontiers of the Arab empire.

According to the Quran, Muslims may forcibly convert adherents of polytheistic religions to Islam. The first conquered peoples of the Arab empire, however, were mostly Jews and Christians. Islam teaches that Judaism and Christianity were founded by authentic Prophets and are therefore legitimate faiths, even if their followers have distorted God's word. Jews and Christians under Muslim rule were accorded the status of *dhimmis*, nonbelievers who were allowed to practice their religions. They could not be compelled to serve in the army as Muslims were. In return for this privilege, they were required to pay a tax called the *jizya*.

The official religion of the Sasanian empire of Iran was Zoroastrianism. After the Arab conquest of Iran, Zoroastrians were added to the list of dhimmis. Muslim theologians justified this on the grounds that, although Islam does not recognize Zoroaster as a Prophet, his followers are like Jews and Christians in that they are monotheistic and have a holy book. With the conquest of Sindh, large numbers of Hindus and Buddhists came under Muslim rule, and the category of dhimmi was further enlarged to accommodate them. This was probably more for pragmatic than theological reasons, in that the Sindhis were simply too numerous to convert forcibly. Nevertheless, though Muslims were prepared to tolerate nonbelievers as dhimmis, Muhammad had declared the worship of images to be a grave sin. The Arabs accordingly often destroyed the statues in Hindu temples in Sindh, and they occasionally demolished Hindu and Buddhist holy places altogether.

Between the eighth and tenth centuries, the Muslim Arab empire disintegrated as provincial governors established themselves as independent rulers, regarding the khalifa as a purely religious leader with no political authority. In Iran, the new monarchs were called sultans. The sultans replaced Arab culture in their courts with a blend of Islamic and Iranian traditions, projecting themselves as semidivine monarchs in the old Iranian style and sponsoring Persian literature and art.

Sultans in Iran often used slaves as advisers and military officers, on the assumption that a master could count on the loyalty of his slaves. Most of the slaves were Turks from Central Asia, who were converted to Islam by their masters. They were not always as loyal as expected, and in the ninth and tenth centuries many Iranian sultans were overthrown by their Turkish slave officers. At the same time, free Turkish nomads entered Iran, became Muslims, and founded dynasties of their own. The result was that most of the eastern Islamic world came under the rule of Turkish sultans, who continued to use fellow Turks as slaves.

In 962, a Turkish slave founded the Ghaznawid sultanate in eastern Afghanistan. Sultan Mahmud (997–1030) expanded the Ghaznawid territories to the west and east. He conquered the Hindu kingdom of Kabul (which comprised northeastern Afghanistan and the northern half of Pakistan), and northern Sindh. Like the Arabs in Sindh, the Ghaznawid sultans recognized the Hindus under their rule as dhimmis. Mahmud made seventeen raids into India. Like many later Muslim warrior kings, Mahmud claimed to be acting in the spirit of jihad, although his real goal was to acquire plunder. The raids destabilized the North and East, and the Gurjara-Pratiharas ended after Mahmud sacked their capital Kanauj in 1019. Among the new dynasties that arose from the wreckage were the Gaharwars in Kanauj, and the Senas in Bengal (c. 1097–1223).

The Ghaznawids were eventually conquered by the Ghauris, a people from central Afghanistan who had been converted to Islam by Mahmud. In the twelfth century, the Ghauris made themselves the rulers of all Afghanistan. The Ghauri ruler Muizz ud-Din Muhammad (1173–1206) subjugated modern Pakistan. Desiring plunder, he decided to move on into India. At this time, three Hindu kings were warring for supremacy in North India: Prithviraj Chauhan, Jaychand Gaharwar, and Parmal Chandel. In 1192, Muizz ud-Din and his mounted Turkish slave archers defeated Prithviraj. They followed this up with further campaigns in

India. By 1206, a chain of Ghauri forts extended from the Afghan border to northwestern Bengal and ensured the submission of the Hindu kings of North India to their new overlord Muizz ud-Din.

THE DELHI SULTANATE

In 1206, Muizz ud-Din was assassinated. His Turkish slave generals divided up his territories, and many of the Hindu monarchs who had accepted his supremacy regained their independence. One of the slaves, Qutb ud-Din Aybeg, made himself ruler of Lahore, now the largest city of northern Pakistan. From here, he controlled much of Pakistan and North India. Aybeg died in 1210, when his own slave Shams ud-Din Iltutmish established himself at the city of Delhi. Delhi, which had been part of the kingdom of Prithviraj Chauhan, was an economic and administrative center but had never before been the capital of a major state. Iltutmish apparently chose it as his seat because it was a central point in North India. Delhi has been one of the principal cities of India ever since.

Iltutmish defeated other Muslim rulers in Pakistan, North India, and Bengal, and forced many Hindu kings into submission. He was the first ruler of the Delhi sultanate, which for 200 years was the leading—and often the only—Muslim-ruled state in India. Iltutmish's Shamsid dynasty (1210–1266) set a pattern for the Delhi sultanate. Each royal family produced one or two capable rulers. Their reigns were followed by turmoil as their relatives and nobles struggled for control until a new dynasty came to power. Iltutmish died in 1236. Over the next ten years, his nobles installed and then overthrew four Shamsids. The most noteworthy of them was Iltutmish's daughter Raziyya (1236–1240). Raziyya was a capable ruler but was deposed by the nobles after only four years.

The main external threat to the sultanate came from the Mongols. In 1206, the Mongol ruler Genghis Khan began a campaign to subjugate the entire world. He invaded what is now Pakistan in 1223–1224. He did not, however, attack Iltutmish, who may have forestalled him by recognizing Mongol supremacy. In the late 1230s, Genghis Khan's son Ögödei conquered Afghanistan, acquiring a frontier with the Delhi sultanate. He captured Lahore, and the Mongols soon seized most of Pakistan. By the mid-1240s, whatever arrangements Iltutmish had made had broken down, and there were annual Mongol incursions into North India.

The Shamsids were succeeded by the Ghiyasids (1266–1290). The first monarch of the new dynasty, Iltutmish's slave Baha ud-Din Balaban, restored order in the Delhi sultanate. The Mongol attacks continued, however, and in 1285, Balaban's eldest son Muhammad was killed in battle against the Mongols. Balaban himself died two years later. Family quarrels ensued until a noble named Jalal ud-Din became sultan. Jalal ud-Din came from the Khalaj people of Afghanistan, and founded the Khalji dynasty (1290–1320). He dispatched his nephew Ala ud-Din on a great raid through south India. The campaign served both to obtain wealth to defend the sultanate from Mongol attacks, and to keep the army in training. Ala ud-Din returned to Delhi victorious, murdered his uncle, and became sultan (1296–1316).

As ruler, Ala ud-Din both repelled Mongol invasions and continued his campaigns within India. Between 1299 and 1305, he secured the submission of Hindu kings in Gujarat, Rajasthan, and Central India, and he apparently tightened the sultan's control in the region east of Delhi where petty kings had hitherto enjoyed considerable autonomy. In 1307, his general Malik Kafur, a Hindu convert to Islam, launched a second great expedition to the south, which ended in the defeat of all the major kings of the Deccan and the Tamil country.

Sultans, in India and elsewhere, often paid their civil and military officials with *iqtas*, the right to taxes from a given region. This resembled the system by which Hindu kings made over land revenue to their subordinates. As in pre-Muslim times, the revenue was normally remitted by local chieftains, often of Hindu warrior castes, who remained dominant at the lowest level of the administration. *Muqtas*, or recipients of iqtas, were often also responsible for governing the area included in their grants, which required them to establish good relations with the chieftains. Ala ud-Din feared that his muqtas might use their holdings as territorial bases from which to challenge his authority. He created a network of spies to watch for discontent, and confiscated iqtas and began to pay officers with cash rather than land grants. If he was to keep his army content with cash wages, however, Ala ud-Din had to ensure that the cost of living remained low. He therefore set maximum prices for essential commodities and instituted harsh punishments for merchants who broke the price law or cheated customers. He also prohibited the production of wine and narcotics, perhaps partly to boost grain cultivation as a further means of keeping prices down.

Ala ud-Din's son Qutb ud-Din Mubarak Shah (1316–1320) abolished the network of spies, abandoned the price controls, and raised military wages. If he hoped that this would secure his throne, however, he was wrong. The Delhi sultanate was torn by unrest until Ala ud-Din's Mongol or Turco-Mongol officer Ghiyas ud-Din Tughluq made himself sultan and founded the Tughluq dynasty (1320–1414).

Tughluq too campaigned in the south, and apparently conquered the whole of the Deccan and Tamil country except for the southernmost part of the Pandya kingdom. He also recovered Bengal, which had been independent of Delhi since the death of Balaban. Tughluq was now the overlord of Hindu and Muslim kings in all four regions of the subcontinent, and controlled more of South Asia than any previous monarch. In 1324, he was killed in the collapse of a new building. It was widely believed that the accident was engineered by Tughluq's son Muhammad, who now became sultan (1324–1351).

Muhammad's reign started well. He drove out a Mongol army that had reached the regions east of Delhi, and he strengthened his authority over the local kings who had submitted to his predecessors. In some places, he deposed Hindu monarchs and replaced them with Muslim governors. About 1326/1327, he established a new capital at Daulatabad in the Deccan. He sent the leading Muslim residents of Delhi to live in Daulatabad and transformed the old capital into a base for a huge army with which he intended to drive the Mongols from Khurasan (northern Afghanistan).

Now, things began to go wrong. To clear a route to Khurasan, Muhammad sent a large force through passes in the Himalayas, where his men were wiped out by mountaineers. Meanwhile, the sultanate was reeling, as military costs and the expense of ruling the newly conquered south apparently worsened an economic slump that had hit all of Muslim Asia. Because he was now the overlord of most of India, Muhammad could not plunder his neighbors to replenish his treasury. He experimented with several alternatives: reinstituting the use of iqtas as salaries; paying his troops with coins made of bronze rather than precious metals, which provoked inflation and may have caused trade to shift out of the sultanate; and collecting taxes at unprecedentedly high rates. This in turn led to a revolt by peasants on the royal estates near Delhi, which was met with heavy punishment. The resulting disruption of agriculture joined with a drought to produce famine in Delhi and elsewhere in North India.

Peasants were not the only source of trouble. Muslim nobles resented the sultan's infringements on their prerogatives and his seeming preference for high-ranking Hindus. At the same time, nobles born in India disliked the favoritism shown to Turks, Mongols, and other foreign Muslims. The revolts in the North apparently spurred uprisings across the sultanate. Unfortunately, the Himalayan disaster and epidemics of disease had weakened the army, which could not be rebuilt because of the economic difficulties. As a result, Muhammad was unable to suppress discontent. In the 1330s, Muslim nobles in the Tamil country and in Bengal broke away to become independent sultans, and in 1336 the whole southern half of the Deccan seceded as the Hindu-ruled kingdom of Vijayanagara.

As territory was lost, tax demands increased on what remained, causing further revolts by Hindu kings and Muslim governors. About 1335/1336, Muhammad apparently tried to regroup. He allowed all who wished to leave Daulatabad to return to Delhi. But the 1340s saw risings in the Deccan and Gujarat, and the governor of what remained of the Deccan declared his independence. Muhammad campaigned in Gujarat and Sindh, where he died in 1351. By then, he had lost most of what he had inherited, and his dominions were confined to the North and its dependencies in Central and Western India.

The new sultan, Muhammad's cousin Firuz Shah (1351–1388), tried to win support through openhanded generosity to Muslim religious leaders, nobles, and army officers. Despite fierce campaigning at the beginning of his reign, however, he was unable to regain the lost territories, and he could not stop the continuing Mongol attacks. When Firuz Shah fell seriously ill in 1384, his family and nobles began the familiar struggle for power. The sultan died in 1388. Infighting continued for ten years, until India was invaded by one of the great conquerors of the Middle Ages, the Turco-Mongol Temür, called Tamerlane in English.

Temür had already made himself master of Central Asia and Afghanistan, South Russia, Armenia, Georgia, Iraq, and Iran. He claimed that he was motivated by the desire to spread Islam, but scholars agree that in actuality he wanted either plunder or to reestablish the Mongol empire of Genghis Khan. Temür crossed the Indus in September 1398 and advanced on Delhi. On December 16, he defeated Firuz Shah's grandson sultan Mahmud Shah, who fled. For three days, Temür's troops looted Delhi, massacring both Hindus and Muslims. Then, the invaders circled through the districts east of the Yamuna before returning across the Indus.

In the wake of Temür's incursion, the Delhi sultanate quickly broke up. The governors of Gujarat, Malwa (western Madhya Pradesh), and other provinces raised themselves to the rank of sultans, and Hindu kings in Rajasthan and elsewhere regained their independence. Delhi itself was dominated by a succession of nobles until one of them, the Afghan Khizr Khan, made himself sultan and founded the Sayyid dynasty (1414–1452). For thirty years, the Sayyids recognized the overlordship of Temür's descendants in Afghanistan and Central Asia. In 1448, the last Sayyid sultan left Delhi for the town of Badaun. Three years later, Bahlul Lodi, another Afghan noble, seized the capital. He inaugurated the Lodi dynasty (1451–1526), which gradually restored Delhi's supremacy over the Muslim and Hindu kings of North India.

Bahlul's son Sikandar (1489–1517) moved the capital down the Yamuna river from Delhi to Agra, so that he could better watch his outlying dependencies. The next sultan, Ibrahim (1517–1526), antagonized his nobles by trying to curb their power. Daulat Khan Lodi, the governor of Punjab and a member of the sultan's own tribe, rebelled and sought the assistance of Babur, the ruler of Kabul. Babur, who was a direct descendant of both Temür and Genghis Khan, had already invaded India three times in an effort to reestablish his family's supremacy there. He welcomed Daulat Khan's invitation, captured Lahore in 1524, and two years later advanced on Delhi. The armies of Babur and Ibrahim met at Panipat north of Delhi on April 20, 1526. The sultan had the larger army, but Babur's combination of artillery and mounted archers won the day, and Ibrahim was killed in battle. Babur and his successors became the most powerful dynasty in Indian history, the Mughal emperors. Before we turn to them, however, we must examine several aspects of religious interaction during the period of the sultans of Delhi.

MUSLIM RULE IN INDIA

Although the sultans of Delhi were Muslims of foreign origin, the state that they ruled was similar in structure to the dominions of regional overlords in India before the conquests of Muizz ud-Din Muhammad Ghauri. Only the area around the capital, and a few major fortresses elsewhere, were under the direct rule of the sultan. Outlying areas were administered either by Muslim governors appointed from Delhi, or by Hindu kings who recognized the sultan's supremacy. Across most of the sultanate, local power remained in the hands of petty Hindu chieftains. In return for paying the land revenue to muqtas, subject kings, provincial governors, or sultans, the chieftains were allowed to rule their tiny kingdoms more or less as they pleased. Governors and kings alike assumed independence whenever the sultanate was too weak to keep them in check. This happened during the decay of almost every dynasty at Delhi, under Muhammad Tughluq, and after Temür's invasion.

At least in the eyes of Muslims, formal recognition by the khalifa was a great asset for a sultan who wanted to ensure the loyalty of his subordinates. In 1258, however, Genghis Khan's grandson captured and put to death the khalifa of the day, who lived at Baghdad in Iraq. For several generations, the sultans of Delhi continued to recognize the executed man as their nominal master. Then, in 1317/1318, Ala ud-Din Khalji's son Qutb ud-Din Mubarak Shah proclaimed himself khalifa. He may have hoped to enhance his authority by adding spiritual legitimacy to his temporal power, but he seems merely to have scandalized many Muslims. His claims were abandoned by the Tughluqs. The latter recognized the primacy of a line of khalifas who had lived in Egypt since the Mongol invasions. In the fifteenth century, the office of khalifa seems to have declined in importance for Indian Muslims, although it regained its significance for a time in the twentieth century.

Association with a class of Muslim holy men called Sufis also enhanced the authority of sultans. Orthodox Muslims regard the study of the Quran and obedience to Islam as the keys to salvation, but Sufis believe that with meditation, trances, and other techniques, it is possible for their souls to enter the presence of God himself. Many Indian Muslims believed that God had conferred both religious and secular government on the Sufi shaikhs, or holy men, who were closer to Him than other mortals. The shaikhs, however, might delegate their temporal jurisdiction to sultans. Many sultans of Delhi therefore sought the goodwill of shaikhs, and Muslim chroniclers often blamed disasters on sultans who treated Sufis badly.

The Delhi sultanate, and the Muslim states that seceded from it, had a Muslim religious elite comprising Sufi shaikhs, the ulama or interpreters of Islamic law, Islamic judges, and preachers. There was also a Muslim secular nobility of top administrators and army generals. In the time of Iltutmish, it included slave and free Turks, Arabs, Khalaj, Ghauris, and Iranians. These were later supplemented with Mongols and Africans, and a growing number of Indian-born Muslims. By the fourteenth century, the nobility also included Hindus, mostly local chieftains by background. Except during and immediately after the reign of Ala ud-Din Khalji, nobles were usually paid with iqtas. Iqtas and administrative offices were originally held for a stated term, sometimes as little as two or four years, but under Firuz Shah Tughluq, hereditary tenure became the norm. This paved the way for governors and muqtas to transform themselves into independent rulers after Temür's invasion.

Without the support of the nobility, no sultan could hope to hold the throne for long. At least from the accession of Raziyya in 1236, new monarchs sought to assure themselves of that support by exacting a pledge of allegiance from the nobles and leading men of Delhi, although Raziyya herself found the limits to loyalty when she was deposed by her nobles. After taking power, both Balaban and Ala ud-Din replaced the existing nobility with trusted supporters, but most sultans promoted their own men alongside the older aristocracy rather than eliminate it.

It was noted previously that the creation of the Muslim Arab empire joined the economies of the Mediterranean and the Indian Ocean. Beginning with Mahmud the Ghaznawid, Muslim rulers used the plundered silver of Hindu kings and temples to mint coins that circulated throughout the Muslim trading world. As Turkish and Mongol invasions disrupted the Middle East, and Europeans gained commercial supremacy in much of the Mediterranean, India became increasingly central to the Indian Ocean economy. Meanwhile, the conquests of Muizz ud-Din Muhammad Ghauri gave the trade of North India access to the great Eurasian empires. These were dominated by first the Turks and then the Mongols, and linked the expanding economies of Europe and China. All the while, Muslim rule in India fostered urbanization, as centers of trade and administration—Delhi among them—grew into cities.

HINDUISM, BUDDHISM, AND ISLAM IN INDIA

When Muizz ud-Din first invaded North India, most of the people of South Asia were Hindus, Buddhists, or followers of Tribal beliefs. Over the succeeding centuries, Buddhism almost completely disappeared from its homeland. Hinduism, however, flourished and continued to absorb Tribal religions. At the same time, large numbers of Indians became Muslims, and since then, Hinduism and Islam have been the two main religions of South Asia.

Its historical importance may give an exaggerated picture of how well rooted Buddhism actually was in Indian society. For 1,500 years, many Indians were undoubtedly influenced by Buddhist teachings, but most of them also worshipped the local deities of their own communities. Along with many other folk beliefs, their practices gradually merged into Hinduism. The process was helped by the fact that Indian Buddhism had no rituals or priests, and Buddhist laymen often relied on Brahmins to perform marriages and funerals. Purer forms of Buddhism depended on the patronage of kings and merchants. Early medieval kings increasingly sought legitimation through Hindu rituals, however, and it has been suggested that the growing foreign domination of India's long-distance trade eroded the number of wealthy Indian Buddhist laymen.

By the time of Muizz ud-Din Muhammad Ghauri, Indian Buddhism was largely confined to an ever-shrinking number of monasteries in North India. Hinduism was vibrant enough not to be seriously affected

by the occasional demolition of temples by iconoclastic Muslim conquerors, but the destruction of Buddhist monasteries apparently brought
about a rapid—and almost total—disappearance of Buddhism from
North India. Seven centuries later, in 1954, many Untouchable Hindus
converted to Buddhism. They believed that Buddha opposed the caste
system, although in fact caste apparently did not even exist in any recognizable form in Buddha's time. Buddhists in India today total only 8
million, or less than 1 percent of the total population.

In Delhi and the sultanates that broke away from it, sultans and the
highest nobles were almost invariably Muslim. So too was a large part
of the urban population. In much of South Asia, however, the rural people were overwhelmingly Hindu. They were often governed by their
own kings and chiefs, and except perhaps in wartime had little contact
with their Muslim overlords. It has been seen that the Arab rulers of
Sindh recognized Hindus as dhimmis. Most sultans in India followed
this principle, but they never consistently collected the jizya tax required
of dhimmis. This could be justified under Islamic law on the grounds
that the jizya was ostensibly a payment in lieu of military service, and
Hindus (unlike Jews or Christians) could and did serve in the army.
Perhaps more importantly, at least outside of cities, it was difficult to
exact the jizya from a population composed largely of non-Muslims,
many of whom were under the immediate administration of fellow Hindus.

It appears that sultans often determined their treatment of Hindus
according to the political needs of the moment. For example, Ala ud-Din
Khalji was firmly in control for much his reign. He therefore did not
need the backing of Muslim theologians, so he could safely disregard
the Islamic law banning the construction and repair of dhimmi places of
worship. Muhammad Tughluq, however, was in constant fear of his
Indian-born Muslim nobles. He sought to counter them by securing the
support of both Hindus and foreign-born Muslims. This explains such
seemingly contradictory actions as his alleged participation in Holi, the
Hindu spring festival, and a call that he made for Muslim theologians
from Central Asia to settle in Delhi. His successor Firuz Shah looked on
orthodox Muslims as a source of strength, and accordingly collected the
jizya, destroyed Hindu temples that had been built since the time of
Muizz ud-Din, and suppressed heretical Muslim sects.

Nevertheless, Hindus always predominated in the armies, the building
crews, and the lower administration of the sultanates of India. Hindu
castes with traditions of bureaucratic service adapted themselves by
learning Persian, the language of government in most sultanates, and it

has been noted that Hindu chieftains retained power at the local level. Despite the occasional insistence of orthodox theologians that no non-Muslim should be admitted to the ruling class, an increasing number of Hindus entered the ranks of the nobility in Delhi and the other sultanates. At least in part, this was because there were never enough Muslims in India for any sultan to be able to dispense with Hindu assistance, for while much of North India was under Muslim rule for 600 years, and the Deccan for 400 years, the majority of the people of South Asia remained Hindu.

This is not to say that Hinduism was unaffected by Muslim rule. Such Hindu regional overlords as the Gurjara-Pratiharas and the Senas had often been generous patrons of Hindu temples. This royal patronage ended with the establishment of Muslim domination, and few great temples were built in the North and the East after the time of Muizz ud-Din Ghauri. Monumental temple construction was henceforth largely confined to the Deccan and the Tamil country. It has been suggested that in some areas, the end of independent Hindu kingship helped strengthen the ever-changing caste system, as individual castes assumed what had been the king's duty of keeping society in order.

Devotional Hinduism, or bhakti, originated long before the Muslim conquest but became more popular than ever in the sultanates of medieval India. With their use of vernacular languages rather than Sanskrit, and their acceptance of worshippers of all castes, bhakti movements appealed particularly to the common people. Their followers felt an overpowering love for God, which they often saw in the light of the love between men and women. For example, the Bengali Brahmin Chaitanya (1486–1533) founded a sect devoted to the worship of God in the form of Krishna. He compared the love of humans for God with the love of the milkmaid Radha for Krishna.

With few exceptions (the most notable being Firuz Shah Tughluq), sultans made no sustained efforts at converting Hindus to Islam. Nevertheless, 120,102,000 Indians are now Muslims, 12 percent of the total population. If Pakistan and Bangladesh are added, 30 percent of the people of South Asia practice Islam. Whatever official policy may have been, many Indians clearly adopted the religion of their Muslim rulers. A clue as to how this came about lies in the fact that the majority of Muslims in South Asia fall into several concentrations. Of these, by far the largest are in Pakistan and Bangladesh. Before becoming Muslims, most of the inhabitants of Bangladesh apparently practiced Tribal religions. In what is now Pakistan, many people once regarded themselves as Hindus or Buddhists, but they did not follow the orthodox forms of those religions.

For example, Sindhi Hindus did not regard the cow as sacred. It is therefore simplistic to say that most South Asian Muslims are descended from Hindus and Buddhists who adopted the Muslim religion.

Islam spread very gradually in India. Most Sindhis were apparently not yet Muslims in the eleventh century, 300 years after the Arab conquest. Even more striking is the case of Bangladesh, the eastern half of the historic region of Bengal. By the time it was conquered by the Mughal successors of the sultans of Delhi in 1574, West Bengal was more or less part of the Indian cultural world, its people largely Hindus and peasants. Most of East Bengal or Bangladesh, however, was still covered in dense forests and inhabited by Tribals.

In the seventeenth century, the Mughals instituted a policy of clearing the forests of Bangladesh, and transforming Tribals into peasants. A "pioneer," often from the lower levels of the secular or religious nobility of Bengal, would settle on a tract of forest land, and either bring in peasants, or teach the neighboring Tribals how to cultivate rice. Once his men had cleared the land, the pioneer would go to the authorities, and obtain title to his settlement. The process both cemented the loyalty of petty nobles who now held productive parcels of land by royal grant, and through the pioneers brought the former Tribal areas under effective Mughal control.

The pioneers included Hindus, but a majority of them were Muslims. Many were, or said they were, holy men, especially Sufis. It was useful to be a holy man for two reasons. First, if he claimed the need to support a mosque or shrine, the pioneer could secure for himself the land revenue of his tract. Pioneers therefore often either made sure they were already custodians of a holy place or built one on their new lands. Second, the Tribals seem to have been prone to accepting the leadership of men who claimed personal knowledge of God and professed a faith based on immutable written Scriptures such as the Quran. Without abandoning their own beliefs, they listened to the preaching of their new leader and turned to him to perform marriages, funerals, and other ceremonies. They soon inducted the holy man's God, angels, saints, and prophets of Islam into their pantheon, praying to the new divinities alongside their old ones.

Such a pairing of Islamic and Tribal beliefs offended the holy men, or at least those among them who knew something of Islamic theology. Muslim teachers tried to persuade their followers to worship only those superhuman beings found in the Quran. After several generations, the effort succeeded, but only at the cost of a compromise: The former Tribals now prayed to divinities who bore Quranic names but had all the characteristics of their non-Islamic predecessors. Finally, in the nineteenth and twentieth centuries, reformers taught the beliefs and practices of orthodox Islam. Rural Bengali Muslims henceforth prayed exclusively to God rather than to saints and angels. They also adopted such customs as the seclusion of women that many theologians regarded as integral to true Islam. Bangladesh had completed its long journey from Tribal to Islamic beliefs, and 88 percent of its population is now Muslim.

OTHER SULTANATES AND KINGDOMS

South Asia therefore became a land of two principal religions, Hinduism and Islam. This was reflected in the politics of the Delhi sultanate and its neighbors. The latter included Kashmir, which for centuries was ruled by Hindu kings. Kashmir lay on a major trade route, and its people actively traded with the Islamic world. In the thirteenth and fourteenth centuries, many Muslims settled in Kashmir, and in 1339 a Muslim immigrant, Shah Mir, seized the throne and made himself the first sultan of Kashmir. This was followed by the spread of Islam in Kashmir, which now has a largely Muslim population.

It has already been seen that in the 1330s, sultans in Bengal established their independence from Tughluq Delhi. Eighty years later, a Bengali Hindu named Raja Ganesh rose to power. Raja Ganesh knew that as a non-Muslim, he would never be accepted as sultan by the Bengali Muslim nobility. In 1415, however, he had his son Jadu converted to Islam, and installed the boy as sultan under the name of Jalal ud-Din Muhammad. Jalal ud-Din secured noble support with displays of his Islamic credentials. He built mosques, financed a college in Mecca, even proclaimed himself khalifa. At the same time, he did not forget his father's coreligionists. Many of his coins, for example, depict a lion, symbol of the Hindu deity Shiva's wife Durga. Bengal was subsequently ruled by a succession of Turkish, African, and Arab Muslim sultans, some of whom openly funded Hindu preachers and scholars.

Ala ud-Din Khalji and Ghiyas ud-Din Tughluq conquered the Deccan and the Tamil country, but South India broke away from the control of Delhi during the troubled reign of Muhammad Tughluq. It did not, however, revert to the political structure that had been disrupted by the Muslim invasions of the late thirteenth and early fourteenth centuries. Rather, two entirely new states arose, the Hindu kingdom of Vijayanagara in the Tamil country and the southern Deccan, and the Muslim Bahmani sultanate in the northern Deccan.

The city and kingdom of Vijayanagara were established in 1336. Their monarchs claimed sovereignty over all India south of the Krishna River

and for 200 years compelled many of the kings within that area to recognize their overlordship. The early sovereigns of Vijayanagara were not
of royal blood. They accordingly sought to legitimize their rule by declaring themselves the protectors of Hindu and Jain shrines against Muslim desecration, instituting the rituals connected with traditional Hindu
kingship, and generously patronizing temples. Frequent wars with the
Muslim rulers to the north suggest that the Vijayanagara kings really
were defenders of Hinduism against the menace of Islam. Their true
goal, however, was political supremacy. To obtain it, they fought Hindus
as well as Muslims, and if it served their purposes, they allied themselves
with Muslims against other Hindus. From the mid-fifteenth century onward, the Vijayanagara armies included many Muslim soldiers, particularly artillerymen, who were allowed to build their own mosque in the
capital of the kingdom.

Eleven years after the foundation of Vijayanagara, Ala ud-Din Bahman
Shah, Muhammad Tughluq's governor of the Deccan, broke away and
founded the Bahmani sultanate. His successors dominated the northern
half of the Deccan, often ruling from coast to coast. The Bahmanis
claimed to be the guardians of Islam in south India and depicted their
frequent conflicts with Vijayanagara as attempts to spread the true faith.
In reality, they were no more motivated by religion than their southern
neighbors were, and the wars between the Bahmanis and Vijayanagara
in some ways merely continued the old rivalry between the overlords of
the Deccan and the Tamil country. Muslims formed a tiny minority
among the subjects of the Bahmanis, who depended on the support of
Hindu officers, bureaucrats (usually Brahmins), headmen, and local
chieftains. Indeed, some sultans sought to check the rivalry between immigrant and Indian-born Muslims by promoting Hindus to high office.

In 1498, a new era in maritime history began when the Portuguese
navigator Vasco da Gama sailed around Africa and established direct
sea contact between Europe and India. This greatly eased the interchange
of products, technology, and ideas. In 1509, a Portuguese force defeated
the combined fleets of the sultans of Egypt and Gujarat, which secured
Portuguese control of the Indian Ocean. For the next century, Portugal
dominated both the trade in spices and other goods between Asia and
Europe, and local traffic in the Indian Ocean. From 1510, the Portuguese
headquarters in Asia were at Goa on the west coast of India.

Meanwhile, the Bahmani kingdom had begun to fragment, and by
1512 its territory was divided into five sultanates. Of these, the most
powerful were Ahmadnagar in northwestern Maharashtra, Bijapur in
southern Maharashtra and northern Karnataka, and Golkonda in north-

ern Andhra Pradesh. These Deccan sultanates regularly warred with one another. Often, two of them joined forces against a third, and one side or the other made and broke alliances with Vijayanagara and the Portuguese. If anything, Hindus enjoyed greater prominence in the successor sultanates than under the original Bahmani sultans. The Ahmadnagar dynasty was of Hindu ancestry, and—as in the Delhi sultanate—the bureaucracy and the local administration in all the sultanates were largely in the hands of Hindus. In Ahmadnagar and Bijapur, the Hindu village headmen, local chieftains, and petty kings coalesced into a caste called the Marathas, who corresponded to the Rajputs of North India; in Golkonda, as in Vijayanagara, local power was monopolized by Telugu-speaking Hindu warriors belonging to a number of castes.

In 1564, the sultans of Ahmadnagar, Bijapur, and Golkonda formed a rare triple alliance. Their goal was to curb Ramaraya, the regent of Vijayanagara, who in his machinations to uphold his power had recently fomented revolt in several sultanates. In January 1565, the allies met Ramaraya's army on the banks of the Krishna. The battle ended in a crushing defeat for Vijayanagara. Ramaraya was killed. The victorious sultans looted Vijayanagara city, and the Vijayanagara dynasty never returned to its old capital. Ramaraya's successors styled themselves kings until 1650, but they had little real power in what was now a fragmented kingdom. Since the mid-fifteenth century, the Vijayanagara monarchs had rewarded their generals with land grants that resembled the iqtas of the Delhi sultanate. These grandees enjoyed considerable autonomy, and after 1565 the greatest of them assumed complete independence.

The Deccan sultans soon resumed their wars with one another. Bijapur and Golkonda expanded southward into the former Vijayanagara territories. Their dynasties were eventually extinguished by the Mughals who had established themselves at Delhi in 1526.

4

The Rise and Fall of the Mughal Dynasty

THE ESTABLISHMENT OF THE MUGHAL DYNASTY

As a descendant of Temür and Genghis Khan, Babur was called a Mughal, or Mongol. The dynasty that he founded on conquering the sultanate of Delhi in 1526 is also called Mughal. When Babur died four years later, his son Humayun inherited an empire that extended from Central Asia in the west to Bihar in the east. The Afghan nobles who had plagued Ibrahim Lodi remained restive, however, and one of them, Shir Khan Sur, rebelled. In 1539 he defeated Humayun and made himself sultan of Delhi under the name of Shir Shah.

Shir Shah made administrative and financial reforms, among them establishing the rupee as the basis of the Indian currency. But his successors were weak, and in 1555 Humayun returned from exile in Iran and restored the Mughal empire. He survived only six months before dying in January 1556. The new emperor, his thirteen-year-old son Akbar, became the greatest of the Mughals. Like many of his family, Akbar was a military genius. Between the 1560s and the 1590s, he subdued the Tribal region of Gondwana in Central India and the Rajput kings of Rajasthan, conquered Gujarat and Bengal, and established Mughal rule over much of Himachal Pradesh, Kashmir, the tribes of the present

Afghan-Pakistani border, and Sindh. In 1595, the Iranian governor of the city of Qandahar defected to Akbar, who thus acquired control of southern Afghanistan. South of the Mughal dominions, in the Deccan, were the sultanates of Ahmadnagar, Bijapur, and Golkonda. They invited conquest, both to round out Mughal rule in India and as a source of wealth. Akbar conquered much of Ahmadnagar, and by the time of his death in 1605, he ruled one of the great empires of the Muslim world.

Akbar began his reign as a devout Muslim. He credited his victories to a long-dead Sufi holy man named Khwaja Muin ud-Din Chishti, and made an annual pilgrimage to the saint's tomb. He became a devotee of another Sufi, Shaikh Salim Chishti, who lived at Sikri near Agra. When Shaikh Salim died in 1571, the emperor honored him by moving his capital from the Lodi city of Agra to Sikri, which he renamed Fathpur (Town of Victory) Sikri. Akbar's Fathpur Sikri centered on a huge mosque and the tomb of Shaikh Salim, which showed the world that he was a good Muslim king and thus entitled to the throne.

All this was to change. An interest in his religion led Akbar to organize debates on Islamic theology. Then, he brought Jain, Hindu, and Zoroastrian teachers into the discussions, and finally Jesuit missionaries. As he listened to their arguments, Akbar concluded that Islam did not have a monopoly on the truth. At the same time, he was clashing with the Muslim religious elite. For centuries, Muslim rulers in India had supported Islamic holy men with hereditary grants of land. Akbar, however, confiscated all grants where title could not be proved. This angered the ulama, the interpreters of Islamic law, who were further alienated by Akbar's distribution of land to leaders of other religions and by his refusal to suppress unorthodox Muslims. They were particularly incensed at Akbar's removal of long-standing restrictions on non-Muslims, culminating in 1579 with the abolition of the jizya, the tax on non-Muslims. Although the jizya had never been consistently collected in India, its existence had always been regarded as a mainstay of an Islamic state.

The same year, 1579, Akbar more or less rendered the ulama superfluous when he assumed their function of deciding how Islamic law would be applied. Unfazed by an unsuccessful revolt among orthodox Muslim officers, the emperor next removed Islamic motifs from coins, stopped worshipping Sufi holy men, and apparently ended his weekly appearance at the mosque. By the early 1580s, he had invented his own form of worship, centering on fire, sun, and light. In 1585, Akbar left Fathpur Sikri to campaign in the northwest. When he returned thirteen years later, it was to Agra, not Fathpur Sikri. There were strategic reasons, for Agra fort was easier to defend than Fathpur Sikri. But Akbar probably also went to Agra because Fathpur Sikri symbolized the now-departed days when he had exemplified Muslim kingship. In place of Islam, Akbar now sought to legitimize his rulership with what has been called a Mughal "dynastic ideology." This held that the emperor, his ancestors, and his descendants were particularly close to God, who had both given them special knowledge of religious truth and chosen them to govern.

To reinforce the dynastic ideology, the emperor was glorified as never before. Akbar spent lavishly on architects, poets, dancers, and musicians, including the Hindu singer-musician Tansen who created classical North Indian music. Ignoring the orthodox Muslim view that portraiture is a sinful attempt to imitate God's creativity, Akbar sponsored Iranian and Indian painters. In their pictures, he and his successors were painted with haloes, a borrowing from European art. Dynastic ideology merged with Akbar's own beliefs when he initiated most of his nobles into his fire worship. This ensured their loyalty by transforming them into disciples who recognized the emperor as an intermediary between themselves and God. And every morning at dawn, Akbar appeared on the balcony of the palace, where (like a Hindu deity) he gave divine grace to all who glimpsed him.

Under Babur and Humayun, the majority of high-ranking Mughal nobles were Central Asian Muslims, like the emperors themselves. In 1564 the Central Asians rebelled. Akbar defeated them and decided to dilute their strength with men from other backgrounds. Most of these newly minted nobles were Iranian Muslims, but Akbar introduced another new element into the upper Mughal nobility. Early in Akbar's reign, Raja Bharamall Kachhawaha, a Rajput king from Rajasthan, had obtained the emperor's help in resolving difficulties with a local Mughal official. He showed his gratitude by giving Akbar his daughter in marriage, and in return was enrolled as a noble. This opened a century and a half of warm relations between the Mughals and the Rajputs. Most Mughal emperors took Rajput wives, and Rajputs reached the highest levels of the nobility. Never before had a Hindu community been so closely tied to a Muslim dynasty. This secured for the Mughals the loyalty of the Rajput kings and chiefs who dominated much of northern and western India, and let the imperial government draw on their military and administrative skills.

At the same time, Akbar reorganized the nobility with a system of ranks (*mansabs*) that had originated under the Mongols. He assigned a rank to every noble, or *mansabdar*, reserving for himself the right to create, promote, or demote as he saw fit. In return, each mansabdar was to maintain a standing body of troops, trained and equipped to imperial standards. The number of men varied according to the rank of the mansabdar. So did salary, although Akbar reinforced the loyalty of his nobles by paying all of them generously. Mansabdars filled the higher positions in both the army and the administration. To ensure that they could not build up power bases, they were frequently transferred to new appointments, and Indian-born nobles were kept away from their home regions.

Efforts to block the emergence of rivals also underlay Akbar's administrative reforms. He abolished the powerful office of prime minister in favor of four senior ministers, equal in authority and each in charge of a separate branch of the imperial government (such as finance or war). The system was replicated in the provinces into which Akbar divided his dominions, where a governor oversaw law and order, a *diwan* collected taxes, and so on. This ensured that, for example, the governor could not amass the finances to revolt, and the diwan would lack the soldiers. The whole edifice was firmly under the control of Akbar, who daily received and acted upon reports from all over the empire.

All this was underpinned by the efficient system of taxation established by Akbar and his talented finance ministers, notably the Hindu Raja Todar Mall. The land revenue remained the principal tax in India, as it had been for centuries. Between one quarter and one third of the taxes collected each year was retained by the emperor for his household, his soldiers, his clerks, and the like. Most of the rest was used to pay the salaries of the mansabdars. A Mughal noble's pay was usually in the form of a *jagir*. Like the iqta of the Delhi sultanate, a jagir was the right to the revenue from a specified parcel of land, although it did not carry with it the administrative rights to the tract that were normally conferred on recipients of iqtas. Frequent confiscation and redistribution of jagirs gave Akbar yet another means of maintaining control over his mansabdars.

Building on a base laid by Shir Shah, Akbar and his financial advisers remodeled the system of revenue collection. Todar Mall's agents surveyed yields and prices across the empire. Then, taking a ten-year average as their base, they prepared tables for groups of neighboring villages, showing how much tax every possible crop should pay. Depending on the crop, the rate ranged from one fifth to one third of the value. Every year, local chieftains and village headmen ascertained the acreage devoted to each crop and used the tables to calculate the land revenue. The rates were periodically revised with information supplied by village accountants. This rationalized a haphazard system, in which tax collectors had had to negotiate with chieftains or headmen to decide how much land revenue each village would pay. And to simplify the transmission of land revenue to the treasury, peasants were now required to pay their taxes in cash. This forced them to sell their produce, and so channeled agricultural wealth into the general economy.

JAHANGIR AND SHAH JAHAN

The greatest blot on Akbar's generally successful reign was probably his son Salim, named for the Sufi shaikh. While the emperor was campaigning in Ahmadnagar, Salim unsuccessfully tried to seize the throne. This set a pattern for the Mughal Empire: From then on, almost every emperor was challenged by a son who wanted to hurry his own ascension to power. The next installment came in 1605, when Akbar lay dying. This time, it was Salim's seventeen-year-old son Khusrau who attempted a coup. He too failed. Akbar effected a deathbed reconciliation with Salim, who became the fourth Mughal emperor under the name of Jahangir.

Unlike his father, Jahangir remained a devotee of Sufi saints, and he was willing to suppress religious leaders who were likely to provoke unrest. But his mother was the daughter of Raja Bharamall Kachhawaha, and he celebrated the major Hindu festivals and occasionally visited a Hindu holy man. He also maintained the imperial cult, with himself as the master and his nobles as disciples. Jahangir, however, is best remembered for the artistic patronage that he exercised with his favorite wife, Nur Jahan. The imperial couple were particular connoisseurs of painting. They encouraged artists to experiment, and they oversaw the creation of a unique Mughal style. This is one of the great classical schools of art, and its models—a blend of Iranian, Hindu, and European traditions—were followed in India through the nineteenth century.

Jahangir's principal military concern originated in his father's campaigns in Ahmadnagar. What remained of that sultanate passed under the control of Malik Ambar, an African slave and sometime commander in the Ahmadnagar army, who fought the Mughals with guerrilla warfare. In 1608, a Mughal army defeated Malik Ambar. The former slave submitted, but revolted as soon as the imperial force had moved on. This scenario was regularly repeated until Malik Ambar died eighteen years later. Meanwhile, at the other end of the Mughal realm, the Iranians recaptured the frontier town of Qandahar in 1622. Jahangir, by now addicted to a mixture of opium and wine, never recovered from the shock. He died in October 1627, touching off a struggle for succession that ended when his third son Shah Jahan became emperor in January 1628.

Shah Jahan moved the Mughal empire away from Akbar's religious eclecticism. He restored the canonical ban on the construction or repair of non-Muslim places of worship, and ended the imperial cult as un-Islamic. He encouraged the support of his mansabdars through a sense of hereditary noble loyalty to the dynasty, rather than discipleship. But he was by no means illiberal. Hindus, particularly Rajputs, remained prominent in the nobility, and with his favorite wife Mumtaz Mahall, Shah Jahan presided over a flowering of arts and literature.

The emperor's principal interest was architecture, and two of his projects illustrate the union of his Muslim faith with his keen aesthetic sense. After Mumtaz Mahall died in childbirth in 1631, the grieving Shah Jahan commemorated her with the Taj Mahal at Agra, regarded by many as the most beautiful building in the world. The Taj is set in a walled complex, and the whole allegorically represents God sitting in judgment over humanity. While the Taj was being built, Shah Jahan decided to leave Agra and return the capital to Delhi. Grief may have played a part, but the move also had a religious significance, for Delhi was the old seat of Muslim rule in India and was surrounded by the tombs of Islamic holy men. Between 1639 and 1648, Shah Jahan oversaw the construction of Shahjahanabad, now called Old Delhi, the Mughal seat till the dynasty ended in 1857. Its centerpieces are the Red Fort, a great walled palace on the Yamuna river, and the Jami Masjid, the largest mosque in India.

Shah Jahan was as keen on conquest as he was on building. He failed in his attempts to recapture lost ancestral territories in Central Asia and Qandahar, but enjoyed success in the Deccan. He went to war against the remnants of Ahmadnagar, whose defenders came under the command of a Hindu noble named Shahji Bhonsle. Shahji belonged to the Maratha caste, which for generations had served the sultans of Ahmadnagar and Bijapur as administrators and soldiers. In 1636, however, Shahji surrendered, and all of Ahmadnagar was annexed to the Mughal empire. For most of the next fifty years, a shaky peace subsisted between the Mughals and the remaining Deccan sultanates, Bijapur and Golkonda. This allowed the sultans to expand southward into Carnatic, the eastern Deccan coast that once formed part of Vijayanagara. At the same time, the Mughals tried to destabilize their southern neighbors by fomenting discontent among their subjects. Bijapur was badly undermined, as Mughal intrigue sapped the ties of loyalty between the Maratha chieftains and their sultans.

AURANGZEB

The most capable of the four sons of Shah Jahan and Mumtaz Mahall were Dara Shikoh, the eldest and his father's favorite, and Aurangzeb, the third son. These two brothers were not only rivals for the throne but also opposites in temperament and religion. The lazy and arrogant Dara Shikoh had a gift for alienating others. Like his great-grandfather Akbar, he enjoyed theological discussions with Hindus and Jesuits, and believed that all religions contained an identical truth. Aurangzeb was hard-working and a devout Muslim. When Shah Jahan fell seriously ill in September 1657, the four princes began to maneuver for the throne. As they assembled their armies, Shah Jahan unexpectedly recovered, but preparations had reached the point of no return and the brothers went to war.

Aurangzeb defeated Dara Shikoh in May 1658, took Agra, and announced the deposition of Shah Jahan. He went on to Delhi, where he was crowned emperor under the name of Alamgir. When Dara Shikoh fell into his hands a few months later, Aurangzeb decided that he must die. The unorthodox Mughal prince was tried for apostasy and idolatry, convicted, and executed. Another brother, Murad Bakhsh, was later executed on charges of murder; the remaining brother, Muhammad Shuja, fled to what is now Burma and met his death there. Shah Jahan lived out his days in captivity in Agra fort.

Aurangzeb resolved to complete Shah Jahan's transformation of Akbar's empire into a Muslim state. He eliminated the surviving vestiges of the imperial cult, ending his daily public appearances and patronage of secular artistic projects. Nobles and members of the imperial family continued to sponsor the arts, but the withdrawal of the emperor's lavish support closed the great age of Mughal culture. The ulama regained the power that they had lost in the 1580s, and Aurangzeb reiterated his father's orders for the destruction of all newly built or repaired non-Muslim places of worship. The process culminated in 1679, when the jizya was restored. None of these measures was thoroughly enforced, but the mere fact that imperial policy now treated non-Muslims as second-class citizens provoked resentment.

But there was more to Aurangzeb than philistinism and religious bigotry. He supported architects and intellectuals whose work was compatible with Islam—for example, the builders of the Pearl Mosque at Delhi and the Imperial Mosque at Lahore, or the philosopher Danishmand Khan who was equally familiar with Hindu thought and the works of René Descartes. Political considerations probably outweighed the emperor's unquestionably sincere faith in such incidents as the execution of Dara Shikoh. Aurangzeb's troubled relations with the Sikh religion show the same mixture of religious and secular causes. Sikhism was founded by Nanak (1469–1539), a Punjabi Hindu belonging to a merchant caste. In a long quest for religious truth, Nanak probably talked with Hindus and Muslims, and traveled to holy places inside and outside India. He was strongly influenced by the teachings of Kabir, a weaver who asserted that neither the Hindu Vedas nor the Muslim Quran was true. Kabir dismissed image worship, fasts, and pilgrimages as irrelevant to salvation, and instead advised worshipers to build their love for God until they lost themselves in Him.

Nanak eventually developed his own theology and preached it to a growing circle of disciples or Sikhs. It centers on a loving God with the power to intervene and save us from the rebirth that, Sikhs agree with Hindus, is our natural fate. In return, we must love and fear God at all times, and live honestly and charitably. God reveals Himself to us when we envelope ourselves in His Word and His Name, which are embodied in the sacred verses composed by such teachers (*gurus*) as Kabir and Nanak. Our ultimate goal must be to overcome our blinding self-centeredness so that we can recognize the handiwork of God in everything in the universe, whether natural forces, inanimate objects, living beings, or emotions. As a corollary to this, we must not treat people differently according to their caste, sex, or nationality, for all are created equal.

When Nanak died, his chosen successor Angad became the second guru of the Sikhs (1539–1552). He was followed by Amar Das (1552–1574), Ram Das (1574–1581), and Arjan (1581–1606). Their tenures saw the spread of Sikhism among Punjabis of all religions and classes. The faith now has 19 million adherents in India, most of them in Punjab, forming 1.9 percent of the total population of the country. Meanwhile, a distinct Sikh identity emerged. One of its pillars was Amritsar, "the essence of the nectar of immortality," a sacred pool built by Ram Das. The Golden Temple, the spiritual center of Sikhism, was afterwards built in the pool, and the city of Amritsar grew up around it. Another pillar was the Adi Granth (First Book) or Granth Sahib (Honored Book), the Sikh scriptures, compiled in 1604 from the writings of Kabir, the Sikh gurus, and other holy men.

Arjan had good relations with Akbar, who met him in 1598. But the gurus were not without enemies. Some of these were schismatic Sikhs, who followed such gurus of their own as Arjan's brother Prithi Chand. Others were Mughal officials who were jealous or fearful of the wealth and power of the gurus. In 1606, Arjan was arrested and executed by Jahangir. This was supposedly because the guru had blessed the emperor's rebellious son Khusrau, although it has been suggested that the emperor was actually influenced by slanders against Arjan, or that he disliked the Sikhs because of their active proselytization.

The gurus Hargobind (1606–1644), Har Ray (1644–1661), and Har Krishan (1661–1664) generally avoided confrontation with the secular authorities by living in the Hindu kingdoms of Himachal Pradesh, which paid tribute to the Mughals but enjoyed considerable autonomy. After the death of Har Krishan, political and religious quarrels took relations between Sikhs and emperor to a new low. Aurangzeb, who was now emperor, wanted to see Har Krishan's brother, his friend Ram Ray, as the new guru, but the position instead went to Hargobind's son Tegh Bahadur (1664–1675). The bad feelings between Aurangzeb and Tegh Bahadur were worsened by the emperor's religious policy, which among other things led to the demolition of at least one Sikh temple. In the end, Tegh Bahadur decided to uphold his faith through martyrdom. After naming his son Gobind Das as his successor, he allowed himself to be arrested in 1675, and through his defiance of both the emperor and Islam ensured his own execution at Delhi.

SHIVAJI

After Shah Jahan's conquest of Ahmadnagar in 1636, Shahji the Maratha entered the army of the sultan of Bijapur, whom he served in the campaigns in Carnatic. He made over his lands in the Pune area of northern Bijapur to his young son Shivaji. Shivaji afterwards took advantage of the long illness of the sultan, and the effects of destabilization by the Mughals, to acquire suzerainty over hilltop fortresses and rural Maratha chieftains on both sides of the border between Bijapur and the old Ahmadnagar sultanate. He adopted the administrative forms of the sultans who had ruled before him, and like them governed through a bureaucracy composed largely of Brahmins.

Shivaji's expansionism led to war with the Mughals in 1659. Four years later, after the Marathas raided the principal imperial military camp in the Deccan and sacked the great port of Surat in Gujarat, Aurangzeb sent a huge army into Maharashtra. The Marathas and Mughals were fighting different wars, for Shivaji relied on guerrilla tactics and Aurangzeb on sieges and battles, and this meant that neither side could win. Eventually, Shivaji agreed to enter Aurangzeb's service and surrender the majority of his forts in return for recognition of his title to his remaining possessions. In 1666, the Maratha was summoned to the imperial court. The visit went badly. Aurangzeb regarded his guest as an upstart chieftain, not the regional overlord he had become, and after a few months an angry Shivaji returned home. After consolidating his power, he reopened the war. He recaptured his lost forts, sacked Surat again, and raided Mughal territory, and in 1674 had himself crowned king in a Hindu ceremony. This represented a formal declaration of independence from the Mughals and Bijapur, and also ensured the legitimacy of his authority in the eyes of his Brahmin officials and Maratha chieftains.

On Shivaji's death in 1680, his son Sambhaji assumed the Maratha throne. The new king soon acquired an unexpected ally. The previous year, several Rajput clans in Rajasthan had revolted against Aurangzeb. As Hindus, the Rajputs were unhappy with the new Islamic policy (although Rajput mansabdars were exempted from the reimposed jizya), but they were more concerned over infringements of their privileges: a sharp fall in the proportion of Rajputs in the high nobility, a reduction in their lucrative jagir holdings, and the emperor's interference in a succession dispute in the Rajput kingdom of Jodhpur. Aurangzeb despatched his youngest son Muhammad Akbar to quell the uprising. The prince, however, first joined the revolt, then fled to Sambhaji in Maharashtra.

For the next twenty years, skirmishes continued between Mughal troops and Rajput warriors. To Aurangzeb, however, a greater danger lay in the possibility that Muhammad Akbar might forge an alliance of the Marathas, the Rajputs, and the Bijapur and Golkonda sultanates. To forestall it, he decided to bring the south under Mughal rule. He therefore assumed personal command of his army in the Deccan, and led it to victory after victory. He conquered Bijapur in 1686 and Golkonda in 1687. Then, Muhammad Akbar fled to Iran, and in 1689 Aurangzeb captured and executed Sambhaji. The old Mughal now ruled the greatest empire in Indian history, covering the whole of the subcontinent except its southernmost tip.

THE ECONOMY OF MUGHAL INDIA

In the late seventeenth century, the Mughal empire had between 100 million and 150 million people. The relative peace and security that followed the establishment of Mughal rule in most of India, the reduction of taxes on internal trade, and government encouragement of the cultivation of waste and forested lands, all had contributed to a vigorous commercial and agricultural economy across much of the subcontinent.

Foreign trade also flourished. During the reign of Jahangir, the Portuguese were driven from their hundred-year-old command of the Indian Ocean by two merchant firms, the English and the Dutch East India Companies, founded in 1600 and 1602 respectively. In 1664, they were joined by a French East India Company. On the coasts and inland, the European companies built trading posts, or "factories," where their agents purchased export goods to ship to Europe, the Far East, and America. India's exports ranged from indigo to saltpeter, but they were dominated by cotton cloths. These had long been sent to Indonesia, and they became phenomenally popular in Europe after their introduction there by the English and Dutch companies near the beginning of the seventeenth century. The Europeans paid for most of their purchases with silver, much of it from the Spanish colonies in the New World.

THE DECLINE OF THE MUGHAL EMPIRE

The execution of Sambhaji marked the beginning of the end of the Mughal empire. For the next six decades, much of India was torn by warfare, and the Mughal administrative system collapsed. Despite year after year of campaigning in the Deccan, Aurangzeb was unable to capture the new Maratha king, Sambhaji's brother Rajaram, whose men carried on a guerrilla war. After Rajaram's death, the struggle was continued by his widow Tarabai. All the while, local chieftains in Maharashtra continually changed sides in search of favorable terms, until neither the imperial nor the Maratha government could exercise authority over large parts of the countryside. The spiraling anarchy, and the efforts of the two administrations to collect taxes and military supplies, severely disrupted trade and agriculture. Trade through Surat virtually dried up, and Bombay, an old Portuguese station that now belonged to the English East India Company, gradually replaced Surat as the principal port on the west coast. Maratha warrior bands took advantage of their newfound freedom to raid further and further afield for plunder. During the first decade of the eighteenth century, they poured out of Maharashtra into Andhra Pradesh, Madhya Pradesh, and Gujarat.

Meanwhile, from 1685 the area around Agra was torn by a rebellion among the Jats, members of a large cultivating community of North India, who disrupted the main road linking Delhi to the Deccan. In the following decade, the guru Gobind Das (1675–1708) showed the strength of the Sikhs when his men helped defeat Mughal troops who had been sent to collect tribute from refractory kings in Himachal Pradesh. Gobind Das also sought to make good his claim to be the only true living guru in the face of rival claimants, and in 1699 he united his military and religious endeavors. Before a great body of Sikhs who had gathered to celebrate the spring festival of Baisakhi, Gobind Das established his Khalsa or Pure Ones, a body of Sikh men who underwent an initiation of his own devising. The guru and his initiates took the name of Singh ("lion"), Gobind Das becoming Gobind Singh. Members of the Khalsa were required to bear arms and were forbidden to cut their hair, and were unquestionably loyal to the guruship of Gobind Singh, who insisted that they were the only authentic Sikhs. Himachal Pradesh kings, fearful of the growing power of the guru in their midst, persuaded Aurangzeb to send an army against Gobind Singh. This touched off a war between the Mughals and the Khalsa.

By now, wars, bad harvests, and a reluctance of local chieftains to cooperate with a government that could no longer maintain order had made the collection of the land revenue increasingly uncertain. This hit at the salaries of the mansabdars, whose consequent demoralization was increased when Aurangzeb sought to secure the adherence of Muslim and Maratha nobles from the Deccan by promoting them over the heads of North Indians who belonged to families that had served the Mughals for generations. Inevitably, the mansabdars' loyalty to the emperor began to fray.

Aurangzeb died in the Deccan in 1707. The usual war of succession among his three surviving sons was won by Bahadur Shah, who tried to restore order. He released Sambhaji's son Shahu, who had lived at the Mughal court since 1689 but now returned to Maharashtra to claim his father's throne. This split the Marathas between the supporters of Shahu and of his sister-in-law Tarabai. Bahadur Shah also ended his father's quarrel with Gobind Singh. But peace was short-lived. In 1708, Gobind Singh was murdered. He had indicated that the Granth Sahib and the will of the Khalsa could jointly lead the Sikhs, rendering a living guru unnecessary. The human guruship therefore now fell vacant. Meanwhile, despite the truce between Gobind Singh and Bahadur Shah, Mughal officials in Punjab had continued to persecute the Sikhs. Not long before his death, the guru told a Sikh named Banda Bahadur to lead the Khalsa against their oppressors. Banda Bahadur launched a revolt that ended Mughal control over much of eastern Punjab and northern Haryana. A desperate Bahadur Shah led his army to Punjab, where he died in 1712. Yet another war of succession ended in the accession of Bahadur Shah's son Jahandar Shah. The new emperor was drunken and frivolous, and left the administration to Zu'l-Fiqar Khan, a mansabdar who had helped him defeat his brothers. Zu'l-Fiqar Khan desperately tried to win support for his regime: He abolished the jizya; showered titles and lands on Rajput kings; even appointed Sambhaji II, Tarabai's candidate for the Maratha kingship, as a mansabdar.

Within months, however, Jahandar Shah's nephew Farrukhsiyar laid claim to the throne. He obtained the support of the brothers Sayyid Husain Ali and Sayyid Abdallah Khan, members of an old noble Indian Muslim family. With an army supplied by the Sayyids, Farrukhsiyar seized power and executed Jahandar Shah and Zu'l-Fiqar Khan. The following years saw several victories for Mughal arms and diplomacy. In 1715, Banda Bahadur and 700 of his fellow Khalsa warriors were captured and executed, and in 1718 Sayyid Husain Ali ended the Mughals' war with the Marathas by concluding a treaty with Shahu. The agreement recognized Shahu as ruler of the Maratha conquests in the Deccan and granted him a share of the imperial revenues that had been claimed by the Maratha kings since Shivaji (amounting to 35 percent of the revenues in the Deccan, and 25 percent in Madhya Pradesh and Gujarat). In return, Shahu agreed to supply the Sayyid brothers with tribute and soldiers.

Meanwhile, Farrukhsiyar lived in constant terror that the Sayyids would turn on him, and devoted himself to intriguing against them rather than to ruling his empire. In 1719, the standoff ended when the combined armies of Husain Ali and Shahu overthrew Farrukhsiyar. The Sayyids installed three grandsons of Bahadur Shah as puppet emperors in rapid succession, Rafi ud-Darjat, Rafi ud-Daula, and Muhammad Shah. But Husain Ali and Abdallah Khan were unpopular among many mansabdars of Iranian and Central Asian background on account of their Indian origins and the pro-Hindu tendencies that the alliance with Shahu seemed to demonstrate. In 1720, the Central Asian Nizam ul-Mulk defeated the Sayyid and Maratha armies. The new emperor Muhammad Shah quickly transferred his support to Nizam ul-Mulk, and the two Sayyids were murdered.

MUHAMMAD SHAH

Under Muhammad Shah, the Mughal empire disintegrated. Like Farrukhsiyar, he spent more time plotting against his nobles than governing. Left to their own devices, Mughal governors and mansabdars drifted into independence. Murshid Quli Khan was a textbook case. A Brahmin slave who had converted to Islam, he rose to the office of diwan (head of the revenue collection) for Bengal, Bihar, and Orissa. In the time of Farrukhsiyar, he acquired the additional position of governor, violating

Mughal practice that had always kept the two functions separate. Now, Murshid Quli Khan could apply the revenues of his provinces directly to his own administration, although he continued to send his surplus funds to Delhi where they formed a bulwark of the imperial finances.

Muhammad Shah's lack of interest in his eastern provinces allowed Murshid Quli Khan to consolidate his position. He reduced the power of local chieftains and filled the administration with his dependents (often his own relatives or Bengali Hindus). He maintained stability, so that trade flourished, and conducted the first reassessment of the land revenue since Raja Todar Mall's survey. On his death, it seemed natural for the government of Bengal, Bihar and Orissa to pass to his son-in-law Shuja ud-Din Muhammad Khan (1727–1739). Shuja ud-Din still sent funds to Delhi, but by the time he died, he was effectively an independent monarch paying tribute rather than a governor remitting the revenue. Finally, Allahwardi Khan (1740–1756) began to retain all the revenues of Bengal and Bihar for himself, severing the last real bond between Delhi and eastern India. It was much the same story in the province of Awadh in Uttar Pradesh, under the governorships of Saadat Khan (1722–1739) and his nephew Safdar Jang (1739–1754), of whom the latter extended his control over the neighboring province of Allahabad.

Nizam ul-Mulk, the Central Asian nobleman who had overthrown the Sayyid brothers, found that he could not dominate the government at Delhi. He retired south to the old Golkonda capital of Hyderabad, from where he ruled much of the Deccan until his death in 1748. At first, peninsular India was a patchwork of territories controlled by Nizam ul-Mulk and the Marathas. The situation gradually solidified, so that Nizam ul-Mulk dominated the eastern Deccan, and the Marathas the western.

Nearer to Delhi, the Rajput kings asserted their autonomy in Rajasthan, and seized Mughal districts that bordered on their lands. The Ruhela and Bangash clans of Afghans took control of the region between Delhi and Awadh, and the Jats established themselves as masters of much of Agra province. Punjab headed toward independence under the governor Abd us-Samad Khan and his family. They were challenged by a hard core of the Khalsa that went into outlawry after the execution of Banda Bahadur, plundering and killing anyone associated with the Mughal government. By 1748, the Khalsa ruled much of East Punjab, including Amritsar.

By the time that Farrukhsiyar came to the throne, Maharashtra was torn by civil war between the rival members of Shivaji's family, Shahu and Tarabai. Bands of Maratha peasants and soldiers turned to banditry and indiscriminately raided the lands of the two claimants and the

Mughals. Order was gradually restored by Balaji Vishvanath Bhat, a member of the Chitpavan subcaste of Brahmins. Beginning as a clerk, Balaji rose to become Shahu's peshwa or prime minister in 1713. He won over many of Tarabai's supporters, defeated several Mughal armies, and in 1718 negotiated the treaty with Sayyid Husain Ali that recognized Maratha rule in the Deccan. Balaji filled his bureaucracy with fellow Chitpavans and other Brahmins, whose hereditary experience of administration went back to the days of the Deccan sultans. He also established good relations with the great Brahmin banking families of Maharashtra, and from them borrowed sufficient money to create an effective administration. Balaji died in 1720. By then, anarchy had given way to a functioning Maratha government in much of Maharashtra. Shahu named Balaji's son Bajirav to be the new peshwa. Bajirav made the peshwa the real head of the Maratha kingdom, which for the next century was ruled by his family; Shahu and his successors were reduced to symbolic kings.

During the 1720s, Bajirav incorporated the independent bands of part-time Maratha warriors into a professional army, commanded by men of unimpeachable loyalty. He turned this force on the Mughal provinces to the north, and by his death in 1740, the Marathas had replaced the Mughals as the rulers of much of Madhya Pradesh and almost all of Gujarat. Expansion came at the price of increasing decentralization. In 1731, Bajirav ended the Maratha civil war by recognizing Tarabai's candidate Sambhaji II as ruler of the Kolhapur area in southern Maharashtra. Looking to this precedent, Maratha commanders in Gujarat and Malwa demanded a share of the conquests. Bajirav agreed to divide the new provinces, keeping some districts for himself and allocating others to his commanders in return for their continued allegiance to his government.

Under Bajirav's son Nana Saheb or Balvantrav (1740–1761), the Marathas ranged even further afield. In the 1740s they began incursions into Rajasthan, often at the invitation of Rajput princes who gave them lands and tribute in return for help in seizing the throne. To the east, a Maratha warrior named Raghuji Bhonsle first acquired mastery over the Gond (Tribal) kingdom of Nagpur, and then began to raid the territories of Allahwardi Khan of Bengal, Bihar, and Orissa. In 1751, he compelled Allahwardi Khan to transfer Orissa to Maratha rule.

Meanwhile, in 1736, the emperor of Iran was overthrown by an officer named Nadir Shah. The new monarch moved on to conquer what is now Afghanistan, including the Mughal province of Kabul, then invaded India, and in February 1739 defeated a Mughal army outside Delhi. When some of his soldiers were killed after entering the capital in search of loot, Nadir Shah ordered a general massacre. Twenty thousand Delhiites were slain. The Mughal emperor Muhammad Shah was compelled to pay an indemnity of 20 million rupees and to cede all his territories west of the Indus. Carrying a fortune in gold, silver, and jewels, Nadir Shah returned to Iran in May 1739, after vividly demonstrating the utter impotence of the Mughal empire. Muhammad Shah died nine years later, in 1748. By then, imperial authority was confined to Delhi and the surrounding territories to a distance of fifty miles.

5

A Century of Realignment

MUGHALS AND MARATHAS

Under Muhammad Shah's son Ahmad Shah (1748–1754), the Mughal empire no longer existed. Nevertheless, the governors who had made themselves independent in Bengal, Awadh, and elsewhere continued to recognize the nominal supremacy of the emperor. Most called themselves not king but *nawab*, the plural of *naib* or "deputy." Across India, new dynasts maintained Mughal forms of government and issued Mughal-style coins. Even the Marathas and Sikhs looked to the phantom emperor for recognition of their titles and conquests. The Mughals also enjoyed spiritual authority over many Indian Muslims, particularly after Muhammad Shah resumed the function (renounced by Aurangzeb) of interpreting Islamic law.

Yet whatever their attitude to his office, the regional rulers had little respect for the person of the emperor. Ahmad Shah was dominated by nawab Safdar Jang of Awadh, until Imad ul-Mulk (a grandson of Nizam ul-Mulk) and a Maratha army replaced him with Alamgir II (1754–1759). After Imad ul-Mulk murdered Alamgir II, the latter's son Shah Alam II (1759–1806) lived in Awadh under the protection of Safdar Jang's successor Shuja ud-Daula. In 1771, the Maratha warlord Mahadji Scindia took Delhi, and the following year Shah Alam returned to the capital as his puppet. These powerless emperors sought to boost their self-respect by taking the names of their more illustrious ancestors: Alamgir I had been Aurangzeb, and Shah Alam I was Bahadur Shah.

Meanwhile, the nawabs, peshwas, and other inheritors of Mughal power were establishing orderly states. By the mid-eighteenth century, the near anarchy that parts of India had seen since the time of Aurangzeb was over. This allowed the economy to grow rapidly, which both enriched the new states and drew the European East India Companies deeper into Indian trade.

In the 1750s, the most powerful ruler in India was the Maratha peshwa Nana Saheb. His empire extended across the western Deccan, Orissa, Madhya Pradesh, Gujarat, Rajasthan, and Punjab. He might have become master of all India, but this was prevented by a series of events that began with the assassination of Nadir Shah of Iran in 1747. What is now Afghanistan was seized by an officer named Ahmad Shah Durrani, who raided India several times and in 1756–1757 imitated Nadir Shah by sacking Delhi. In 1759–1760 Durrani drove the Marathas from Punjab, and then moved into Haryana. Skirmishing between the Afghan and Maratha armies culminated in 1761 in a battle at Panipat, the place near Delhi where Babur had defeated sultan Ibrahim Lodi. Durrani won a crushing victory, and he and his men took whatever they could carry back to Afghanistan.

The 50,000 dead at Panipat included several Maratha leaders, and Nana Saheb died soon after the battle. Maratha power in north India evaporated. The Marathas were further weakened by struggles between the new peshwa, Nana Saheb's son Madhavrav I, and his uncle Raghunathrav. Maratha warlords used the situation to make independent states of the provinces that they had shared with the peshwa since the 1730s. Madhavrav died in 1772. The next year, his heir Narayanrav was killed by partisans of Raghunathrav, who challenged Narayanrav's son Madhavrav II. This touched off a civil war, which pitted Madhavrav's guardian Nana Phadnis against Raghunathrav.

Nana Phadnis secured the support of the warlords. Raghunathrav obtained troops from the British East India Company in return for territory and money (British rather than English, because since 1707 England had been joined with Scotland in the kingdom of Great Britain). In 1779, however, Nana Phadnis and the warlord Mahadji Scindia defeated Raghunathrav. Phadnis and Scindia then vied for control of the Marathas until Scindia's death in 1794.

In the wake of the Maratha defeat at Panipat, Sikh warriors overran

Punjab and northern Haryana. By the 1770s the region was divided into over sixty principalities, most of them ruled by Khalsa Sikhs. These chieftains employed non-Khalsa and even non-Sikh administrators and soldiers, and gave their patronage to religious persons and institutions of all religions. Nevertheless, the late eighteenth century saw the steady absorption of schismatic Sikhs into the Khalsa.

Meanwhile, in the 1750s, a Muslim army officer named Haidar Ali had risen to power in the Hindu kingdom of Mysore in south India. After Panipat, he extended his sway over all Karnataka. In 1782 he was succeeded by his son Tipu Sultan, who conquered Kerala. Haidar Ali and Tipu Sultan were among the greatest Indian rulers of the eighteenth century. They boosted their collection of land revenue, often eliminating local chieftains and dealing directly with peasants, and controlled the trade of southwestern India. With their wealth, they created a modern army, with European training and tactics, which they used to good effect against the British. In 1790–1792, however, the British, now allied with the nizam (ruler) of Hyderabad and the Marathas, defeated Tipu Sultan. The victorious allies annexed half of Mysore's territory.

THE BRITISH EAST INDIA COMPANY

In the eighteenth century, the ships of the British East India Company and the British Royal Navy dominated the Indian Ocean, and the governors of the Company's three main factories at Madras, Calcutta, and Bombay presided over a flourishing trade. The six months' voyage to Britain made them virtually independent of their directors in London. After 1750, Company agents in India profited by this autonomy to acquire territory.

They began in the Deccan. The French and British Companies were bitter rivals in the dominions of Nizam ul-Mulk, the ruler of Hyderabad. In 1744, war broke out between Britain and France. The French captured the British post at Madras. They returned it after the coming of peace in 1748, but now the Companies competed by entering local power struggles. For several years, two families had been dueling for the post of nawab of Carnatic, the Hyderabad governor on the southeast coast. Then, the death of Nizam ul-Mulk in 1748 touched off a succession dispute in Hyderabad itself.

Joseph Dupleix, governor of the French factory at Pondicherry, used Indian mercenaries, trained in European tactics, to install on the thrones of Carnatic and Hyderabad rulers who were friendly to French interests. Robert Clive of the British Company now imitated Dupleix, using Indian troops to support pro-British claimants in Carnatic and Hyderabad. Both Dupleix and Clive adopted the Indian practice of subsidiary alliance with their new friends: The pro-French or pro-British rulers agreed to pay tribute (called a "subsidy") in return for military protection. The French and British used the subsidies to build up powerful armies, which they employed against each other during the Seven Years' War of 1756–1763. The British won the war all across the globe, and virtually ended French activity in India.

Meanwhile, trade with the British, French, and Dutch Companies helped make Bengal and Bihar wealthy. This invited attacks by the Marathas, the Afghans, and the nawab of Awadh. To meet the danger, nawab Allahwardi Khan of Bengal and Bihar pressed nobles, bankers, zamindars, and the Companies for money. (Zamindars, literally possessors of the land, collected the land revenue from cultivators or local chieftains, and passed it on to the government. They usually also administered justice and maintained order, and were the descendants of Hindu petty rulers or Muslim officials appointed by the Mughals and nawabs.)

In 1756, Allahwardi Khan was succeeded by his great-nephew Siraj ud-Daula. The new nawab dismissed most of his predecessor's civilian and military officials, including a general named Mir Jafar. This lost him much support among the nobility. Then, Siraj ud-Daula's demands for money alienated the powerful banking firm of Jagat Seth (Banker of the World), the zamindars, and the European Companies. When the British rejected his demands, Siraj ud-Daula seized their factory at Calcutta. It has been suggested that the nawab engineered the episode so that he could destroy Calcutta's new fortifications: Though these were directed primarily against the French, they might one day allow the Company to defy the nawab's authority.

At Madras, Clive had assembled British and Indian soldiers to use against the French in the Seven Years' War. He took them to Bengal instead and recaptured Calcutta. There, he learned that the firm of Jagat Seth was plotting to replace Siraj ud-Daula with Mir Jafar. Clive joined the conspiracy and agreed to supply troops. On June 23, 1757, the armies of the Company and Siraj ud-Daula met at Plassey. The nawab was captured and killed, and Mir Jafar was installed on the throne. He rewarded the British Company with money and privileges (including immunity from customs payments in his territories), and abolished the trading rights of the French Company. Almost immediately, however, he found that he could pay neither the promised rewards nor the expenses of a Company army that protected him. His impotence was made obvious when Company soldiers—not his own—defeated invasions of Bengal by the emperor Shah Alam and the Marathas. A resentful Mir Jafar began to plot, until in 1760 the British deposed him in favor of his son-in-law Mir Qasim.

Mir Qasim wanted to leave coastal Bengal to the British and exclude them from the rest of his territories, but this was impossible. The Company let its employees (and other Britons) trade within Asia for their own benefit, so long as they did not infringe on the Company's monopoly of commerce with Britain. After 1757, British traders spread through Bengal and Bihar and applied Mir Jafar's concession of freedom from customs to their own as well as Company business. Meanwhile, the Company continually demanded more money from the nawab. Conflict was inevitable. The Company won, deposed Mir Qasim, and restored Mir Jafar. Mir Qasim fled, and in 1764 he joined with Shuja ud-Daula of Awadh and the emperor Shah Alam to invade Bihar. They were defeated by the Company's army. Mir Jafar died soon afterwards, and the British chose his successor.

In 1765, Robert Clive became the Company's governor at Calcutta. To ensure sufficient revenues, he secured from Shah Alam the Company's appointment to the old Mughal post of diwan of Bengal and Bihar. This made the Company responsible for collecting the revenues of the two provinces. In return, Clive undertook to pay tribute to Shah Alam, although remittances ceased after the emperor came under Maratha domination on his return to Delhi seven years later. As in Mughal times, the offices of governor and diwan of Bengal and Bihar were separate, after having been united in the person of the nawab since the beginning of the eighteenth century. Moreover, the nawab, now reduced to the single post of governor, was compelled to hand over his remaining duties to a deputy, chosen by the Company, which gradually assumed his functions. By 1790, when the position of deputy nawab was abolished, Bengal and Bihar were fully under British rule; and Calcutta had replaced the nawab's seat as the capital.

The Company moved into government to increase its revenues and allegedly because of a feeling on the part of many Britons that Indian officials were inherently oppressive. Company employees, however, were no better. After 1765, Clive began to restrain extortion by his subordinates, but their mismanagement and corruption helped ensure a constant shortfall in revenues. The return to Britain of once-penniless men with fortunes from India seemed to confirm that misrule was rampant in the Company's territories. When the Company requested a loan to cover its expenses, the British prime minister, Lord North, saw an opportunity for rectifying matters. His price was governmental control over the Company, instituted by Parliament in 1773 through the Regulating Act and strengthened with the India Act of 1784 and the Charter Act of 1793.

To consolidate the channels of communication between London and India, the 1773 act gave the Company's governor at Calcutta the title of governor-general and put the foreign relations of his counterparts at Madras and Bombay under his supervision. The autonomy of Madras and Bombay was later further curtailed. The first governor-general was a Company employee, Warren Hastings, but (in an effort to ensure impartiality) his successors were usually British aristocrats with no experience of India. The 1784 act placed the Company directors in London under the supervision of a Board of Control, composed of British politicians, which made the British government the ultimate master of the Company.

Britons almost universally agreed that the primary purpose of the Company was to make money and that Bengal and Bihar could be used to this end. Profits required law and order, which allowed trade to flourish and taxes to be collected. The Company therefore built up its Bengal army. Indian troops were supplemented with British soldiers of the Company and the regular British armies. At the same time, the Company disbanded the potentially rival armies of the nawab, zamindars, and chieftains.

Even before 1757, the Company occasionally bypassed Indian middlemen and bought export goods directly from producers. This practice now increased. Political power let the Company control production. For example, peasants were compelled to grow such crops as indigo and to accept low prices for them. After Plassey, the French and Dutch Companies stopped trading in Bengal, but the British had no objection to individual private foreign traders in their new dominions and American, Danish, Portuguese, and French merchants testified to the vitality of Indian commerce.

The acquisition of the office of diwan changed trade between India and Britain. Unlike previous diwans, the Company did not spend its revenues solely on the administration of Bengal and Bihar. It began to use local taxes—rather than the imported silver used before 1765—to buy exports in Bengal, and applied profits from the sale of Indian goods in London towards its expenses in Britain. These expenses ranged from supplies to shareholders' dividends. The result was that the new diwan was constantly in need of money. Some of the need was filled through government monopolies over salt and opium, which were widely consumed in India. Much of the opium was also exported, to Britain and especially China and Southeast Asia, and in the 1820s opium sales provided 10 percent of the revenues of the Bengal government.

The land revenue remained the principal tax, however. The Company initially contracted collection to Indian entrepreneurs. The yield was never satisfactory, though, and in the 1780s it fell precipitously. For reasons that are unclear, there was a crisis in the rural economy of Bengal and Bihar. Some have pointed to a famine that killed between one fifth and one third of the population of Bengal in 1769–1770; others to a breakdown in law and order after the establishment of British rule; still others to a general economic decline that affected the Middle East and South Asia in the mid-eighteenth century.

Lord Cornwallis, governor-general from 1786 to 1793, sought to solve the revenue crisis. He believed that corruption among the Company's Indian and British employees was partly to blame. In his mind, Indians were irremediably dishonest, and he banned them from higher posts in the Company's administration and trade. Indeed, Cornwallis exemplified a new racist climate of opinion that soon virtually ended the once-close business and social ties between Company employees and Indians, as well as sexual relationships between British men and Indian women. To replace the supposedly corrupt Indians and Britons, Cornwallis recruited educated men from good families in Britain, selected by patronage and later by competitive examination. In return for generous salaries, they were barred from private trade. They formed a corps of elite administrators, eventually known as the Indian Civil Service, and oversaw a huge body of Indian and British subordinates.

In 1793, Cornwallis appointed a British "collector" in each of the districts into which Bengal and Bihar were divided. As the designation implies, the collector received revenues, but he also headed the district administration, which was now firmly in British hands. The same year, the governor-general implemented the Permanent Settlement, so called because it set the land revenue assessment forever. Henceforth, each zamindar in Bengal and Bihar was to remit the annual land revenue at the level collected in 1789–1790. If he paid, he owned the land outright. Otherwise, it was sold. As a corollary, cultivators were now regarded as tenants of the zamindar, and the payments they made were treated as rent.

For many years, supporters had argued that a Permanent Settlement would encourage zamindars to promote agricultural improvement among their cultivators: By setting the land revenue in perpetuity, it would make the zamindars want to maximize productivity, because they (rather than the government) would pocket its fruits. And recognizing zamindars as owners of the land, rather than merely of the right to receive and remit its revenue, would make land a salable commodity, whose value its new owners would want to increase. The ensuing rural prosperity would ensure that the Company never received less than the assessed revenue. This, and the creation of an aristocracy that owed its position to British rule and would presumably support its continuation, were held to be sufficient compensation for the fact that the land revenue would never increase.

The first result of the Permanent Settlement, however, was the breakup and sale of virtually all the large estates in Bengal and Bihar, as the great zamindars defaulted on their payments. This was largely because the nawabs and the British had undermined the power that zamindars required to collect revenue from thousands of peasants, especially by abolishing private armies. Some land was bought by wealthy Indian merchants or Company employees from Calcutta. Most of the purchasers, however, were zamindars of existing smaller estates, who already had to be efficient at collecting, or employees of great zamindars.

At the beginning of the nineteenth century, inflation raised the value of agricultural produce. Zamindars who had survived thus far could now enhance rents without needing to encourage improvement, and the peasants of Bengal and Bihar were increasingly exploited. This, however, was due not so much to the Permanent Settlement as to population, which had always governed the relationship between cultivators and the recipients of their dues. When peasants were scarce, a zamindar attracted them with favorable terms. In case of a population surplus, he offered bad terms (such as high rent), which peasants had to accept if they wanted land. In the nineteenth century, the population of Bengal and Bihar grew fast, thanks to the absence of great famines or floods, and this let zamindars increase rents without any fear of losing tenants.

LORD WELLESLEY

In 1798, Lord Wellesley, the brother of the Duke of Wellington, was appointed governor-general. He launched a half century of expansion which ended in Company supremacy over the entire Indian subcontinent. Wellesley desired glory and was also convinced that Indians were better off under British rule than under that of their compatriots. The war between Britain and Revolutionary France, which had begun in 1793, aroused his fears of French officers who served in the Maratha and Hyderabad armies, and of Tipu Sultan of Mysore who had sought an alliance with France. Moreover, Wellesley realized that Indian resources could serve British interests worldwide.

Wellesley first went to war with Tipu Sultan, who was defeated and killed in 1799. Part of his kingdom was restored to its old Hindu royal family, now under British supremacy. The remainder was divided between the Company and Hyderabad. Then came the subsidiary allies, by now Carnatic, Hyderabad, and Awadh. Subsidiary alliances invariably undermined Indian rulers. To pay the subsidy, they either squeezed their subjects for revenue or borrowed money. In the latter case, repayment again necessitated extortion. Either way, the result was oppression, revolt, and administrative collapse. Wellesley annexed Carnatic, then forced the rulers of Hyderabad and Awadh to accept tighter British control and to cede much of their territory.

Meanwhile, Maratha power was collapsing. In 1795, the peshwa Madhavrav committed suicide. This touched off a Maratha civil war, in which the new peshwa, Bajirav II, and the warlords constantly switched sides. Wellesley used the conflict to bring the Marathas under British control. The first Maratha state to fall was that of the Gaekwad family, in Gujarat. In 1802, the Company helped the ruling Gaekwad against a rival, at the price of a subsidiary alliance. The same year, Bajirav II signed a treaty that placed all the Maratha territories under British supremacy, in return for military support. The warlords Holkar, Scindia, and Bhonsle refused to recognize the agreement and went to war with the Company. In 1803, the British defeated Scindia and Bhonsle, who entered subsidiary alliances and ceded territory. The Company's acquisitions included Delhi from Scindia and Orissa from Bhonsle. The war continued, however, draining Company revenues. When Wellesley refused to make peace, the directors dismissed him in 1805.

The Maratha war ended the following year, but its effects were felt for another decade. War debts cut deeply into the Company's revenues. The defeated Maratha rulers also experienced shortfalls. The peshwa responded by oppressing peasants, and Scindia and Holkar by plundering other states. Pindaris, former cavalrymen in the Maratha armies, lived by raiding Madhya Pradesh and Rajasthan. The Company felt threatened by the consequent instability on its borders. The governor-general Lord Hastings (1813–1823) (not related to Warren Hastings) sought to solve these problems by resuming expansion. A war with Nepal ended in 1816 with British rule over Uttaranchal and much of Himachal Pradesh. In return, the Company recognized the independence of Nepal and allowed Nepalese soldiers to enlist in its well-paid army. Even today, Britain and India maintain regiments of Nepalese Gurkhas. Hastings also suppressed the Pindaris, and brought the kingdoms of Rajasthan under British supremacy.

In order to strengthen British control, Hastings ordered the peshwa to renounce what remained of his overlordship over the Marathas. This so angered the peshwa and Bhonsle that they rebelled. They were defeated in 1818. Bhonsle's state of Nagpur was given to a new ruler under British domination, and the peshwa's territories were annexed by the Company. Hastings' successor, Lord Amherst (1823–1828), rounded out British rule with a victory over Burma, which ceded to the Company the modern states of Assam, Meghalaya, and Manipur, and territory on the east coast of the Bay of Bengal.

THE COMPANY STATE

When the Company took over Delhi from Scindia in 1803, it became the guardian of the Mughal emperor. Many Indian rulers recognized the nominal suzerainty of Shah Alam, his son Akbar II (1806–1837), and his grandson Bahadur Shah II (1837–1857), although in 1827 the Company gave up the pretense of subordination to the Mughal throne. Long before this, however, the Company's governor-general in Calcutta had become the real ruler of India. He was assisted by an executive council. Its members met collectively with the governor-general to set policy, and later were individually placed in charge of government departments.

The territories that were annexed by the Company formed what was called British India. This was divided into provinces. The original provinces—Bengal, Madras, and Bombay—came into being as the Company placed newly acquired areas under the administration of the governors of its principal factories. From 1834, new provinces were created. Madras, Bombay, and later the other provinces had their own governors and executive councils. Provinces were divided into districts, on the model of Bengal and Bihar. Governors, councillors, district collectors, and other senior officials often belonged to Cornwallis's creation, the Indian Civil Service or ICS. In 1833, the British Parliament banned discrimination against Indians in government employment. Nevertheless, there were no Indians in the ICS till the 1860s, and governors and executive councillors were all British until the twentieth century.

Much of the subcontinent, however, was not annexed to British India, and formed what was known as Indian India or the Indian states. These areas retained their own monarchs, under indirect British rule. The first Indian states were the territories of rulers in subsidiary alliance with the Company. Local kings who had been subordinate to the Marathas or Nepal were later put in the same category. In some areas, the British recognized hundreds of petty chieftains as rulers of their own tiny states. The monarchs of Indian India, styled princes or chiefs by the British, headed their state governments but were required to follow the orders of a British representative (often called a resident).

Company domination affected India's economy as well as its administration. By the early nineteenth century, the Industrial Revolution meant that British factories could turn out endless quantities of cheap cotton cloth. Manufacturers secured the domestic market by getting the British government to impose prohibitive duties on imported textiles, which quickly wiped out sales of Indian cottons in Britain. Then, between the 1820s and the 1840s, as its price fell with the expansion of production, British cloth drove Indian textiles from the Americas, Portugal, and East Asia, and in the 1840s it began to take over in India too. All this created unprecedented unemployment among Indian cotton spinners and weavers and eliminated what had been the focal point of Company trade for 200 years.

Ever since its establishment, the Company had enjoyed a monopoly on trade from South and East Asia to Britain. In 1813, however, Parliament gave in to the demands of British merchants and opened trade between India and Britain to all. In 1824, the Company stopped importing goods into India, and nine years later Parliament barred it from trade altogether. Its sole function was henceforth ruling India, which required substantial revenues. The army was particularly costly, absorbing 42.5 percent of the Indian government's expenditure under Lord Wellesley, and about a third from the 1820s onward. Indian troops did not merely establish and maintain British rule in their homeland. In 1811, they helped conquer Java from the Dutch, marking the first use of the Indian army for British interests outside of India. Indians fought in British campaigns in Asia, Africa, and Europe until World War II.

The land revenue remained the Company's principal source of income. The Permanent Settlement was never implemented outside of Bengal and Bihar, which meant that revenue assessments could be raised. In some areas, local chieftains were made landowners along the lines of the Bengali zamindars. This was not possible everywhere—for example, in Mysore, where Haidar Ali and Tipu Sultan had eliminated most of the chieftains. The British followed their lead and collected the land revenue directly from headmen or peasants in much of the south and west.

THE ECONOMY OF THE COMPANY STATE

The Indian economy unquestionably changed during the first half of the nineteenth century, although the nature and extent of the transformation are debated. Some Indians saw their status decline. Village elites were often undermined. This might be unconnected with British rule, as when the division of lands among the heirs of deceased headmen left properties so small that owners could not hire labor and had to cultivate the land themselves. Just as often, however, the Company *was* responsible. For example, rural notables often traditionally supplemented their incomes through part-time military service. This became impossible with the abolition of all armies in British India except the Company's force of professional soldiers. Similarly, with the end of the rule of the nawabs, the Muslim administrative elite that had dominated urban life in Bengal and Carnatic disappeared. It was replaced by a new class of Hindus who owed their position to participation in the Company's commercial and bureaucratic activities.

A long-standing trend that continued through the nineteenth century was the incorporation of Tribals and nomads into settled society. Peasants might escape heavy land revenue assessments by founding agricultural colonies among the inhabitants of forests and grazing lands. Company rule also played a part—for example, by introducing the commercial logging of such woods as teak. The consequent destruction of forests made the Tribal way of life impossible. This opened lands to settled farming, either by peasants from elsewhere or by Tribals themselves. Partly because of this, a greater proportion of Indians than ever before were peasants. The destruction of Tribal and nomadic communities, however, eliminated sources of food and goods that many peasants had relied on after bad harvests or in times of unrest.

After the loss of textile markets, India's exports shifted from manufactures to agricultural raw materials. The result was increasing cultivation of such crops as sugar, tea and coffee, and jute (which was used to make sacking). This particularly benefited wealthier peasants who held enough land to devote some acreage to nonfood crops and the assets to borrow start-up money on favorable terms.

British merchants dominated the long-distance trade of Company India. Nevertheless, many Indians enjoyed success in commerce and banking. Moreover, export trade was always dwarfed by local trade, which remained in Indian hands. The Company's centers grew as they evolved from commercial cities to administrative capitals. Madras and Calcutta were probably the largest cities in India in 1800. The end of the Company monopoly on trade was followed by the rapid growth of the European population of the major cities as private merchants flooded into India; in 1837, there were over 3,000 Europeans in Calcutta.

Many individual Europeans made fortunes through business in India in the eighteenth and nineteenth centuries. Despite what is sometimes said, however, Indian wealth played only a minor role in the Industrial Revolution. Indian cash and raw materials formed a relatively small proportion of total imports into Britain. Moreover, until 1813, during the crucial years of Britain's economic transformation, the Company controlled the India trade, and it used its profits to pay its home expenses, not to feed British industry.

THE SIKH EMPIRE

While Wellesley and Hastings were creating the Company state, a Sikh chieftain named Ranjit Singh was carving out an empire in the northwest. Ranjit Singh fought Afghan invasions of Punjab in the 1790s, and in 1799 took Lahore and made it his capital. Between then and 1836, he conquered the modern Northwest Frontier Province, Pakistani Punjab, Kashmir, and parts of Indian Punjab and Himachal Pradesh. He owed his success to his army. To keep his troops up-to-date, he recruited deserters from Company regiments, and from the 1820s engaged European officers. Partly because of Sikh military strength, mutual respect subsisted between Ranjit Singh and the British.

Ranjit Singh's 12 million subjects included 1.5 million Sikhs. Although there were Hindus and Muslims in the ruling class, Sikhs were dominant, and the army was probably over half Sikh. Ranjit Singh was a member of the Khalsa, but he did not discriminate against Sikhs who followed their own gurus.

Ranjit Singh rewarded agricultural productivity, gave loans to support the digging of wells, and generally encouraged cultivation. He fostered commerce, making trade routes secure and imposing low taxes on trade. He also supported industry, including the weaving of Kashmiri shawls. The Sikh empire was peaceful and prosperous, and—like the great Mughal emperors—Ranjit Singh sponsored architecture, painting, and Persian and Punjabi literature.

CRISIS AND REFORM

The Company's successive annexations of territory were intended to provide security and revenues. Conquest was expensive, however, and necessitated heavy taxes from British India and tribute from Indian states. This often created a vicious circle: Increased revenue demands provoked revolts, which (if British rule was to continue) had to be suppressed at further expense. Moreover, taxation and the consequent unrest limited the growth of the Indian economy. For various reasons, including the destruction of the textile industry, the economic situation became even worse in the 1830s and 1840s.

To this was added military disaster. In 1835, Shah Shuja, the ruler of Afghanistan, was overthrown. To prevent Iranian or Russian expansion into Afghanistan, a Company army accompanied the deposed monarch to Kabul and restored him as a British puppet. In 1841, however, the Afghans revolted, killed Shah Shuja, wiped out the Company force, and regained their independence.

Meanwhile, Ranjit Singh had died in 1839. Soon afterwards, a power struggle broke out between two of his Hindu nobles, the brothers Raja Dhyan Singh and Raja Gulab Singh. In 1841, Raja Dhyan Singh triumphed when he helped Ranjit Singh's son Sher Singh seize the throne.

The unrest in the Sikh empire caused instability across the northwest. The chieftains of Sindh had submitted to the Company before the Afghan campaign, but now they rebelled. This led to war and the British annexation of Sindh in 1843, at further expense to the Company. The same year, Sher Singh and Raja Dhyan Singh were murdered. Ranjit Singh's youngest son Dalip Singh was installed on the Sikh throne at the age of five. His mother, Maharani Jindan Kaur, feared the Sikh army, which she could not control, and asked for British help. The Company obliged: It invaded, and defeated the army in 1846. Raja Gulab Singh, who had helped the conquerors, was made maharaja or king of Jammu and Kashmir. The remainder of the Sikh empire was divided between the British and Dalip Singh, who held his portion as an Indian state.

Besides conquest and crises, the Company state was characterized by reform, a term that covers changes that occurred as a result of British rule. The best known reforms were enacted by the governor-general Lord William Bentinck (1828–1835). He suppressed the *thags*, gangs who robbed and murdered travelers, and made a criminal offense of *sati*, a custom by which Hindu widows burned themselves to death on their husbands' funeral pyres. Though dramatic, however, these reforms affected few Indians. For example, sati had never been practiced outside of some upper-caste communities.

More far-reaching changes were often the unintended results of British policy. Thus, Hindus were traditionally governed by custom, which varied according to region and caste. When the Company assumed control of justice in British India, however, its jurists consulted classical legal texts and Brahmin scholars, and applied their findings to all Hindus in the belief that this was authentic Hindu law. Moreover, Muslim and Hindu law were interpreted by Company judges in accordance with British principles. This created a new legal system, followed across British India and blending Indian and British justice.

Another set of changes occured in the field of education. In the late eighteenth century, Company employees began to take a scholarly interest in Indian culture. They established the Asiatic Society to study Indian literature and antiquities, and the Company government later founded Muslim and Sanskrit colleges at Calcutta. In 1813, Parliament ordered the Company to promote education among its subjects. Meanwhile, elite Indians in Calcutta, Madras, and Bombay had begun to learn English to further careers in business and administration. In 1817, Indian merchants in Calcutta founded the Hindu College for their sons, who studied literature, politics, and sciences in English.

The Company long barred Christian missionaries from its territories, on the grounds that they brought instability. From the 1790s, however, missionaries defied the ban or settled just outside British India, and in 1813 Parliament forced the Company to admit them. The missionaries made few converts, but like the Calcutta merchants, they founded English schools for Indian children. From 1823, the Company government supported English-language private schools, and in 1835 it began directly providing English education. This was accompanied by the substitution of English for Persian in official correspondence and the higher law courts. English thereafter became essential for Indians who sought work in the professions and the bureaucracy, and in 1857 three English-language universities were founded. Nevertheless, throughout the nineteenth century, the number of Indians affected by Western education was tiny.

LORD DALHOUSIE (1848–1856)

Lord Dalhousie, who became governor-general in 1848, devoted himself to remedying the problems of the Company state. To obtain revenues and security, he enlarged British India at the expense of the Indian states. With his Doctrine of Lapse, he annexed seven states after their rulers had died without heirs. A revolt by two provincial governors gave him the excuse to annex what remained of the Sikh empire in 1849. Three years later, a fresh Anglo-Burmese war ended in the acquisition of Lower Burma. And in 1856, Dalhousie annexed Awadh, claiming misgovernment by its ruler. When Dalhousie left India the same year, the Company state embraced virtually all of modern India, Pakistan, and Bangladesh. Awadh alone added 5 million British pounds to the revenues, and further money was saved by ending the pensions paid to royal families that had been dispossessed by Wellesley and Hastings. For example, when the last peshwa, Bajirav II, died in 1853, Dalhousie refused to continue his allowance to his adopted son Nana Saheb.

By now, the Indian economy had begun to grow, thanks partly to government policy. Except in Bengal and Bihar, the land revenue was recalculated after 1845. The assessment was fixed for a long term, typically thirty years, and often reduced. The annexation of Awadh in 1856 was followed by a revenue settlement that bypassed the rural landowners or *taalluqedars*, and collected directly from the peasants. India's prosperity was further enhanced by the introduction of railways in 1853 and the electric telegraph the following year. The consequent improvements in transportation and knowledge of markets boosted the grain trade within India, and allowed cultivators to take full advantage of the increasing demand for Indian exports abroad, particularly raw cotton.

6

Indians and British Rule

THE GREAT REVOLT

Indians responded to British rule in many ways. One was armed opposition. The nineteenth century saw frequent local uprisings, some by landowners protesting land revenue assessments, others by nomads trying to drive out the peasants who were encroaching on their lands. Occasionally, the East India Company's Indian troops mutinied; in 1806, soldiers at Vellore in Tamil Nadu rebelled, apparently because they felt that the British were infringing on the practice of their religion.

In 1857, a great revolt broke out. It began with a mutiny in the Bengal Army (the Company's forces were divided into three armies based in the original British centers). The soldiers' grievances were economic—for example, a recent decision to deny them foreign service allowances when they were stationed in distant parts of the subcontinent; they were religious, particularly postings to Burma and other places outside of India, which challenged high-caste Hindu soldiers to whom leaving India was religiously polluting; and they were political, especially for the third of the troops who came from Awadh and felt their honor and wealth threatened when that kingdom was annexed to British India in 1856.

The final spark was a rifle introduced in 1857. To load it, soldiers bit the end off a cardboard cartridge. A rumor spread that the cartridges' waterproofing grease was beef or pork fat. If true, this made it a sin for Hindus and Muslims to use the rifles, because the former regard the cow as sacred, and the latter consider the pig unclean. Faced with an uproar, the authorities allowed the soldiers to make their own waterproofing and break the cartridges by hand. The damage was done, however. The fact that some British officers preached Christianity to their men had awakened fears among the soldiers that their religions were under attack, and the rumors about the grease only seemed to confirm them.

In May 1857, eighty-five soldiers at the army camp at Meerut near Delhi refused to use the new rifles. Their inevitable punishment touched off a rising among their comrades, who, after taking control of the camp, marched to Delhi and seized the city. Bahadur Shah II, the eighty-one-year-old heir to the title of Mughal emperor, accepted their request to become their nominal leader. This induced Mughal nobles and other soldiers to join the rising, quickly followed by much of the population of Delhi. A military mutiny had become a rebellion against British rule. In June and July 1857, outbreaks followed across Haryana, Uttar Pradesh, and parts of Bihar and Madhya Pradesh, and British rule collapsed in many areas.

Attempts have been made to explain the whole revolt as a reaction to British interference in religion, an attempt to restore the Mughal empire or deposed chieftains, or an organized Indian war of independence. Actually, Indians rebelled for different reasons, which varied from place to place. Some undoubtedly wanted to end the rule of the foreign conquerors; others felt that they were being taxed too heavily in comparison with their neighbors; still others looked for revenge on old rivals who had profited by establishing good relations with the British. A bandwagon effect played a part, too: Many rebels waited until the rising seemed to be succeeding and then joined in to secure their position in the future. Most risings were led by landholders, chieftains, and members of royal families who had lost their kingdoms to the East India Company. These included Lakshmibai, the widowed queen of Jhansi, which had fallen to Dalhousie's Doctrine of Lapse; her bravery in battle against the British has made her a national heroine of India. In general, the deciding factor was whether or not such leaders felt that their interests and those of the people under their command would be best served by ending British rule.

Nevertheless, the revolt was largely confined to the Gangetic plain. The commercial and educated classes of Calcutta, Bombay, and Madras had prospered under Company dominance, and held back. The same was true of the Bengal zamindars. In the eight years since the annexation of the old Sikh Empire, the people of Punjab had been reconciled to foreign rule by recruitment into the well-paid Company army, low land revenue assessments, and other conciliatory policies. And the men of the Bombay and Madras armies did not share the disgruntlement of their colleagues in the north. Among other reasons, few of them came from the high castes that were particularly sensitive to religious concerns, and none was Awadhi.

Because their leaders had revolted for their own individual reasons, the rebel forces lacked both ideological unity and a coherent strategy. This allowed British troops and their Indian allies to defeat them individually. The British had regained control of most of North India by the spring of 1858, and suppressed the last rebels at the end of the year.

INDIA AFTER THE GREAT REVOLT

The immediate casualties of the British victory included the two institutions that had dominated India for three centuries. The Mughal dynasty had lost all power but was still highly regarded by many Indians. Now, to punish him for accepting leadership of the revolt, the British exiled Bahadur Shah II to Burma and abolished the very title of Mughal sovereign. And rightly or wrongly, many Britons blamed the uprising on the policies of the East India Company. Control of the subcontinent was transferred from the Company to the "Crown," the British government, through a newly appointed member of the British cabinet called the Secretary of State for India. The Secretary of State lived in London, where he headed a government department called the India Office. Like all cabinet ministers, he was chosen by the prime minister, and answerable to parliament. In India, the governor-general assumed the additional title of viceroy (vice-king), to show that he represented the British monarch. He too was chosen by the prime minister, and reported to the Secretary of State. As in Company days, the capital of British India was Calcutta.

All this showed that the British intended to keep India. They wanted to do so for many reasons. The former Company armies, now called the Indian Army, included half of all the troops in the British Empire in the late nineteenth century. It was paid for by Indian taxpayers, as were the salaries of Britons who found jobs in the administration and military in India. Up to the 1930s, more than one fourth of all the taxes collected in India flowed into Britain in the form of "Home Charges," which paid for military supplies, pensions for British retirees from Indian services, the expenses of the India Office, and interest on money that India had borrowed in London. India was the world's largest market for British exports, and supplied raw materials, foodstuffs, and manufactured goods in return. Indian laborers worked for minimal wages on British plantations around the Indian Ocean and the Caribbean, and on railway construction in British East Africa.

Nevertheless, the British did not want India simply for economic reasons. The subcontinent would probably have imported just as many British goods if it had been independent. Nor did Britain monopolize India's exports; in the 1870s, central Europe bought more Indian cotton than Britain did. Psychological considerations were probably as important to the British as economic ones. India symbolized Britain's status as a great power, and provided a large population of "backward" people who, many Britons believed, could absorb superior Western habits from their foreign rulers. By the end of the nineteenth century, many people in Europe and the United States believed that inculcating such habits in other parts of the world was a moral duty.

For the British to enjoy the various benefits of ruling India, they had to guard it against external and internal enemies. They were preoccupied with fears that the Russians would spread from Central Asia to India. This was probably militarily impossible in the nineteenth century. Nevertheless, it underlay the establishment of British control over the frontier areas of Pakistan between the 1870s and 1890s, and a fresh unsuccessful attempt to bring Afghanistan under British rule in 1878–1881. In 1886, the eastern border of British India was extended with the annexation of what remained of Burma, which was administered as part of India till 1937.

Internal security required the British to prevent a repetition of the revolt of 1857. The Indian Army stopped recruiting soldiers from communities that had mutinied, and turned instead to Punjabi Muslims, Sikhs, and other groups that had sided with the British. In case even these men might one day rebel, the number of British troops stationed in India was increased, and British soldiers were given exclusive control of the artillery.

Fears engendered by the revolt led the British to execute tens of thousands of real or suspected rebels in 1858, heightened racial prejudice on the part of many Britons, and furthered their tendency to segregate themselves from Indians. Nevertheless, the British knew that their dominance was only secure so long as most Indians at least passively accepted it. A strong police force, soldiers who could be stationed in troubled areas, and controls on the press were all employed to damp down discontent, but the priority was making Indian community leaders, bureaucrats, and the army feel that their interests were served by British rule.

The princes and chiefs of "Indian India" accordingly received land, titles, and a guarantee that their states would never be annexed to British India. This ensured that for the next ninety years, one third of the subcontinent's area and one quarter of its population were included in Indian states rather than British provinces. The elites of British India were also courted. Rural chieftains and notables were recognized as landowners, on the model of the zamindars of Bengal, and received judicial powers over the inhabitants of their estates. In Awadh, peasants were put back under the control of the taalluqedars, whose authority had been curtailed on the British annexation. The merchants and educated classes of the cities were made magistrates and knights, and rural and urban leaders alike were allowed to enhance their local standing by using connections with the British to help families and neighbors. This may not have made Indian leaders unquestioning devotees of colonial rule in their country, but it did give enough of them a stake in the system that they would want to think very carefully before trying to eject the British.

THE ECONOMY AND SOCIETY, 1858–1914

Between the revolt and the outbreak of World War I in 1914, the economy and society of India were affected by both British rule and changes that had begun centuries earlier. The introduction of the steamship and the opening (in 1869) of the Suez Canal reduced the journey between Britain and India to three weeks, which tightened the bonds between South Asia and the West. Within India, the railway, the telegraph, and a cheap postal service enabled even the poor to travel around the subcontinent and correspond with faraway friends and relatives. The effects of improved communications were mixed, however. For example, rail lines were laid to move troops and passengers, to send food to famine-prone areas, and to ship exports and imports to and from seaports, but not for the benefit of internal trade. As a result, although they enriched producers of export commodities, they did little to unify the subcontinent's economy.

The period saw gradual economic growth, helped by a low rate of population increase. By 1914, India showed some features of a "developed" Western economy, such as technological modernization and capital accumulation. Others were absent, however, notably increased productivity and more equitable distribution of wealth. Thus, although landowners, the rich peasants who grew cash crops, businessmen, and professionals all became wealthier, the poor experienced little change. This has contributed to a debate as to whether British rule on the whole impoverished India or enriched it. A simple answer is impossible, although it is safe to say that the incomplete "development" of India owes much to both British and Indian practices and decisions.

Agriculture remained at the heart of the Indian economy, employing over 70 percent of the population. Many cultivators could do no more than feed themselves and pay the land revenue, but those who could grow export crops might profit handsomely. The second half of the nineteenth century saw a decline in exports of indigo and opium, but this was balanced by a phenomenal expansion in overseas sales of raw cotton, jute, and grain (between 1902 and 1913, India met almost one fifth of Britain's demand for wheat). India also exported tea, and at the beginning of the twentieth century supplied 59 percent of the tea drunk in Britain. Unlike other export crops (which were grown by peasants), tea was raised mainly on British-owned plantations.

Mechanized industry first appeared in India among the Indian cotton merchants of Bombay. Since the eighteenth century, they had bought raw cotton from cultivators and exported it to Europe and the Far East where it was spun into yarn and woven into cloth. In 1856, Asia's first steam-powered cotton mill opened at Bombay, but the industry did not really get off the ground till the 1870s. By then, improvements in transportation around the world had allowed other suppliers of raw cotton to edge Indian exporters out of markets in Europe and the Far East. The Bombay merchants responded by shifting their emphasis away from unprocessed cotton. They built mills to spin yarn themselves for the Indian and East Asian markets. British-made yarn had dominated in China and Japan since the 1840s, but it was now driven out by Indian competition. By 1900, Indian mills supplied 68 percent of all the yarn sold in India, and had destroyed much of whatever domestic hand-spinning had survived the coming of the British. Mechanized weaving grew more slowly than spinning, but from the 1890s more and more power looms were installed in the mills. In 1913, the textile factories in Bombay and elsewhere in western and southern India constituted the subcontinent's most important manufacturing industry.

The principal mechanized industry of eastern India was jute processing. The first steam-powered jute mill was opened at Calcutta in 1855, and by 1928, jute mills had almost as many workers as the cotton factories. In the east more than in the west and south, business was dominated by British firms, but there was a substantial Indian presence. In

1907 an Indian merchant family, the Tatas, opened an iron and steel plant at Jamshedpur in Jharkhand. It was so successful that the population of Jamshedpur grew from nothing in 1907 to 218,000 in 1951. Still, the textile and jute mills and the Tata plant notwithstanding, handicraft production dominated Indian manufacturing, and in 1901 fewer than one manufacturing worker in twenty was employed in a modern factory.

SOCIORELIGIOUS REFORM MOVEMENTS

From 1854, the British supported primary and secondary education in Indian languages, which helped slowly to raise the literacy rate. English higher education, however, had a more obvious impact, by creating an English-speaking Indian elite. Its members were concentrated in Calcutta, Bombay, and Madras, and belonged mainly to high-ranking Hindu castes with traditions of literacy and government service. They used their skills to obtain lucrative and prestigious employment in the administration, or in such professions as law and teaching.

Knowledge of English united educated Indians, whose exposure to Western culture and institutions led them to seek changes in Indian customs or British policy. To that end, they formed voluntary associations on British lines, with paid memberships, bylaws, regular meetings, and fund-raising drives. These associations proliferated in the second half of the nineteenth century, and it is sometimes said that after 1858 they replaced armed resistance as the primary Indian response to British dominance. Actually, armed revolts were endemic until the end of British rule in India, and the activities of voluntary associations began in the early nineteenth century.

Movements to reform society and religion inherited a tradition that went back millennia. Typically, their goal was to eliminate "wrong" beliefs and practices. This ironed out many of the regional and caste variations that had existed within Hinduism, Islam, and Sikhism. For example, in the early nineteenth century, Sahajananda Swami founded the Swami Narayana Sampradaya, or Community of Lord Vishnu. He and his missionaries traveled around Gujarat, calling on Hindus to stop eating meat and drinking alcohol, to abandon the obscene songs that featured in their religious gatherings, and to become devotees of Vishnu (in his incarnation of Krishna) rather than the female power that they then worshipped. In what is now Bangladesh, Sahajananda's contemporary Hajji Shariat Ullah led the Faraizi movement, which persuaded Bengali Muslim peasants and artisans to erase the Hindu and Tribal beliefs that had survived the adoption of Islam.

Improved communications helped the reformers spread their message, but also brought them into conflict with one another. They often disagreed as to which practices and beliefs were excrescences and which were the essentials of their religions. This became apparent in the 1820s, when Western education, and criticisms leveled at Hindu society and religion by Christian missionaries, provoked debate among the English-educated elite of Calcutta. One faction founded the Hindu Dharma Sabha, the Association of the Hindu Religion, to defend such existing practices as *sati*. Opposed to the Hindu Dharma Sabha were the followers of Henry Louis Vivian Derozio, a Calcutta college teacher of mixed Indian and European ancestry. A rationalist, Derozio felt that his beloved Indian homeland had been held back by religion, and his student disciples epitomized their rejection of Hindu mores by eating beef.

Rammohun Roy lay between the Hindu Dharma Sabha and Derozio. Although a devout Hindu, Roy was convinced that Brahmin priests had corrupted the true religion that he found in the Upanishads. Roy's Hinduism had one loving God, Brahma (the name of the Hindu creator), and no place for polytheism, image worship, or the subordination of women. Roy believed that if his coreligionists returned to this faith, no Hindu would be tempted to convert to the Christianity of the missionaries. He acquired a growing band of followers, and in 1828 organized them into the Brahmo Sabha (Association of Brahma). Two years later, he went to England to give evidence against attempts by orthodox Hindus to overturn the criminalization of *sati*, speak in Parliamentary hearings on the East India Company, and represent the Mughal emperor in negotiations with the Company. He died in England in 1833, and the Brahmo Sabha soon faded.

The Hindu Dharma Sabha, Derozio, and Roy had little influence except among educated Hindus of Calcutta. Perhaps out of necessity, Muslim reform movements had a wider impact, as they sought both to explain how Islam had ceased to be the religion of the subcontinent's masters and to remedy the consequent fall in status of Indian Muslims. Shah Wali Ullah, who lived in Delhi during the decline of the Mughal empire in the eighteenth century, blamed the political and moral decay of Muslim India on the ulama, arguing that they had let incorrect beliefs and practices creep into Islam. He insisted that nothing outside of the Quran and the Hadith (a collection of stories about Muhammad) was Islamic, and that the principles contained in those works should be ascertained by the use of reasoning rather than the current interpretations put forth by the ulama.

In the nineteenth century, Shah Wali Ullah's spiritual heirs split. One group tried to reestablish Muslim rule by force of arms, warring against both the Sikh Empire and the British. Others sought a new ulama, with the skills to interpret Islam correctly. In 1867, some of them founded the Deoband School to train theologians. Unlike other Muslim seminaries, it followed Western models, with a full-time teaching staff, fixed curriculum, and regular examinations. Students at Deoband received a thorough grounding in scripture, which they were trained to apply to modern life.

Sir Syed Ahmed Khan agreed that the ulama had misinterpreted Islam. Rather than wanting a reformed ulama, however, he believed that the future of Indian Muslims lay in regaining political power. The British would not leave, and so members of old noble Muslim families like himself had to join them in ruling India. To secure British agreement to this, he tried to build friendly relations between Muslims and their rulers. To qualify young Muslims for their new position, he encouraged them to acquire Western learning, especially science and technology. When the ulama asserted that this was un-Islamic, Sir Syed retorted that God Himself had created the natural laws underpinning science. In 1875, he founded the Mohammedan Anglo-Oriental College at Aligarh (now Aligarh Muslim University) to teach Western learning in an Islamic environment.

The Deoband School, Sir Syed, and Muslims who accepted the then-current practices of Indian Islam agreed that Muhammad was God's last prophet, and that his teachings (however interpreted) embodied truth. At the end of the nineteenth century, however, Mirza Ghulam Ahmad, a Punjabi lawyer, said that he had received divine messages to supplement the revelations given to Muhammad. Ghulam denounced many Indian Muslim customs, such as worship at the tombs of holy men, and urged an acceptance of British rule. He and his missionaries made many converts to what became known as the Ahmadi movement, both in Punjab and in the West. Ahmadis and other Muslims denounced one another as purveyors of falsehood. Ahmadis insisted that it was incumbent on all Muslims to accept Ghulam's completion of Muhammad's work, and other Muslims held that as Muhammad was the last prophet, Ghulam must be a fraud.

By this time, many Indian Muslims considered themselves part of a worldwide Islamic community. Early Muslims had regarded the khalifa or successor of Muhammad as their spiritual leader, but the importance of the khalifa in India had long since declined. In the sixteenth century, the sultan of Turkey had assumed the title of khalifa, and now many Indian Muslims emphasized his primacy as a link among all Muslims. This furthered their distance from Hindus. Coupled with this was an apparent threat from Hinduism, symptomized by a movement that began in the 1880s to replace Urdu (associated with Muslims) with Hindi (associated with Hindus) as the language of the local administration and courts in what is now Uttar Pradesh.

This was connected with the activities of Hindu reformers. The Brahmo Sabha was revived by Debendranath Tagore, from a family of Bengali zamindars, who in 1841 renamed Roy's organization the Brahmo Samaj (Society of Brahma) and wrote a statement of its beliefs. He sent out missionaries who made many converts to his teachings in rural Bengal. For some time, Tagore's closest associate was an English-educated bank employee named Keshub Chunder Sen. However, Tagore's main interest was the modernization of theology and rituals, whereas Sen wanted to concentrate on abolishing what he regarded as social evils, such as the caste system, drinking, and inequality between men and women.

In 1865 the Brahmo Samaj split. Tagore and his followers took the name of Adi (original) Brahmo Samaj. Sen founded the Brahmo Samaj of India and preached all over the subcontinent. In 1872, he persuaded the government to recognize Brahmo marriages that were performed without Hindu rituals. As this amounted to an exemption from Hindu law, it implied that Brahmos were not Hindus. In the late 1870s, Sen lost interest in social reform. By this time, he claimed to be receiving divine messages that contradicted Brahmo teachings, and when he obeyed one command and married his thirteen-year-old daughter to a Hindu prince, many of his followers had had enough. They formed the Sadharan (General) Brahmo Samaj, which to this day runs hospitals, orphanages, and girls' schools. Sen became more and more mystical. In 1881 he founded a cult with himself as leader, called the Nava Vidhan (New Dispensation), but he died three years later.

Sen's Bengali contemporary Sri Ramakrishna taught that all religions were true. This included Hinduism in its current forms, which meant there was no need for reform. On his deathbed in 1886, Ramakrishna chose as his heir Narendranath Datta, later called Swami Vivekananda (joyful conscience). In 1893, Vivekananda left India to attend a gathering in Chicago called the World Parliament of Religions. He spent four years in North America and Europe. On his return home in 1897, he founded the Ramakrishna Mission to propagate his ideas, which combined social service (such as helping the poor or organizing relief after earthquakes) with teaching the Upanishads and running spiritual retreats. The Ramakrishna Mission was active in India and the United States from the time of Swami Vivekananda, and later spread to other countries.

Another reformer, Swami Dayananda Saraswati, found true Hinduism in the Vedas. He called on middle-class Hindus in Bombay to renounce post-Vedic accretions (such as image worship, the intercession of priests, and pilgrimages) and to worship his one all-knowing and merciful God. In 1875, Dayananda founded the Bombay Arya Samaj (Society of Aryans) to spread his ideas. Two years later he moved to Lahore in Punjab, where he established a new Arya Samaj. By the time of Dayananda's death in 1883, local Arya Samajas existed across northern and western India. They commemorated their founder with the Dayananda Anglo-Vedic College, a high school and college at Lahore that taught English literature, science, and social studies alongside Sanskrit and Hindi. (The Arya Samaj encouraged Hindus to speak Hindi, leading many of its members to join the campaign against Urdu in the administration and the courts.)

The Arya Samaj had great influence, especially in Punjab, and by 1947 there were between 1.5 and 2 million Aryas. From 1893, they were split into two groups. One devoted itself to education and social service, the other to a Hindu equivalent of the Christian missions. As part of their effort to understand India and thus foresee potential trouble, the British conducted a decennial census. By the late nineteenth century, the census showed a sharp increase in the number of Christians and Sikhs in Punjab, and the goal of the Arya missionaries was to win back to the Hindu fold those who had converted to other religions.

By now, there was a growing interest in Indian religions among Europeans and Americans. In 1875, the Russian Helena Petrovna Blavatsky and the American Henry Steel Olcott founded the Theosophical Society in New York. Theosophy, or the Wisdom of God, began as an offshoot of Western occultism, but Blavatsky and Olcott became increasingly interested in Hinduism. They corresponded with Dayananda Saraswati, declared the Theosophical Society to be a branch of the Arya Samaj, and moved to India. The alliance with Dayananda did not last, mainly because Theosophists rejected Arya criticisms of modern Hindu practices. In 1882, Blavatsky and Olcott withdrew from the Arya Samaj and settled near Madras. By now, Theosophy taught the existence of a universal soul, like Brahman in the Upanishads, which our individual souls left to come down into the world. The secret of how we can return to the universal soul is guarded by spirits called Mahatmas (Sanskrit for "great souls"), who communicated it to mortals through their medium, Blavatsky.

In 1884, Blavatsky left India following accusations that her séances with the Mahatmas were rigged, and Olcott became leader of the Theosophists. He traveled around India and made many converts, including

Britons and Hindus. In 1907 he was succeeded by an Irishwoman named Annie Besant. Besant focused on social work, such as education and the elimination of child marriage. The movement flourished under her leadership, but eventually declined after an Indian named Krishnamurti renounced the role of Messiah that Theosophy had accorded him. Nevertheless, by attracting Westerners to beliefs that drew on Hindu motifs, Theosophy gave many Hindus a renewed confidence in their culture.

The line between Hinduism and Sikhism had always been ill-defined. Many Sikhs considered themselves to be followers of a Hindu sect rather than a distinct religion, and united the teachings of their gurus with polytheism, image worship, and a reliance on Brahmin priests to perform their rituals. Partly in response to the claims of Hindu reformers that Sikhism was simply one more corrupt form of Hinduism, some nineteenth-century Sikh teachers sought to harden religious boundaries by purging their faith of Hindu elements. In 1873, a group of prominent Sikhs in Amritsar founded the Amritsar Singh Sabha. Its goals were to teach their people about their religion, to win back Sikhs who had converted to Christianity and Islam, and to provide Sikh children with Western education. From 1879, Singh Sabhas were founded in other cities.

The Singh Sabhas insisted that all Sikhs accept the teachings of the last human guru, Gobind Singh. This was successful, and the percentage of Sikhs who identified themselves as members of Gobind Singh's Khalsa rose from seventy in 1881 to ninety in 1931. The Singh Sabhas also published historical and literary works that emphasized the distinctiveness of Sikhism, and campaigned against practices that were not sanctioned by the Sikh scriptures. In 1905, reformers took over the chief Sikh temple, the Golden Temple at Amritsar, and expelled the Brahmin priests, removed the images of Hindu gods, and stopped the use of Hindu rituals. The census reveals a measure of their success in separating Sikhism from Hinduism: In 1881, 54 percent of Punjabi Jats (the main peasant caste of Punjab) identified themselves as Sikhs, and most of the rest as Hindus. In 1931, however, 80 percent of Jats called themselves Sikhs. This was not because they formally converted from Hinduism to Sikhism, but because the reformers convinced them that the two faiths were mutually exclusive.

This points to a major effect of Indian socioreligious reform movements: They sharpened religious divisions. At the popular level, Hinduism, Islam, and Sikhism had often shaded into one another. Nineteenth-century Jats were not alone in being vague about their religious affiliation; Hindus and Muslims in Eastern Bengal often shared more customs and beliefs with one another than they did with their nominal coreligionists elsewhere. Thanks to the Faraizis, the Arya Samaj, the Singh Sabhas, and other likeminded groups, however, Indians increasingly identified themselves as Hindus, Muslims, or Sikhs, different from people of other religions (even near neighbors), while having something in common with all members of their own religion. This consolidated communal identities, the idea that no matter where they live, the followers of a religion form a distinct community.

INDIAN NATIONALISM

Caste was another identity that changed under British rule. With few exceptions, Hindus traditionally saw their own castes in relation to the communities that they lived among rather than as part of a wider group. By the late nineteenth century, however, improved communications and other factors often produced a sense of fellowship with people elsewhere who had similar caste names or occupations. Many castes established voluntary associations, which encouraged a sense of solidarity among their members. The lowest castes across India began to consider themselves part of an Untouchable community.

Caste associations increasingly lobbied the government in pursuit of their interests. For example, the Non-Brahmin Movement in southern and western India fought the supposed overrepresentation of Brahmins in higher education and government employment. This blending of identities with politics became particularly important with the emergence of identities embracing all India. For centuries, Hinduism had given a sense of unity to some Indians. So too did the shared experiences of Mughal and British rule, and the nineteenth-century improvements in communications. These bases of unity were now joined by Indian nationalism.

Nationalism is based on the idea that individuals are part of a group called a nation, united by a common history, language, and culture. It originated among eighteenth-century European intellectuals, who argued that the ideal country was built around a nation rather than a dynasty or a church. In the following century, nationalism spread across Europe, where it led to the unification of Italy and Germany and to calls to dismantle the multinational Austrian and Russian empires.

Familiarity with Western political thought introduced nationalism to English-educated Indians. Some saw separate nations in speakers of each Indian language and wanted political boundaries to reflect this. For example, Oriya nationalists demanded a homeland for speakers of their language, who were spread across three provinces. The British granted this request when they established the province of Orissa in 1936. Many speakers of Dravidian languages in South India came to see themselves as a nation, oppressed by the Hindu religion of the North and its Brahmin agents.

Subcontinental nationalism had a problem in that India lacks the common language or culture that defined nation in Europe. Some nationalists sought to bind the Indian people with a shared commitment to political liberalism, which they believed could only be instilled by continued British rule. Others looked to the very diversity of India as the basis for the nation and found among their compatriots a unique tolerance that allowed different cultures to coexist and to enrich one another in a composite Indian civilization. For example, *Jana Gana Mana*, now the national anthem of India, was written by modern India's greatest poet, Rabindranath Tagore. Rabindranath, the son of Debendranath Tagore of the Brahmo Samaj, was the winner of the 1913 Nobel Prize in Literature. *Jana Gana Mana* celebrates the common Indian-ness of the whole subcontinent:

> Punjab, Sindh, Gujarat, Maharashtra, the South, Orissa, Bengal;
> The Vindhyas, the Himalayas, the Yamuna, the Ganges;
> The waves of the Indian Ocean.

Opposing these secular nationalisms, Hindu nationalists asserted that Hinduism was a foundation for not merely the cultural unity of the subcontinent but a modern Indian nation. The differences among all these strains of nationalists are illustrated in their attitudes to the seventeenth-century Maratha king Shivaji. To non-Brahmins, Shivaji was a valiant enemy of upper-caste privileges. To Maharashtrian regionalists, he fought for the independence of Maharashtra. Secular nationalists saw him as an Indian patriot, and Hindu nationalists as the founder of a Hindu state.

With its assumption that a country is tied together by its inhabitants, nationalism implies that the people have a shared interest in the country and are therefore entitled to a say in its government. In the 1860s, Indians were admitted to the formal structures of government in British India with the establishment of local boards. These had the power to impose taxes, and spend them on schools, drains, and other local purposes. Their members were mostly Indians, initially named by the government but from the 1870s elected by men wealthy enough to pay the property tax. The boards served as a safety valve, giving Indians real power but at a level where they could not threaten British interests.

English-educated Indians, including many nationalists, wanted more than control of local boards. One of their concerns surrounded the highest level of government employment, the Indian Civil Service or ICS. ICS officers enjoyed good salaries and considerable prestige. The British parliament had banned discrimination against Indians in government appointments in 1833, but there were practical barriers. Since 1855, the ICS had recruited officers with an examination that was offered only in London. A greater hurdle came when the maximum age for taking the examination was lowered to 23 in 1858 and to 19 in 1876. This was intended to let successful candidates attend a British university before going on to India. However, the examination was based on the English school curriculum, and anyone who had not spent several years at school in England found it difficult to pass. The lower the age, the harder it was for Indians to obtain the necessary prior education.

The educated also wanted a part in lawmaking in British India. By the early 1860s, the viceroy and provincial governors each had legislative councils to discuss proposed new laws. All their members were chosen by the viceroy or governor. Most were British government officials, but there were also a few private citizens or "unofficial members." These included princes, landowners, and urban community leaders. Many educated Indians felt that nominated unofficial members did not represent them. They wanted "unofficials" to be elected, and to enjoy the right to initiate legislation as well as discuss it.

The power to reform the councils and the ICS lay with the central government in Calcutta and the British parliament in London. In 1866, a group of Indians in Britain founded the East India Association to discuss Indian affairs and bring their grievances before the British authorities. In India, such bodies as the Poona Sarvajanik Sabha or Association of All the People of the city of Poona petitioned the government on the ICS, the councils, and other issues.

THE INDIAN NATIONAL CONGRESS

In 1883, the government of India unveiled the Ilbert Bill, a proposal to rescind the right that Europeans in rural Bengal enjoyed not to be tried by an Indian judge if they landed in court. Bengal's British businessmen and planters were outraged, claiming that Indian judges did not share Western conceptions of right and wrong. They launched a campaign of petitions, speeches, and lobbying, until the government watered down the Ilbert Bill to their satisfaction. The episode showed Indians the power of public opinion, if it was channeled properly.

In 1885, members of the educated elite from all over India met in Bombay to discuss means of bringing pressure to bear on the government. They called themselves the Indian National Congress, or Congress, and from then on met in a different city each year during the Christmas vacation. (It must be made clear that in India, Congress is the name of an organization, which became a political party, and not a law-making branch of government like the United States Congress.) The principal organizers of Congress included Allan Octavian Hume, a British Theosophist and retired officer of the ICS, who supported the demands of educated Indians; Pherozeshah Mehta, a Bombay lawyer; and Surendranath Banerjea, a Bengali and one of the first Indians to pass the ICS examination. Mehta and Banerjea were disciples of Dadabhai Naoroji, a London-based businessman and intellectual from Bombay whose books and articles are some of the clearest expositions of nineteenth-century Indian nationalism.

Congress set itself two tasks: to raise money with which to publicize its grievances in Britain, and to drum up Indian support for reforms. Its weapons included passing resolutions at the annual meetings, because a successful vote showed the British that the issue in question had widespread support among educated Indians. In their effort to retain the loyalty of leading Indians, the British went some way toward meeting Congress demands. In 1892, the age limit for the ICS examination was raised to 23, and in 1892–1893 "indirect election" to the legislative councils was introduced: Local boards, universities, and other bodies chose unofficial Indian members of the provincial councils, which in turn picked representatives on the viceroy's council. Nevertheless, British officials still formed the majority on all councils.

The early Congress came to life only during its annual meetings. To many members, nationalist concerns were less important than establishing friendships that would help them in local or provincial politics. Most meetings attracted fewer than a thousand delegates, and the largest number of them were Brahmin lawyers from the big cities of the Bengal, Bombay, and Madras provinces, classic members of the English-educated elite but hardly typical of Indians in general.

THE PARTITION OF BENGAL

In 1903, the viceroy Lord Curzon announced that to simplify the administration and aid economic development, the huge province of Bengal would be divided in two. English-educated Bengali Hindus were enraged at the move, which many believed was punishment for their support of Congress. They foresaw a decline in opportunities for advancement, as they would constitute minorities in both new provinces: Eastern Bengal (modern Bangladesh and northeastern India) would be inhabited mainly by Assamese and by Muslim Bengalis; most of the people of the western province (West Bengal, Bihar, Jharkhand, and most of Orissa) would be Biharis and Oriyas.

The Calcutta elite fought partition with meetings and petitions, but the British were undaunted, and Bengal was divided in 1905. The same year, the protestors opened a drive to replace British-made cloth with Indian-made, or *swadeshi* (of one's own country). In the hopes of forcing the British to listen by hurting them economically, they burned imported fabric and picketed shops that sold it. They drummed up wider support for swadeshi with newspapers, pamphlets, and traveling theatrical troupes and sent volunteer speakers (especially students) into the Bengal countryside. The movement was phenomenally successful and led to a boom in sales of Indian cloth.

At the 1906 session of Congress, a dissident faction under Bal Gangadhar Tilak saw a chance to hijack Congress from its leaders Surendranath Banerjea and Gopal Krishna Gokhale (Pherozeshah Mehta's successor). Tilak moved for an endorsement of not only swadeshi but also a campaign for self-government within the British Empire. Thanks to the excitement over the situation in Bengal, Tilak's resolutions passed. This split Congress. The Moderates under Banerjea and Gokhale opposed the partition of Bengal, but saw good relations with the British as the key to resolving Indian grievances. They feared that a premature demand for self-government would jeopardize those relations. Tilak, on the other hand, insisted that only a mainly Indian administration could resolve Indian concerns, and took his Extremists in an increasingly confrontational direction. He first called on Indians to make British rule impossible by refusing to work in the army or the government, or pay taxes, then penned articles that seemed to endorse a terrorist movement that had launched bomb attacks in Bengal. This, however, was overplaying his hand. Tilak and many of his followers were arrested; other Extremists realized the futility of his methods, and returned to the Moderate fold. Gokhale consolidated his position as the dominant politician in India.

THE ALL-INDIA MUSLIM LEAGUE

For various reasons, Congress had never attracted many Muslims. Muslims were poorly represented among the English-educated classes of Bengal, Bombay, and Madras from which Congress drew much of its support, and were further alienated by the fact that Hindu supporters of Congress were prominent in the movement to replace Urdu with Hindi. Many agreed with Sir Syed Ahmed Khan that participation in Congress would earn Muslims nothing but British hostility.

In 1906, the viceroy Lord Minto met a group of prominent Muslims to discuss the Indian policy of the newly elected government in Britain. Perhaps as a ploy to secure support against the agitation in Bengal— perhaps not—Minto promised that any reforms in India would take account of Muslim interests. Soon afterward, the Muslims who had met the viceroy formed the All-India Muslim League, modeled on Congress. Their main goal was separate electorates for Muslims. This meant that Muslims would vote separately from other Indians, and for their own candidates, as a means of guaranteeing representation even in areas where they were a minority. Separate electorates already existed in elections for some local boards, and the League wanted them made general.

THE MORLEY-MINTO REFORMS

Electoral questions were important because Lord Morley, the Secretary of State for India in the new British government, was planning the most far-reaching constitutional changes that India had seen since 1858. The resulting Morley-Minto Reforms link his name with that of the viceroy, but the Congress leader Gokhale seems to have influenced the Secretary of State more than Minto did. Probably thanks to Gokhale, Morley went far to meet the demands of the Moderates, to show India that there was no need to adopt Tilak's methods. In 1909–1910, Indians were appointed to advise the viceroy and governors on the central and provincial executive councils. The provincial legislative councils were also reformed. A majority of their members would now be Indians, most of them elected by such interest groups as landowners and Muslims (who obtained their separate electorates). The viceroy's legislative council would still have a majority of British officials, but its unofficial membership was increased. The unofficial members of the legislative councils also gained the right to introduce legislation.

Besides the Moderates, Morley and Minto courted the princes and chiefs, the rulers of the third of the subcontinent that formed Indian India. The assumption was that if these monarchs were content under British rule, their subjects would follow suit. Since the 1860s, the British had often pressured princes to reform their administrations along Western lines, or to abolish social practices that were considered backward.

The princes saw this as an abridgement of their power as sovereigns. In 1909, Minto eliminated this source of friction when he informed the princes that they would henceforth be allowed to rule their states more or less as they saw fit.

Finally, in 1912 the British reunited the Bengali-speaking region. This abolished the mainly Muslim province of East Bengal. To compensate the subcontinent's Muslims, the capital of India was moved from Calcutta to the old Muslim center of Delhi, where a planned city of New Delhi was built. This did not satisfy the Muslim League, but the policy of Morley and Minto showed that in British eyes, the two principal forces in Indian public life were Congress and the princes. Efforts to balance British interests with their demands were the main feature of Indian politics for the next thirty years.

7

The Struggle for Independence

WORLD WAR I

Britain's declaration of war on Germany in 1914 brought the whole British empire into World War I. Indian princes and politicians gave their support to the Allied war effort, to which India supplied money (£146 million sterling) and men (1.5 million Indians served as soldiers and laborers against Germany and her ally Turkey in Europe, Africa, and the Middle East). Indian industry expanded to fill shortfalls in everything from cloth to steel, as British production was diverted to military needs. At the same time, the war led to increased taxes, and shortages and high prices of basic goods. By 1918, this had produced riots and strikes.

Many Indian politicians felt that, with improved access to the ICS and councils already achieved through the Morley-Minto reforms, their wartime sacrifices should be rewarded with self-government or home rule. This did not mean they wanted independence, but rather what Canada, Australia, and other British "dominions" enjoyed: internal affairs run by a ministry answerable (or "responsible") to an elected parliament, while Britain handled foreign affairs. The Muslim League had already declared itself in favor of self-government in 1913. Its members were angry over the reunification of Bengal (which eliminated the mainly Muslim province of Eastern Bengal) and Britain's refusal to help Turkey against attacks by Italy and the Balkan states shortly before the oubtreak of World War I. In 1915, Congress too approved a call for self-government.

The same year, Pherozeshah Mehta and Gopal Krishna Gokhale, two principal leaders of Congress since its establishment in 1885, both died. The rising stars of the new Indian freedom movement were Annie Besant, leader of Theosophists, who believed that self-government would restore the Hindu India that so influenced her religion; and Bal Gangadhar Tilak, Gokhale's old Extremist opponent, who had been released from prison in 1914. In 1916, Besant and Tilak both founded Home Rule Leagues. They planned to build enough popular support for self-government that the British could not refuse their demand. Thanks to Besant's Theosophical links and Tilak's popularity among former Extremists, the two Leagues grew rapidly. They attracted people who had not hitherto been involved in nationalist politics—non-Brahmins, petty merchants, rich farmers, students—and drew them into Congress, to which Besant and Tilak both belonged.

The war increased British fears of subversion. In 1915, the government of India supplemented its powers of repression with the Defense of India Act, which allowed it to ban books deemed seditious, control newspapers, and intern critics of the government. Among those interned were Annie Besant, and Mohamed Ali and Shaukat Ali, two brothers who were among the leading Muslim politicians in India.

The deaths of Mehta and Gokhale, and the influx of supporters from his Home Rule League, allowed Tilak to take center stage when Congress held its annual meeting in 1916. The gathering was in Lucknow in Uttar Pradesh, where (by prior arrangement) the Muslim League was meeting simultaneously. Under an agreement called the Lucknow Pact, the two parties presented joint demands to the British: an increase in the number of voters; refashioned legislative councils, with four fifths of the members elected rather than appointed, and executive councils on which half the members were responsible to the legislative councils; equality between Indians and other inhabitants of the British Empire, particularly the right to live anywhere in the empire (including the dominions that excluded them) and to receive military commissions on equal terms with Britons.

Both parties gained by the Pact. The alliance with the League allowed Congress to claim to represent Muslims, and so enhanced its right to negotiate with the British on behalf of all Indians. The League secured Congress recognition that Muslims were different from other Indians, as in the Pact Congress accepted separate electorates and "weighted" representation. This meant that in the legislatures at the center and in most provinces, where Hindus formed the majority, Muslims would have more seats than their population warranted; in Punjab and Bengal, with their slight Muslim majorities, Hindus would be overrepresented.

Lord Chelmsford, the British viceroy of India, and the Secretary of State in London were meanwhile trying to defuse the demand for home rule with concessions to Indian opinion. In 1917, the two principal forces in Indian public life were admitted to a meeting of the British and dominion prime ministers in London, in the persons of Satyendra Prasanna Sinha, a former president of Congress, and Maharaja Ganga Singh of Bikaner, a leading prince. On August 20, 1917, after consulting Sinha, Bikaner, and his colleagues in the British cabinet, the Secretary of State, Edwin Montagu, announced that Indian participation in the administration would gradually increase, until the government of India was fully responsible to an elected legislature.

Montagu and Chelmsford now toured India to hear the opinions of Indians and Europeans, then drafted a scheme to set the country on the path to responsible government. Their Montagu-Chelmsford Reforms were enacted by the British parliament in 1919. They remodeled both the central and provincial governments. At the center, the legislative council was replaced with a bicameral legislature, where elected nonofficials outnumbered government officials. The viceroy's executive council remained independent of the legislature, whose functions were to discuss and advise rather than set policy; but the number of Indians on the executive council was increased, giving Indians a real voice on foreign affairs, communications, and other matters judged to be of All-India importance.

Other powers of government were devolved to the provinces, which were allocated the land revenue so that they could finance their new responsibilities (the center kept the income tax for itself). Provincial governors and their appointed executive councillors undertook the administration of law and order, justice, and the like. India acquired its first experience of responsible government with the transfer of such subjects as agriculture, public works, and education to Indian ministers who answered to mainly elected provincial legislatures.

This met many (though not all) of the demands of the Lucknow Pact, with which the Montagu-Chelmsford Reforms also accorded in increasing Indian representation among military and ICS officers, and enlarging the electoral franchise. For men, the right to vote was now based on property ownership and education, which allowed one in ten adult males to vote in provincial elections (the proportion was smaller in elections to the central legislature). Provincial legislatures set their own qualifications for female voters, but most enfranchised only minuscule numbers of women. The new voters included many illiterates. To allow them to identify candidates, ballots were printed with symbols beside each name. This is still done in India, where every party has an emblem that appears on ballots—for example, a flower or a hand. Muslims kept the separate electorates that had been granted in 1909 and approved by Congress in 1916.

The princes also obtained concessions. Following discussions between the viceroy and leading princes, the British further limited their power to infringe on princely sovereignty. In 1921, in accordance with a suggestion made by Montagu and Chelmsford, a Chamber of Princes was established, in which the princes met periodically both to discuss matters of common concern and to advise their British overlords.

In an effort to maintain Indian support for British control, the Montagu-Chelmsford Reforms gave unprecedented power to Indian politicians and accorded the princes greater autonomy than at any time since the early nineteenth century. In December 1919, the members of Congress approved the reforms and voted to participate in the next year's legislative elections. Over the following twelve months, however, Indian politics were transformed.

MAHATMA GANDHI

Unlike the men who dominated Congress during its first thirty years, Mohandas Karamchand Gandhi was a product of Indian India, born in 1869 in a small kingdom in Gujarat. He qualified as a lawyer in England, but after returning home, he was unable to establish a practice. In 1893 he moved to South Africa. The South African Indian community had been founded by plantation laborers, who were later joined by merchants and professionals. All Indians were subject to discrimination at the hands of the ruling white population. Gandhi became his compatriots' spokesman in their struggle for rights, organizing public meetings, petitions, and press campaigns and lobbying governments.

In 1907, however, these lawful methods proved ineffective against new regulations that required Indians to carry identity cards and restricted their movements. Gandhi turned to breaking the laws, leading Indians in burning their cards and taking them into areas from which they were prohibited. He and his followers quietly tolerated harassment, arrest, and imprisonment.

Gandhi called this resistance to unjust laws *satyagraha*, or "insistence on truth." It was part of a philosophy rooted in his belief that an ultimate truth underlies everything in the universe. Our goal is to search for this truth, dedicating ourselves to a life based on self-control, *swaraj*. We should work hard and become self-sufficient (Gandhi called on his followers to spin yarn to make their own clothes); limit our wants for both material goods and such physical pleasures as sexual relations; and welcome people of both sexes and all religions, races, and castes.

Gandhi's mission was to persuade others to devote themselves to swaraj. He felt that such self-control was impossible in modern industrial society, which he held to be inherently selfish. He believed, however, that a new world might grow out of the traditional Indian village, whose inhabitants (he claimed) have few wants and work together. In South Africa, he founded a community, an *ashram* ("refuge"), where he and his followers searched for truth.

No one has yet found the whole truth, though. Disagreements are therefore inevitable, which presents a problem: Disputes normally end with the stronger party forcing its views on the weaker. Satyagraha was Gandhi's method of resolving conflict without violence. If one's opponents are perpetrating a wrong, one first tries peacefully to dissuade them. If this fails, one must be prepared to suffer—for example, accepting punishment for breaking an unjust law. The opponents will then realize that they have unfairly caused another being to suffer. This pricks their consciences, which helps them see the truth. Meanwhile, the person who practices satyagraha preserves his or her integrity and emerges with renewed dedication to the quest for truth. Giving in to injustice, on the other hand, is accepting untruth.

The strength of character that he showed in South Africa earned Gandhi the name of Mahatma, or great soul (the term was also used by Theosophists to refer to their supernatural beings). By the time he returned to India in 1915, Gandhi was experienced in organizing satyagrahas and dealing with governments. Although he associated with Congress, however, he took little interest in politics. Instead, he concentrated on uniting Indians in the search for truth through swaraj. He founded a new ashram and led several satyagrahas against socioeconomic injustice. These campaigns—on behalf of indigo cultivators, cotton-growing peasants, and millhands—earned Gandhi recognition across India. They also brought him into contact with local politicians who joined his satyagrahas. This gave him networks of supporters that stood him in good stead when he entered politics.

Gandhi had always trusted in the benevolence of British rule in India. He did, however, call for satyagraha to protest the internment of Annie Besant and the Ali brothers. This was partly because he saw the internments as an injustice, but he had another objective. To him, the unity of all Indians was a prerequisite to swaraj. Gandhi was a Hindu, but he hoped that his public support for the Alis, the two best-known Muslims in India, would help bring together his country's two main religious communities.

In 1919, Gandhi's political thought was transformed. Worried by the disturbances provoked by economic discontent, the viceroy's legislative council passed the Rowlatt Acts. These continued for three more years some of the repressive powers of the wartime Defense of India Act. They were opposed by every Indian member of the legislative council, and only went through because with the Montagu-Chelmsford Reforms not yet in effect, officials still formed a majority of councillors.

Gandhi was one of many Indians who denounced the Rowlatt Acts. He suggested resisting them with satyagraha, through a national strike or *hartal* ("lock market"). In Punjab, a tense climate arising from economic troubles and communal hostility resulted both in widespread observance of the hartal and in rioting. On April 13, 1919, after disturbances in the city of Amritsar, a British officer ordered his troops to fire on an unarmed gathering; 379 people were killed and a thousand or more wounded.

The Mahatma called off his hartal, and the government of India and Congress both launched inquiries into the Amritsar Massacre. Gandhi served on the Congress inquiry. His experiences there and his conviction that the government report on the massacre was a whitewash changed his mind about British rule, which he now believed was unjust. This meant that seekers of truth must oppose it. In April 1920 he formally entered politics when he took over leadership of Annie Besant's Home Rule League, and in June he suggested that satyagraha could bring self-government to India. Conveniently, the Hindi for self-government is swaraj, the same word that Gandhi used for self-control.

THE NONCOOPERATION CAMPAIGN

With its defeat in World War I, Turkey lost the Muslim holy cities of Mecca, Medina, and Jerusalem. Muslims who regarded the sultan of Turkey as their khalifa felt that this endangered the holy places, and in 1919 the Ali brothers (who had been freed from internment when the war ended) became the leaders of an Indian Khilafat Movement to lobby on behalf of Turkey. (The *khilafat* is the office of khalifa.) The following year, Gandhi announced his support for the movement. He both wanted to further Hindu-Muslim unity and saw the treatment of Turkey as an in-

justice. The Ali brothers agreed to a combined self-government and khilafat satyagraha, and in August 1920 they and Gandhi began promoting
their campaign.

This satyagraha would take the form of noncooperation with the British: Gandhi and the Alis told Indians to withdraw their children from
government schools, refrain from taking disputes to the courts, resign
public office, and boycott elections. They would also give up titles and
medals received for public service, withhold taxes, and practice *swadeshi*,
the use of homemade cloth. Because it required self-discipline, noncooperation would bring Indians closer to Gandhi's swaraj. At the same
time, it would undercut the Indian acquiescence on which British rule
depended.

By the end of 1920, Congress had endorsed noncooperation, thereby
signaling its acceptance of Gandhi's leadership. The Mahatma was
helped by a lack of rivals (Tilak died the day that Gandhi and the Alis
began publicizing their campaign, and Annie Besant's eccentricities had
eroded her support). Moreover, Gandhi managed to pack two Congress
meetings with his followers, among them veterans of the indigo and mill
satyagrahas, and Muslims who appreciated his efforts in the khilafat
movement. The deciding factor, however, was probably political calcu-
lation. National leaders of Congress hoped that Gandhi's khilafat connections would cement the Muslim support that they had pursued since
the Lucknow Pact. Provincial politicians expected rewards for handing
the Mahatma control of Congress. Many saw in noncooperation solutions
to their own dilemmas—for example, candidates who wanted an excuse
not to run in elections that they might lose.

Gandhi took advantage of his newfound dominance to improve Congress's efficiency by creating a full-time party executive or Working
Committee. He also tried to make the organization more representative
by establishing local Congress branches and recruiting members from
outside the English-educated urban classes that still predominated at the
annual meetings.

Most members of Congress did boycott the 1920 elections, and atten-
dance at schools and colleges fell. During 1921, the popularity of swadeshi combined with economic problems to cut into sales of imported
cloth. Nevertheless, satyagraha enjoyed only mixed success. Noncooperation was opposed by Liberals (political heirs of Gokhale, who had left
Congress when Tilak rose to power); the remaining Congress Moderates,
who wanted to work with the Montagu-Chelmsford Reforms; and Hindu
communalists, who disliked the commitment to the khilafat. Few Indians
renounced titles (one of those who did was the poet Rabindranath Ta-

gore, who gave up the knighthood that his writings had earned him several years earlier). Nor did they boycott the courts or resign from the bureaucracy, and students soon returned to their classes. After a time, many Congress politicians wanted to end noncooperation and participate in electoral politics, the only access to power in an India that remained firmly under British rule.

By early 1922, Gandhi was looking for a face-saving excuse to call off a campaign that had grown unpopular and clearly was not working. It came when a mob of noncooperators in Uttar Pradesh burned down a police station, killing twenty-two constables inside. Gandhi announced that the satyagraha was over, and soon after was imprisoned. The noncooperation campaign had not brought self-government to India, a change in British policy toward Turkey, or any indication that Indians were closer to the Mahatma's swaraj. But it had enrolled more people than ever before into a movement directed by Congress, which unquestionably had widespread if not universal support. And it had cemented the position of Gandhi, the man who mobilized this power, as both the best-known man in India and the most important member of Congress.

POLITICS IN THE 1920s

In 1923, legislative elections showed that Congress was strong in much of India. In some places, however, the party was hurt by the enlarged franchise of the Montagu-Chelmsford Reforms. For example, Muslims formed a majority of the population of Bengal. Poverty and low levels of education had hitherto left provincial politics in the hands of urban Bengali Hindus, a powerful force in Congress since its creation. Now, Muslims dominated the electorate of Bengal and excluded Congress from power. Similarly, in Madras province (Tamil Nadu and coastal Andhra Pradesh), the non-Brahmins' Justice Party left the local Brahmin-dominated Congress far behind and won every election between 1920 and 1934. And in Punjab, Muslim, Hindu, and Sikh landowners always ensured that their Unionist Party enjoyed sufficient support in rural areas to defeat the mainly urban Congress.

Indeed, Congress languished after 1922. Following his release from prison, Gandhi pursued swaraj through social work rather than politics. For example, one of the principal obstacles to his dream of Indian unity was Untouchability, discrimination against Untouchables by Hindus of higher castes. The Mahatma joined a satyagraha to win Untouchables the right to walk on a road that passed a Hindu temple. But without his political leadership, Congress's membership and funds dropped, and many local branches ceased functioning. Most of the party ignored Gandhi's ideas about reconstructing society, which threatened the interests of both the small landholders and rich peasants who joined Congress after 1920, and the Indian industrialists who bankrolled their activities. (Fortunately, Gandhi said that the rich *should* use their wealth to help the poor, but he opposed taking it from them against their wishes.) Congress members of the legislatures instead devoted themselves to nurturing power bases, which had to be considerably larger than in the days when electoral politics were confined to local boards. They made concessions to fellow legislators in return for support, and (especially during elections) pandered to voters. By the end of the decade, adepts at this form of politics had established themselves as Congress provincial leaders.

Climatic changes, improved transportation that helped the distribution of food in famine areas, a decline in epidemics consequent on the development of natural immunities, increasing opportunities for poor peasants to enter secure if low-paying nonagricultural work—all this was lowering death rates and leading to a rapid rise in the population of the subcontinent. The annual rate of increase was over 1 percent a year from 1921 to 1951, and thereafter exceeded 2 percent. This strained the available food, jobs, and housing and created a pool of discontent from which politicians could draw support. Frustration extended to the educated classes. Thanks partly to school reforms enacted by the new Indian education ministers, rates of literacy in English and in Indian languages rose through the 1920s. White-collar jobs did not keep pace, however, and the number of unemployed or underemployed educated young men grew. The decade also saw the continued expansion of roads, railways, and the press, and the beginnings of radio broadcasting. Improved communications strengthened class, religious, and national identities and spread both discontent and political movements more rapidly than ever before.

New political movements that entered India after World War I included democratic socialism (modeled on the British Labour Party) and fascism. The success of the Russian Revolution drew educated young people to communism, which also won adherents among factory workers and peasants with its appeal to class identities. Manabendra Nath Roy, the Bengali founder of the Communist Party of India, was so successful in his home province that in 2002 the Indian state of West Bengal was perhaps the only place in the world still under an elected Communist government. Such movements often sanctioned violence to end British rule; Bhagat Singh, an atheist and a militant socialist, sought to free India through bombing and assassination until he was captured and executed in 1931.

The membership of socialist, fascist, and communist organizations in the 1920s was, however, dwarfed by the number of Indians who took part in communal politics. The tendency for people to identify themselves on the basis of religion seemed legitimized when the Morley-Minto Reforms, the Lucknow Pact, and the Montagu-Chelmsford Reforms all accepted separate electorates for Muslims. The enlargement of the electorate extended trends that had appeared with the introduction of elected local boards: Voters looked to elected leaders to protect their religious interests, politicians sought support by appealing to the religious sentiments of the majority of voters, and followers of minority religions became fearful.

Meanwhile, many people saw the activities of Arya Samajists, Ahmadis, and other missionaries as attacks on the community being targeted for conversion. All this meant that long-standing causes of religious tension, such as cow killing by Muslims, or noisy parades near mosques by Hindus, now often led to riot and murder.

The principal Hindu communal party, the All-India Hindu Mahasabha (Great Council), was founded in 1915 to coordinate Hindu organizations in North India and was reorganized as a political party in 1922. Three years later Keshav Baliram Hedgewar, one of the Mahasabha's leading intellectuals, founded the paramilitary Rashtriya Swayamsevak Sangh (RSS) or National Volunteers' Association to defend Hindus and Hinduism. Hindu communalists were particularly active in British Indian provinces where Hindus were the minority (notably Punjab), and in areas of Indian India with Muslim rulers. For some years the Arya Samaj focused its attentions on Hyderabad, where Hindus formed most of the population in a Muslim-ruled state.

In 1924, the Turkish government abolished the post of khalifa. This ended the alliance between Congress and the Muslim League, which had never found common ground beyond the question of the khilafat. The same year, the League voted in favor of a federal form of government for the India of the future, with most powers exercised by the provinces, and continued separate electorates. The first provision would assure Muslims control of provinces where they were the majority, the second would guarantee them representation in mainly Hindu provinces.

But in the 1920s, the League did not speak for all Muslims. A few "nationalist" Muslims stayed in Congress, where they were prized as a sign that the party represented all Indians. Most Muslims supported regional parties such as the Unionists in Punjab. Even within the League, there were disagreements. Muhammad Ali Jinnah, of whom more will be said later, argued that separate provincial electorates were of less value than a guaranteed number of seats in the federal legislature, and the creation of more Muslim-majority provinces. (The British acceded to the latter demand in the 1930s, with the establishment of the Northwest Frontier Province—hitherto administered directly from Delhi—and Sindh.)

The Shiromani Akali Dal, the Supreme Army of the Immortals, which is still the principal Sikh communal party in India, originated in a struggle for control over *gurdwaras* (Sikh temples). In 1920, Sikh reformers established the Shiromani Gurdwara Prabandhak Committee (Supreme Gurdwara Managing Committee) to take over gurdwaras from the Sikh aristocrats and Hinduized custodians who managed them. The Shiromani Akali Dal was the reformers' instrument. It coordinated the activities of Akali Jathas or Immortal Bands, volunteers who braved violence and imprisonment to stage satyagrahas at gurdwaras. All the gurdwaras in Punjab eventually came under their control, and in 1925 the British recognized the Shiromani Gurdwara Prabandhak Committee as manager of the gurdwaras.

THE ROUND TABLE CONFERENCE AND THE SALT SATYAGRAHA

In 1927–1928, the British parliament sent the Simon Commission to India to prepare a further installment of constitutional reform. Two Indians then sat in Parliament and were thus eligible to belong to the commission, but one of them was old and sick, the other a Communist and therefore distrusted. As a result, all seven commissioners were British. Many Indians were outraged at being excluded from a say in their country's future. Congress, Hindu communal parties, and a section of the Muslim League met to discuss their reaction. They agreed not to cooperate with the commission and appointed a committee to draft their own constitutional proposals.

This Indian committee was headed by Motilal Nehru, a leading member of Congress. Its Nehru Report demanded immediate dominion status. The meaning of this term had changed since World War I. From British dependencies with internal self-government, the dominions had become independent countries, linked to Britain only in that they shared the same king. Indian nationalists were now committed to independence.

But the Nehru Report did not please all Indians. Most Muslim politicians objected to its omission of the safeguards that they supported—

strong provincial governments, separate electorates, guaranteed seats. Within Congress, a group of radicals led by Subhas Chandra Bose and Motilal Nehru's son Jawaharlal opposed sharing even a monarch with Britain. This raised the possibility that Congress might split, under circumstances that would be personally painful for the president of its meeting in 1928, Motilal Nehru. To avert this danger, he persuaded Mahatma Gandhi to return to politics, after an absence of almost seven years.

By now, Britain's interests in India had been substantially reduced. Indian revenues still poured into Britain in the form of the Home Charges, and the subcontinent retained its psychological importance as a sign of British power. But India was no longer a source of free men (Britain now paid for Indian troops who served abroad, and recruitment of Indian indentured labor for British plantations had stopped in 1917). Indianization of the officer corps and the administration (including the ICS) reduced the scope for young Britons to obtain employment in India. From 1923, Britain allowed India to impose protective duties on imports that competed with Indian industry. India remained the largest market for British manufacturers till the late 1930s, but mainly for the declining textile industry rather than such growing sectors of the British economy as chemicals and electrical goods. The paradoxical result was that to keep whatever control they could, the British were more willing than before to make concessions to Indian opinion, because they had fewer vital interests in India to safeguard.

In an effort to win back the cooperation of Indian leaders, Lord Irwin, the viceroy, persuaded the British government to confirm that India would indeed become a dominion one day, to shelve the Simon report, and to invite the Indian political parties and princes to a Round Table Conference in London. This worsened the danger of a split in Congress: Within the party, there was disagreement over whether to join the talks in London, and whether to work with whatever reforms emerged from the conference. Gandhi decided on a new satyagraha to unite Congress and ensure his dominance. Assuming that it secured the public support that noncooperation had attracted ten years earlier, it would also remind the British that Congress could mobilize more people than any other organization in the country. After a satyagraha, Gandhi could brush aside Congress opponents of dominion status and the Round Table Conference, go to London, and use his mass support in India to extract a maximum of concessions.

Because the new satyagraha was intended to strengthen Gandhi's hand at the Round Table Conference, there was no need for it to challenge British rule in India. (An unattainable goal of immediate self-government had been one of the flaws of the campaign of 1920–1922.) But it did need a focus that would draw in as many participants as possible. The Mahatma found what he wanted in the salt tax. Salt was a monopoly of the Indian government, which collected a small tax on sales. Gandhi called on all Indians to make their own salt from seawater. This was a brilliant move. Breaking the salt monopoly was a crime, but not violent. A tax on an essential like salt was easy to present as unjust, and thus a suitable target for civil disobedience. And all Indians who made salt would demonstrate that their first loyalty was to the Mahatma rather than to the British who enforced the salt laws.

In March 1930, Gandhi opened the satyagraha by walking to the sea and making salt. Two months later, he was arrested for encouraging lawbreaking. Other Congress leaders organized the next stage of civil disobedience, which included boycotting both imported goods (especially cloth) and the 1930 legislative elections. More and more people joined the satyagraha, which achieved its greatest successes in western India. They included many women, who for the first time played a large part in a political campaign. As in 1920, participants were often motivated by grievances of their own, frequently economic, but the important thing was that they supported a movement directed by Congress. Membership in Congress grew rapidly. Many of the new adherents were local politicians or community leaders, who realized that they could only keep their position by joining the party that had persuaded their dependents to engage in civil disobedience.

Meanwhile, the Round Table Conference had brought together members of the British parliament (led by the prime minister, Ramsay Mac-Donald), the leaders of the political parties of British India with the exception of Congress, and representatives of the princes. By now, the princes' greatest fear was that British authority over them would one day pass to Indian politicians, who were more likely than the British to attack princely sovereignty as a rival to their own power. To forestall this, the princes called for a federation of the British Indian provinces with their states. A federal constitution would demarcate the powers of the different levels of government, leaving the princes secure in whatever it left to them. It would also give the princes a voice in the central legislature and executive of India, which under the Montagu-Chelmsford Reforms represented only British India.

A federation proved equally popular with Muslim leaders, who looked forward to the same autonomy for Muslim-majority provinces that the princes wanted for their states. The other British Indian parties at the conference saw federation as a small price for the support of the princes and the Muslims in constitutional reform. Many British politicians hoped that a federal system would dilute the power of Congress in the central legislature, as the main party of British India as yet had little support in the princes' Indian India. With federation agreed to, the next step was writing a suitable constitution. Irwin and MacDonald had expected the Round Table Conference to discuss general principles, which did not require the participation of Congress. But the federation would not work unless Congress accepted it, and this would only happen if the party were part of the constitutional discussions. Early in 1931, the viceroy therefore approached Gandhi about ending civil disobedience and joining the conference.

The British had jailed thousands of Indians under new laws enacted to repress the satyagraha, and the campaign was running out of steam after nine months. The Mahatma was as keen on negotiations as Irwin. In March 1931, the viceroy withdrew the repressive regulations, legalized the picketing of shops that sold imported goods, and allowed Indians to make untaxed salt for their own use. In return, Gandhi ended the satyagraha, retracted Congress's demand for immediate dominion status, and agreed to attend the constitutional discussions.

Congress and Gandhi enjoyed the support of many Indians, but—as the 1930s showed—not all. When the Round Table Conference reopened, the parties representing communal minorities (including Muslims, Sikhs, and Untouchables) made it clear that the Mahatma did not speak for them. Then, on his return home in December 1931, Gandhi found that many members of Congress were ignoring his pact with Irwin and continuing the satyagraha. This left him with a choice between disowning those who persisted in civil disobedience and thus splitting Congress, or officially resuming the satyagraha so as to reincorporate the dissidents in the party. He chose the latter course, but failed to generate the support seen in 1930. In any case, the Mahatma was arrested only a few days into the campaign. An ever-shrinking core of activists continued civil disobedience for two years, but to little effect.

THE NEW CONSTITUTION

By the end of 1932, the Round Table Conference had hammered out the framework of the new constitution, which now went to the British parliament. After lengthy delays (many of them caused by right-wingers who opposed any loosening of ties between Britain and India), the reforms were implemented after parliament passed the Government of

India Act in 1935. To retain anything in India, the British needed the acquiescence of its elites. This they could obtain only by surrendering the provinces of British India to the elected politicians whom so many Indians now accepted as their rightful leaders.

The constitution divided the powers of government between the federal and provincial governments. The latter were now entirely controlled by wholly elected legislatures. Each province had a prime minister, drawn from whichever party could assemble a majority in the legislature. He appointed the executive council from among his legislative colleagues.

The property and educational qualifications for the franchise were lowered so that the electorate included one sixth of the adult population. Sikhs, Indian Christians, and a number of other communities were granted separate electorates alongside Muslims. MacDonald had also offered separate electorates to the Untouchables. Gandhi opposed this, arguing that it would further divide Untouchables from other Hindus and reduce the incentive for the latter to improve their treatment of Untouchables. The Mahatma went on a hunger strike, until the Untouchable leader Bhimrao Ramji Ambedkar turned down the offer of separate electorates. The two men agreed instead that in constituencies with large populations of Untouchables, the latter would provide all the candidates for elections. This scheme was incorporated in the constitution.

The divided authority that had existed in the provinces under the Montagu-Chelmsford Reforms was now implemented at the federal level: India's internal affairs would be transferred to ministers responsible to a federal legislature, and the viceroy and his appointed executive councillors retained responsibility for defense and external affairs. It has already been noted that the federal government was to have authority over, and include representatives of, the states of Indian India as well as the provinces of British India. In 1929, however, the British had agreed to the princes' contention that supremacy over the states rested with the British monarch, not the government of India. This meant that New Delhi could not unilaterally include the states in the federation. The Government of India Act therefore provided that each prince would negotiate the terms of his accession to the federation. The federal legislature and executive would only come into operation when enough princes had acceded; until then, the central government would operate under the Montagu-Chelmsford system.

While the constitutional negotiations were underway, the economy of India was in turmoil. During the first three decades of the twentieth century, domestic and foreign prices for Indian agricultural produce rose steadily. Then, in 1929, demand suddenly collapsed, and with it prices. The Great Depression was partly responsible, as it compelled millions all over the globe to cut back purchases. Other factors included worldwide overproduction of raw cotton and jute, the principal Indian agricultural exports, and a sudden constriction of the credit networks that had given poorer Indians the wherewithal to buy food. Between 1929 and 1931, the domestic price of Indian crops fell by 44 percent. The burden fell mainly on poor peasants. Not only did their agricultural incomes fall; many of them also lost the opportunity to supplement their earnings with part-time labor for wealthier peasants or landholders, who needed fewer workers with the declining profitability of agriculture. The rural poor had no option but to go ever more deeply into debt, often to rich peasants.

The same rich peasants were the backbone of Congress in rural areas, and among the beneficiaries of the widened electoral franchise of 1935. Many of them were wealthier than ever. During the 1920s and 1930s, protective tariffs were imposed on agricultural imports that could be grown in India, such as sugar. This assured a market to Indian producers of those commodities. Rich peasants who did not enjoy such security might plow their profits into industry rather than the less certain agricultural expansion.

Indian manufacturing enjoyed mixed success between the World Wars. The total percentage of the workforce employed in industry remained unchanged at 12 percent throughout the first half of the twentieth century. The proportion of those in large-scale factories increased, but never exceeded 2 percent of the labor force. From its inception, modern industry in India was hampered by low levels of education and poor training. This partly explains why productivity only grew slowly; in the 1930s, Indian workers produced less per head than their counterparts in Mexico and Egypt. In 1918, an Industrial Commission recommended that the central government encourage technical education and private investment in industry. The Montagu-Chelmsford Reforms, however, transferred industrial policy to the provinces, which lacked the resources to do much.

During the 1920s and 1930s, Indian textiles lost markets at home and abroad to Japanese competitors. The other major export industry, jute processing, was hit hard by the combined effects of the Great Depression and the development of new kinds of packaging in the 1930s. But the picture was not entirely bleak. Industry benefited by the institution of protective tariffs from 1923, and the government's post–Montagu-Chelmsford policy of buying railway and other supplies in India wherever possible. New industries were established to meet growing domestic demand, from automobiles to chemical engineering, and by the mid-1940s India was the world's tenth largest producer of manufactured goods. Some new firms were subsidiaries of Western companies, but many were owned by Indians.

Indeed, during the 1930s and 1940s, manufacturing increasingly came under Indian ownership, as the depression and the political climate forced British firms to sell out. In 1944, Indian-owned firms employed over 80 percent of the workers in large-scale industry. Indian businessmen diversified their interests. The Tatas, who began as traders, went into textiles and then into iron and steel, and in the 1940s inaugurated commercial domestic airline service in India. The Birlas, a merchant family of eastern India, added jute processing in the 1920s and chemical industries in the 1930s. The Tatas and Birlas were among the many Indian businessmen who gave financial support to Congress, while at the same time managing to retain the goodwill of the British.

CONGRESS IN THE LATE 1930s

The first provincial elections under the new constitution were held in 1937. Congress selected candidates whose caste or social status were electoral assets in their constituencies, sent out its best speakers to campaign, and started a Mass Contact program to drum up popular support. Most other parties lacked the resources to reach the millions of newly enfranchised voters and lost heavily at the polls. In the end, Congress dominated the new legislatures of eight of the eleven provinces of British India. Some members argued that the party should not legitimize British rule by assuming office, but they were outvoted by those who wanted to take advantage of the unprecedented power that the new constitution gave to elected politicians. By the end of 1938, Congress prime ministers ruled all the provinces except Bengal, Punjab, and Sindh, which were controlled by regional parties.

There were many reasons for the popularity of Congress, which during the late 1930s enrolled more members than ever before. For over fifty years, Congress had called itself the representative of the Indian people, many of whom had come to accept this claim. The party's record in securing Indian political rights was unimpeachable, and in Gandhi it had the best-known man in all India. Ambitious men joined Congress because it offered the surest route to power and influence, and the eclipse of other parties in 1937 brought new support from politicians and voters. This was a two-way street, however. The rich peasants and urban professionals who joined Congress to secure their own position made themselves indispensable to the party, as legislators and as intermediaries with the mass of the voting and nonvoting population. The provincial prime ministers and national leaders could not afford to alienate these local "bosses," who made sure that Congress refrained from interfering with their interests.

This was partly responsible for the most serious threat to face Congress in the 1930s. Subhas Chandra Bose led a radical faction that wanted to commit Congress to a socialist redistribution of wealth to the poor after the end of British rule. This was a threat to the bosses. For several years, Gandhi avoided a split by postponing any party decision on the question. Meanwhile, Bose's popularity grew among the Congress rank and file, who chose him as party president for 1938. Gandhi made it clear that he would tolerate Bose as president for only one year. When Bose ran for reelection and won, the Mahatma took action to keep the essential support of the conservative bosses. Gandhi's supporters dominated the Congress Working Committee, the party executive, which on his instructions refused to work with Bose. In mid-1939, Bose gave up trying to run Congress on his own and resigned the presidency.

THE MUSLIM LEAGUE IN THE LATE 1930s

Meanwhile, the Muslim League was being transformed by Muhammad Ali Jinnah, a lawyer who was probably born in 1876. Jinnah began his career as one of the comparatively few Muslim members of Congress, and by the time he was elected to the central Legislative Council in 1910 was the right-hand man of the Congress leader Gokhale. Three years later he joined the Muslim League in order to bring the two parties together, and as a member of both Congress and the League he played a central role in negotiating the Lucknow Pact. An old-style Moderate, Jinnah believed in working with the system, and he drifted away from Congress after it approved the noncooperation campaign in 1920. Over the next few years he became increasingly worried by what he saw as a Hindu communal streak in Congress, symbolized when the party endorsed the Nehru Report, which rejected constitutional safeguards for Muslims in an independent India.

In 1935, the impending transfer of provincial power to prime ministers who would inevitably mostly belong to Congress induced Jinnah to accept an invitation to assume leadership of the Muslim League. He believed that a strong League was his community's best defense against discrimination. The party did poorly in the 1937 elections, though, failing to win control of even one of the four Muslim-majority provinces. Fortunately, Jinnah managed to persuade the new prime ministers of Bengal and Punjab (both Muslims from regional parties) to join the League. He could now claim to control the two largest Muslim provinces, although this was more apparent than real. The two prime ministers continued to head their own parties within their provinces, and only identified themselves as Leaguers when they were in other parts of India. The alliance with Jinnah gave them links to a nationwide party, but did not require them to accept its dictation.

The elections did, however, show that most Muslim voters shared Jinnah's suspicions of Congress, which fared poorly in Muslim constituencies. By this time, Mahatma Gandhi was nearly seventy years old. He had no formal office in Congress, and relied heavily on his acknowledged political heir, Motilal Nehru's son Jawaharlal. This probably helped ensure that Jawaharlal did not follow his old comrade Bose in challenging the Mahatma, and made him an important figure in Congress's national leadership. The younger Nehru was thoroughly secular in his outlook, and could not understand people who saw religion as the dominant force in their lives. This made him dismiss the fears of Indian Muslims about being a permanent minority in a democratic country, which in turn increased their feeling that Congress could never represent them.

Other Congress leaders were either insensitive to Muslim concerns, or open Hindu communalists. Some of the new provincial governments promoted the Hindi language at the expense of Urdu. Most treated *Bande Mataram* as an unofficial national anthem (this is a patriotic hymn that speaks to the homeland in terms used for Hindu divinities). Congress's reverence for Gandhi alienated many Muslims, who regarded the Mahatma as a typical Hindu holy man. And in 1937, bosses who wanted the party to remain Hindu in complexion helped scuttle a drive to recruit Muslims to Congress. All this gave Jinnah ammunition with which to persuade Muslims that they were under attack, and that only the League could save them. Thanks partly to this, more and more Muslims came to share Jinnah's conviction that their community would need iron-clad safeguards against discrimination when the British left.

THE FAILURE OF FEDERATION

Meanwhile, the British were negotiating with the princes to secure their accession to the federation. The princes, as ever watchful for their sovereignty, were now afraid that the new constitution did not protect their states against interference by the federal government. Moreover, the constitution had transferred to the provinces a number of lucrative taxes. The central government faced a shortfall in its revenues, without a corresponding reduction in expenditure. To meet this problem, the government of India demanded that acceding princes surrender much of their tax revenue to the federation.

In 1937–1938, for reasons that are unclear, state political leaders who wanted power for themselves unleashed a wave of agitation against many princes. Until now, Congress had confined its activities to British India. Bose and other dissidents realized that if they joined the agitators in Indian India, they might build power bases from which to take over Congress. Gandhi and the Congress leadership defused this danger by formally extending support to the state movements. To prevent Congress from gaining a foothold in the states, the British decided to remove any cause for complaint among the princes' subjects. With this in mind, they began forcing the princes to carry out administrative reforms. Not unnaturally, this increased the princes' fears for their sovereignty. In 1939, it became likely that not enough states would accede for the federal government to become operational, and the viceroy suspended negotiations with the princes.

WORLD WAR II

After 1937, Congress provincial ministers and legislators established good relations with their British governors and the British-controlled central government. Other members of the party, including some national leaders, did not understand that this was necessary if Congress was to enjoy the fruits of its electoral victories. They wanted to obstruct British rule so as to obtain freedom for India as quickly as possible. By mid-1939, Congress was again facing a split.

In September 1939, World War II began when Britain declared war on Germany. The viceroy Lord Linlithgow announced that, as in 1914, India was automatically a belligerent. At the orders of their national leaders, who wanted a breathing space to resolve internal party tensions, the eight Congress provincial governments resigned. Their pretext was that Linlithgow should have consulted Indian politicians before making his announcement.

In August 1940, to secure support for the war effort from the politicians whom so many Indians now regarded as their leaders, Linlithgow offered to appoint representatives of Congress, the League, and other parties to his executive council. This provoked debate in Congress over whether to accept this opportunity for power in Delhi, or hold out for independence as the price of cooperation. Gandhi resorted to his usual method of combatting dissent, a satyagraha. This time, Indians would court arrest through nonviolent resistance to the war effort, demonstrating the mass support that would give Congress leverage in future talks with the viceroy.

This satyagraha accomplished little beyond the imprisonment of the principal leaders of Congress, however. The Muslim League, the Shiromani Akali Dal, and other parties supported the war effort. Linlithgow ignored Congress and appointed new members to the executive council until it was almost entirely Indian in composition.

The viceroy's "August Offer" also promised that India would not be handed over to any body that was opposed by a large part of the subcontinent's population. The meaning was obvious: The British would not transfer power to a purely Congress government, which would assuredly be rejected by most Muslims. Linlithgow wanted to ensure the loyalty of the Muslims who made up a large part of the Indian Army, and the Muslim League had recently endorsed a new policy. At a party meeting at Lahore in March 1940, Jinnah secured approval of a resolution stating that when India became free, its Muslims must have states where they were not under Hindu control. This echoed a call made ten years earlier by the then-president of the League, the poet-philosopher Mohammad Iqbal. Iqbal had urged the creation of a state in northwestern India where Muslims could rule themselves in accordance with Islamic principles. Jinnah's motivation was different. He knew little of theology and had no interest in an Islamic government. Instead, he argued that the Muslims of India formed a nation of their own, which like any nation was entitled to a territorial base.

Neither Iqbal in 1930 nor Jinnah in 1940 made it clear whether their states were to be independent or members of an Indian federation, although it seems that both men inclined to the latter. Jinnah said "states" in the plural, adding the northeast (Bengal and Assam, the latter having a Muslim population of about 25 percent) alongside Iqbal's northwestern state (Punjab, Sindh, the Northwest Frontier Province). This was soon forgotten, as Jinnah and his followers began to speak of the northeast and northwest as a single Muslim state. Their dream was called Pakistan, a punning term coined by Muslim students in England in 1933 (it means "pure land," and also combines letters from the names of the Muslim areas of the northwest: Punjab, the Afghan areas of the Frontier, Kashmir, and so on).

It has been suggested that Jinnah's real goal was a maximum of constitutional safeguards for his coreligionists, and that Pakistan was a bargaining counter that could be given up in return for special protection. But the idea of a state where they were masters would appeal to Muslims who considered themselves victims of discrimination at the hands of Hindus. It was also vague enough to draw in people who conceived of a Muslim state in very different ways. Support for the idea would mean the growth of the League, the only party committed to Pakistan. A strong League would strengthen Jinnah's hand in any negotiations on the constitution of a free India. At the same time, Jinnah's declaration that Indian Muslims were a nation of their own denied Congress any right to speak for them, because Congress's claim to represent Muslims assumed that they were part of the Indian nation whose interests the party advocated.

In December 1941, Japan entered the war on the side of Germany. Japanese troops defeated the British in Malaya and Burma, and reached the frontier of India in the spring of 1942. Winston Churchill, the prime minister of Britain, loathed Indian nationalism (he had been one of the principal obstructionists as the 1935 constitution went through parliament). Nevertheless, he and his cabinet agreed that the danger of a Japanese invasion made Indian support essential. Sir Stafford Cripps, a cabinet minister and an old friend of Nehru, was dispatched to India to make terms with its politicians (the Congress leaders had been freed from prison). Apparently on his own initiative, Cripps promised that in return for support of the war, India would become independent after hostilities had ended. With the Lahore Resolution in mind, he also said that no area would be included in independent India without the approval of its inhabitants.

Possibly overestimating British desperation, Congress rejected the offer, and demanded immediate independence without the provision for any part of India to "opt out." This Churchill and Linlithgow would not grant. Congress, already torn over its reaction should the Japanese invade and now in danger of breaking up over the Cripps Offer, called for satyagraha to force the British to leave. Gandhi, Nehru, and their colleagues were arrested and lost control of their "Quit India movement," which slipped into the hands of local bosses and militants. These drew on the discontent of a population of rural poor who were facing famine on a scale not seen for forty years, thanks to wartime inflation, disrupted communications that interfered with the distribution of food, and poor harvests.

The situation was worst in Bengal, where the loss of Burmese rice fields and grain hoarding by merchants contributed to a million starvation deaths in 1943 (another 2 million Bengalis died from the effects of famine by 1946). All across India, hungry peasants attacked symbols of British power, such as police stations, post offices, and rail facilities. The Quit India satyagraha became the subcontinent's greatest rebellion since 1857, and in some areas, government collapsed. The British used all the force at their disposal against the uprising, which was suppressed by mid-1943.

Meanwhile, Jinnah had been building support for the Muslim League. The party had always been strongest in the mainly Hindu provinces, where Muslims were particularly fearful about discrimination. If Pakistan was to exist, Jinnah needed to extend his authority to the Muslim majority provinces. Congress inadvertently helped him, as the resignations of the Congress prime ministers and legislators in 1939 let League governments take office in Assam and the Northwest Frontier Province.

During the war, Muslim aristocrats and religious leaders in Sindh and Punjab switched their support from regional parties to the League, which they felt would best protect them against a Hindu central government in independent India. In Bengal, the League was helped by the economic crisis, as Muslim peasants looked for its help against Hindu landowners and moneylenders. By now, the League was undergoing the same sort of growth that Congress had seen in the 1930s, with politicians and local leaders flocking to a party that clearly had a future. In 1942–1943, Jinnah had sufficient support in the legislatures of Sindh and Bengal to install members of the League as provincial prime ministers. Because the prime minister of Punjab was also affiliated with the League, the League now controlled the five provinces that Jinnah demanded for Pakistan.

Support for the League almost inevitably meant support for Pakistan. Jinnah skillfully played on the differences that set Muslims apart from other Indians. These had often been negligible before the reform movements of the nineteenth and twentieth centuries, but Jinnah used them to drive home the point that Indian Muslims were a nation. Because the nation is a state of mind, Muslims who accepted Jinnah's thesis really did become a separate nation rather than the minority community that they had considered themselves to be a few years earlier. By the time the war ended in 1945, the Muslim League was a mass party. Jinnah was the acknowledged leader of most Muslims, who looked to him to create Pakistan as a homeland for their nation.

TOWARD INDEPENDENCE

Even if Cripps had not committed them to leaving India, the British in 1945 had fewer reasons for staying than at any time since the eighteenth century. The Home Charges, one of the tangible benefits of imperial rule to survive the reforms of 1920s and 1930s, ceased to exist during World War II. Britain agreed to reimburse much of the expense that India had incurred as a source of men, money, and supplies, and as a base for operations in the Middle East and Southeast Asia. The sums were deducted from the Home Charges, until all of India's debt to Britain was discharged. Britain then issued credits, called the Sterling Balances, and in 1945 it was Britain that owed money to India, rather than vice versa.

By now, too, ordinary Britons were concentrating on making ends meet in the face of postwar economic hardship, and had little interest in holding India. Businessmen felt that their economic interests would fare better in a friendly independent India than a hostile dependency; and intellectuals who a generation earlier would have regarded British rule as an instrument of progress declared their support for colonial nationalism. These sentiments extended to Clement Attlee, the leader of the Labour Party, who in July 1945 replaced Churchill as prime minister.

Willpower aside, the British probably lacked the ability to hold India for much longer. By 1946, units of both the police and the navy had mutinied. During the war, there had been a warning that the army might turn. In 1941, former Congress president Bose made his way through Afghanistan and the Soviet Union to Germany. He met Hitler and—out of either sympathy with their aims or a desire for whatever help he could get against the British—declared his support for the Axis. He then went to Southeast Asia, where he recruited Indian soldiers who had been captured by the Japanese into an Indian National Army. Not all the Indian prisoners of war joined this INA, but Bose found enough men to assemble three divisions that joined an unsuccessful Japanese invasion of India.

Bose apparently died in an airplane crash in 1945, but the INA made it clear that the British could not count on the loyalty of Indian soldiers. The Quit India rebellion was also a warning. It failed because the imprisonment of the Congress leaders left it uncoordinated, and because during the war the British had the will and the manpower to suppress the disturbances. It was unlikely that these circumstances would recur in another rising.

All this meant that after 1945 the principal task of Lord Wavell, who had become viceroy two years earlier, was to make India independent. However much he might have wished to pull out immediately, he could not take a step that might provoke chaos and so tarnish both Britain's name and its remaining interests in India. Rather, Wavell had to find a formula for independence that was acceptable not only to Congress, the most popular party in India, but also to the Muslim League, which represented the Muslims who, thanks to Cripps's promise, were entitled to opt out of any plan they did not like. Congress now needed someone who could negotiate the terms of independence. This cemented the dominance of Jawaharlal Nehru, who had almost thirty years of experience at the top levels of the party and was the Mahatma's political heir. As an English-educated patrician, Nehru shared the schooling and values of the British upper classes and got along well with Wavell.

In 1945, the viceroy made a start by offering to let the Indian leaders choose his executive council. If they accepted, Indian politicians would gain experience in the central government so that there would be no disruption when independence came. Jinnah vetoed Nehru's plan to name a Muslim member to the council, on the grounds that this was mere tokenism directed against the League's claim to speak for all Muslims. Wavell's proposal came to nothing. Elections in the winter of 1945–1946 proved that most Muslims now agreed with Jinnah: The League won every Muslim seat in the central legislature and 439 of the 494 provincial Muslim seats. Congress, meanwhile, garnered massive support among non-Muslim voters, who gave it 91 percent of the non-Muslim seats at the center and returned it to power in eight provinces. The communal polarization of India was almost complete.

In 1946, Cripps returned to India with two fellow British cabinet ministers. This Cabinet Mission proposed to devolve most powers of government to the provinces. If they wished, neighboring provinces could establish federations, called groups, which would belong to a federal India. This permitted the creation of a self-governing Pakistan, though not an independent one, in the northwestern and northeastern groups. Nehru objected that these two groups included large areas where Hindus formed most of the population. He also pointed out that when India became independent, its people could adopt any form of government they pleased. Because the majority of Indians supported Congress, and Congress opposed grouping, this meant that a Pakistan based on the Cabinet Mission proposals would not outlive British rule.

Jinnah therefore rejected the scheme. He now spoke of a Pakistan that would be completely independent, and in August 1946 called on Muslims to do whatever was necessary to obtain it. In Calcutta, this sparked street battles between Hindus and Muslims, and 4,000 people (mostly Muslim) died in the ensuing Great Calcutta Killing. Economic deprivation and rabble-rousing by local political leaders helped spread communal violence across north India. It was particularly severe in East Bengal (where Muslims were the majority) and Bihar (where they were the minority). In early 1947, the center of violence shifted to Punjab, which drifted into civil war between Muslims on one side and Hindus and Sikhs on the other. Most Sikhs gave up the idea (mooted by Master Tara Singh of the Shiromani Akali Dal) of a Sikh state alongside Hindu India and Muslim Pakistan, and the Akali Dal allied itself with Congress.

If Jinnah saw Pakistan as a bargaining counter, he was now over-playing his hand. In September 1946, he refused Wavell's invitation to join the executive council. Nehru and other members of Congress accepted. Jinnah had to backtrack, and his nominees joined Nehru and his colleagues on the council. But the Congress and League councillors could not work together, and the central government slid toward paralysis. In February 1947, Attlee made a fresh start by dismissing Wavell as viceroy. He replaced him with Lord Mountbatten. The new viceroy was a man of great charm and a cousin of the British king, and had been Supreme Allied Commander in Southeast Asia during the war.

Congress was now prepared to call Jinnah's bluff, if it was a bluff. In January 1947, the party executive agreed that no province should be forced to stay part of India against the wishes of its people. This was partly because most of the Congress leaders were prepared to do anything to stop the communal violence. Some, like Nehru, knew that Jinnah's price for staying would be a federal government so weak that it would be unable to rebuild free India. Others, among them the conservative party strongman Sardar Vallabhbhai Patel, were probably happy to give up Muslim-majority areas as a way of reducing the size of a community that detracted from their vision of a Hindu India.

In April 1947, Nehru informed Mountbatten that Congress would accept an independent Pakistan, so long as it did not include territories with non-Muslim majorities. At least for the time being, Nehru also agreed to independence in the form of dominion status. The viceroy still hoped to revive the Cabinet Mission plan, but this was impossible. On June 3 he announced that the British would leave India as soon as they could, and divide the provinces of British India between two independent dominions, India and Pakistan. Lawmakers in Bengal and Punjab agreed to the division of their provinces along religious lines, and the electors of the North-West Frontier Province and the Muslim portions of Assam (both ruled by Congress governments since the last elections) voted in favor of inclusion in a Pakistan that would comprise two wings, separated by a thousand miles of Indian territory. The Muslims of the Hindu-majority provinces, who had always been the League's strongest supporters, were left in India.

There remained the question of Indian India. The Cabinet Mission had stated that all ties between Britain and the princes would lapse with independence. Among other things, this meant that the new dominions would not inherit British supremacy over the states. Some of the leading princes signified their interest in including their territories in independent India by sending representatives to the constituent assembly, which was charged with writing a constitution for independent India. This body consisted mainly of delegates chosen by the provincial legislatures of British India, although the Muslim League refused to participate. Nevertheless, as of June 1947, no ruler had committed himself to joining either India or Pakistan. The following month, Nehru established a Ministry of States, headed by Sardar Patel. Patel promised that if the princes gave the Indian government jurisdiction over their defense, foreign affairs, and communications, they would retain the rest of their sovereign powers. Almost all the major states within the boundaries of the dominion of India accepted these terms by the date of independence.

Independence took effect August 14, 1947, for Pakistan, and August 15 for India. The leaders of India were faced with the enormous task of building a new country on age-old foundations.

8

Building the New India

THE ESTABLISHMENT OF THE REPUBLIC OF INDIA

In 1947, Jawaharlal Nehru's role in negotiating independence won him the post of India's first prime minister. But he had to share the government with his deputy prime minister, Sardar Vallabhbhai Patel, Congress's principal organizer, whose control over the party's pyramid of committees running from Delhi to the villages gave him a solid power base. Nehru led the left wing of Congress, committed to a modern, secular society; Patel represented the conservatives who wanted to rebuild India on its Hindu foundations. The two had usually managed to suppress their differences during the struggle against the British. Now, they dueled to dominate the government and their party, each knowing that victory would determine the country's future.

In the weeks before independence, Patel scored a success when he persuaded the princes of most major states to accede to India. The state of Kashmir (officially, Jammu and Kashmir), however, gave rise to what remains the greatest source of tension in South Asia. In 1947, the mainly Muslim population of Kashmir was ruled by a Hindu prince, Maharaja Hari Singh. His ancestor was Ranjit Singh's nobleman Raja Gulab Singh, who had received the kingdom a century earlier after assisting the East

India Company's invasion of the Sikh empire. The partition of British India gave Kashmir borders with both India and Pakistan, but Hari Singh did not accede to either new country.

Then, in October 1947, a Muslim revolt broke out against the maharaja, perhaps at the instigation of Pakistan. Pakistani volunteers flooded in to join the revolt, and Hari Singh appealed to India for help. This was granted in return for Kashmir's accession to India. Indian troops stopped the Pakistani advance in this first Indo-Pakistani war, but not before Pakistan had won control over about a third of Kashmir. Fighting continued until the United Nations arranged a cease-fire. India and Pakistan agreed that Kashmiris could vote on the future of their state, but they never agreed on the mechanics. By the mid-1950s, India was unwilling to lose Kashmir by either war or votes, and dropped its support for a plebiscite. This was partly a reaction to the creation of Pakistan, which produced a determination on the part of many Indians not to give up any more territory. Equally important was the realization that a vote by mainly Muslim Kashmir to secede from India and join Pakistan might seem to confirm Jinnah's claim that South Asian Muslims formed a separate nation from their Hindu compatriots—a claim that India had never accepted. As a result, to this day Kashmir is divided between India and Pakistan, each of which considers the other to be in illegal occupation of a portion of the state.

A thousand miles to the south, Hyderabad presented a reverse image of Kashmir. There, a Hindu population was governed by a Muslim, Nizam Osman Ali Khan, descended from the eighteenth-century Mughal nobleman Nizam ul-Mulk. India would not accept the nizam's desire for an independent Hyderabad, and in September 1948 invaded Hyderabad to force Osman Ali Khan to accede. This gave India overlordship over the last holdout in what had been Indian India.

By the time of the conquest of Hyderabad, however, Patel had moved beyond accession. Perhaps fearing that the popularity of many princes and chiefs among their subjects threatened the dominance of Congress, he set about ending monarchy in India. Between 1947 and 1949, the rulers were persuaded or compelled to renounce their sovereignty in return for pensions, called privy purses, and a guarantee of royal titles and privileges. Most states were merged into larger units parallel to the provinces of the former British India.

By now, India had lost the man who led its struggle for freedom. After independence, communal hostility exploded into violence on both sides of the new Indo-Pakistani border. This was followed by the largest transfer of population in the history of the world, as fearful Hindus and Sikhs fled Pakistan while Muslims left India. Further violence occurred when Indians and Pakistanis attacked departing refugees. In the end, over 13 million people found new homes in India or Pakistan, and nearly 1 million died. Mahatma Gandhi spoke out against the carnage, particularly when the arrival of Hindu and Sikh refugees in Delhi sparked attacks on Muslims. He tried to defuse communal hostility, which he linked with his government's tardiness in dividing British Indian assets with Pakistan. On January 30, 1948, however, he was assassinated by a Hindu who resented his attempts to accommodate Muslims.

Nehru appealed to Indians to heed the nonviolence preached by their murdered leader. This, and a temporary ban on Hindu and Muslim communal organizations, abated religious warfare. To reassure those Muslims who wished to stay in India that they were welcome, the government committed itself to what it called "secularism." This did not mean the separation of religion and politics, but rather assuring religious minorities the freedom to practice their faiths, even at the cost of exempting them from the law. For example, in the 1950s, new legislation regarding the rights of Indian women to divorce or inherit was explicitly not extended to Muslim women, who remained subject to Islamic law as interpreted by theologians.

The fundamental law of independent India is the constitution, officially the work of the constituent assembly but in fact largely drafted by a small group of men including Nehru, Patel, and the Untouchable leader Dr. Ambedkar. The constitution went into effect with the establishment of the Republic of India on January 26, 1950. Like the 1935 Government of India Act (on which it was based), it provides for a division of the powers of government between the federal "Center" and states (which included both the old provinces of British India and what remained of Indian India). The creation of Pakistan had rendered irrelevant arguments that a weak federal government was essential to keep the Muslim-majority provinces within India. Instead, there was a consensus that only a strong Center could safeguard independence and unity, maintain law and order, and carry out social and economic development. The constitution therefore allocated the more lucrative and important powers to the Center, as well as any powers not specifically named. Moreover, the Center may create new states, abolish existing ones, or dismiss a state government and temporarily assume control of the state through what is called President's Rule. (Partly in order to reconcile its inhabitants to their new Indian nationality, Kashmir was given a special autonomous status that limited the Center's authority within the state.)

There was a general feeling in India that dominion status was not quite independence. The constitution accordingly removed the British monarch from his position as formal head of state. He was replaced with a president, elected by Central and state legislators. The duties of the president of India, however, resemble those of the sovereign of the United Kingdom more than those of the president of the United States, especially in that he normally acts on the advice of the prime minister and cabinet. Like his British counterpart, the Indian prime minister derives his authority from a bicameral parliament, in this case consisting of the Lok Sabha (the "House of the People," elected by popular vote) and the Rajya Sabha (the "Council of States," most of whose members are chosen by state legislatures).

The prime minister must have the support of a majority of the members of the Lok Sabha. If over half the members come from a single party, its leader automatically becomes prime minister. No party has won a majority of Lok Sabha seats since 1984, however, which means that would-be prime ministers must get support from other parties besides their own. If a prime minister loses his majority, he must resign. Then, either someone else assembles a majority and becomes prime minister, or a Lok Sabha election is held.

The prime minister chooses ministers who oversee external affairs, finance, and other government departments. He and his principal ministers form the cabinet, which meets periodically to set government policy. All ministers, including the prime minister, must be members of either the Lok Sabha or the Rajya Sabha. The main function of parliament is, however, to make laws (on the advice of the prime minister, the president can also issue ordinances without parliamentary approval). Like its American counterpart, the Supreme Court of India rules on the constitutionality of laws, although most of its time is occupied in trying cases and hearing appeals.

The president may call a Lok Sabha election at any time, so long as no more than five years pass without one. A popular prime minister may ask the president for an early election in the expectation that his party will sweep the seats, although in recent years all elections have followed the collapse of a prime minister's majority. India is divided into parliamentary constituencies, each with one representative in the Lok Sabha. The constitution replaced the restricted franchise of British times with universal adult suffrage. Congress had long opposed separate electorates for Muslims and other minorities, and they were now abolished. To ensure representation for disadvantaged groups, however, the constitution borrowed the scheme introduced in 1935 following the agreement between Gandhi and Ambedkar: In certain constituencies, all candidates for election must be either Untouchables or Tribals. The Untouchable and Tribal communities are described in a schedule (appendix) to the constitution, from which they are called Scheduled Castes and Scheduled Tribes.

The constitution explicitly bans discrimination against Untouchables. It names other social and economic reforms in its Directive Principles, measures that the government should undertake for the benefit of poor and downtrodden groups. The Directive Principles are desirable but not mandatory, however, and in any case implementing them may infringe on the fundamental rights (to liberty, property, and so on) that the constitution guarantees. So that these rights do not hinder the maintenance of law and order, the constitution allows the president to suspend basic freedoms if he and the prime minister believe that a national emergency has arisen.

Government in the states parallels that at the Center, with a governor (appointed by the president on the advice of the prime minister) corresponding to the president, a chief minister replacing the provincial prime ministers of the 1935 constitution, a legislative assembly, and a High Court. (Until 1956, governors in much of what had been Indian India were called rajpramukhs, and were chosen by former rulers rather than by the president.) Before 1971, elections for state assemblies were normally held simultaneously with Lok Sabha elections.

To strike a balance between diversity and the need for unity, independent India adopted a policy of pluralism, recognizing differences rather than suppressing them. Compromise was integral to the process, as became evident in debates over language. Many Indians felt that with independence, Hindi, the country's most widely spoken language, should replace the English of their former rulers in the Central government, and the constitution accordingly declared Hindi to be India's official language. This meant that Hindi alone would be used in parliament and in all jobs under the control of the Center, from the bureaucracy to publicly owned enterprises.

Indians who spoke other languages objected that this would give Hindi-speakers an unfair advantage, and they secured a constitutional provision that English would be the working language of the Center until 1965. It was hoped that by then, knowledge of Hindi would have spread. This did not happen, however. In 1963, Parliament confirmed that Hindi would become the official language in 1965, but added that English would be used alongside it for at least ten years. Even this was too much for many non-Hindi speakers, who wanted English to be kept in perpetuity. In 1966, a new language law therefore enshrined the joint use of English and Hindi in parliament and provided that all dealings between the Center and non–Hindi-speaking states would be conducted in English. Since then, the huge Bollywood film industry has extended understanding of Hindi, but English remains the principal language of business, the professions, the higher bureaucracy, and elite schools and universities.

The constitution also recognized fourteen regional tongues as "national" languages, the official languages of the states where they are spoken. Examinations for jobs administered by the Center are offered in national languages, whose number has been increased to eighteen since 1950. State and linguistic boundaries did not originally coincide; a given national language might be spoken in several states, or a single state might contain several national languages. Thus, in the old Madras state, Tamil was spoken in the south and Telugu in the north. A campaign for a separate Telugu state culminated in the death of a Telugu leader during a hunger strike in 1952. The resulting anger raised the specter of a Telugu insurrection, and the Center quickly divided the state into Madras (for Tamils) and Andhra (for Telugus). It was obvious that the process could not stop there, and in 1956 state boundaries were redrawn in accordance with language.

This form of pluralism virtually eliminated linguistic separatism in India. The process was not always easy, particularly in Punjab. Sikhs had always been a scattered minority there. In 1947–1948, however, the flight of Muslims to Pakistan and the arrival of Sikh refugees from the same country created a Sikh majority in the western part of India's share of Punjab. There were calls for the creation of a Sikh state, but the Center rejected them on the grounds that India's secularism ruled out political boundaries based on religion. In the now mainly Sikh west of Indian Punjab, Punjabi was the predominant language, while in the east its place was taken by Hindi. Proponents of a Sikh state accordingly pursued their objective by asking for the partition of Punjab into separate Punjabi and Hindi states. In 1966, the Center finally agreed to a linguistic division of Punjab, largely in order to build support among Sikhs for the Congress government. This created a new and much-shrunken Punjab, in which most of the population spoke Punjabi and a bare majority was Sikh, and the Hindi-speaking Haryana.

Meanwhile, a movement for independence had begun among the Naga Tribals of Assam, who felt themselves victimized by the Assamese majority in their state. Naga extremists resorted to armed rebellion, and throughout the 1950s an undeclared war raged between Nagas and the

Indian military. The Center opened negotiations with more moderate Nagas, and the two sides eventually agreed that a separate Naga state would remove the need for independence. The state of Nagaland accordingly came into being in 1963. In the 1970s and 1980s, other Tribal groups in the northeast were given states of their own, and in 2000 the states of Jharkhand and Chhattisgarh were created for the Tribals of Bihar and Madhya Pradesh. In almost all cases, the redrawing of state boundaries showed that adherents of pluralism were correct in their assumption that official recognition in the form of separate states would pacify discontented linguistic and Tribal communities.

POLITICS IN THE 1950s

By 1949, Patel was winning the power struggle with Nehru. He dominated the Congress party's politicians and its "organization" of card-carrying members, and secured the election of supporters as presidents of both India and the party. Patel's sudden death in 1950 allowed Nehru and his followers to regroup. The party president was forced to resign, and Nehru assumed control of the Congress organization. In 1952, the first elections to parliament and the state legislatures were held. Nehru played a large part in leading Congress to victory, and this established his dominance over the party's political wing. For the next ten years, his supremacy was unassailable.

Jawaharlal Nehru was born in a North Indian Brahmin family in 1889. His father Motilal Nehru was a wealthy lawyer, anglicized in habits and ideas, and a Moderate member of Congress. Jawaharlal was educated in Britain, where he acquired a flawless command of English, and followed his father into the law. His upbringing and schooling left him a devotee of progress; convinced of the inherent equality of the sexes, castes, and classes; a religious skeptic; and unable to understand anyone who did not share his views.

Motilal and Jawaharlal Nehru were among the many Indians who turned against the British during and after World War I, and they joined Gandhi's satyagraha of 1920–1922. During the 1920s, both Nehrus served as president of Congress. Motilal wrote the Nehru Report, and engineered Mahatma Gandhi's return to active politics in 1928. But it was Jawaharlal who became Gandhi's political heir, even though they disagreed about everything from religion to violence. Until his death, his relationship with the Mahatma was one of Nehru's greatest assets.

During Nehru's heyday in the 1950s, Congress was the strongest party in India. Parliamentary and state elections were held in 1952, 1957, and

1962; Congress always won majorities in the Lok Sabha, and usually in the state legislatures. This reinforced the trend that went back to the 1930s, by which anyone desirous of power or influence joined the party. Many local and district committees, the lowest levels of the party organization, had long been controlled by rich peasants, who during the 1950s also took over at the state level in much of India. (The national leadership of the party, however, remained in the hands of upper-caste urban professionals like Nehru. This is part of the reason that the rich peasants were never able to get Congress to pursue their interests exclusively.) These party bosses delivered votes to would-be members of parliament and the state assemblies. In return, politicians interceded to obtain favors for friends and dependents of the bosses—for example, preferential access to fertilizers or protection from the police. The bosses thereby increased their own influence and the number of voters under their control. Whatever else may be said of it, this gave Congress politicians genuine grassroots support.

Congress's voting base extended far beyond the party organization. Candidates for parliament and state assemblies were selected on the basis of popular appeal. They included princes running in their former kingdoms, and members of large castes that dominated the population of their constituencies. After independence, Congress secured the electoral support of religious minorities (especially Muslims) and many newly enfranchised poor people, often members of Scheduled Castes and Tribes. Local bosses frequently left these voters little choice but to cast their ballots for Congress. Bosses and politicians alike also bought support with promises of help for the downtrodden, which often remained unfulfilled.

But Congress was never as strong as it looked. It owed its electoral majorities to the fragmentation of its opponents, who in the 1950s ranged across the political spectrum. The Communists, who supported a pro-Soviet foreign policy and a Stalinist crash program of heavy industrialization, were strongest in West Bengal and Kerala, where Congress had never established a firm base. The Socialists were simply a faction of Congress until 1948, when Patel drove them out; their power centered in Uttar Pradesh and Bihar, and they favored neutrality in the Cold War and economic development through small-scale industries. On the right, the Swatantra (free) Party wanted a free market economy and diplomatic alignment with the United States; and the Jan Sangh or People's Organization was devoted to upholding Hindu culture and the Hindi language, and opposed the Congress definition of secularism as special rights for non-Hindus. Swatantra was particularly strong in the old states of Indian India. The Jan Sangh centered in the Hindi-speaking area of northern and central India; it was allied with the paramilitary organization founded by Hedgewar in 1925, the RSS, whose members drummed up support for the party at election time.

Congress's legislative majorities meant that Nehru could normally be generous to politicians from opposition parties, whom he allowed full participation in parliament and the state assemblies. (This was also true of rank-and-file legislators from his own party: Nehru encouraged them to take an active part in lawmaking rather than simply rubber-stamp the decisions made by their leaders.) At the same time, the prime minister was always watchful for non-Congressmen who posed a real threat; he would either undermine them, not always in the most gentlemanly fashion, or lure them into joining his party.

PLANNED ECONOMIC DEVELOPMENT

The keystone of Nehru's economic policy was government-directed development. The prime minister and his colleagues were in agreement on the need for a modern industrial economy in a country where in 1947 over 80 percent of the population was rural. Industrialization would create the wealth to give Indians health care and education and build a modern infrastructure; establish the economic self-sufficiency that would help protect the country's political independence; and end the reliance on trading raw materials for finished goods that had led to the economic crises of the 1930s.

Many politicians, economists, businessmen, and industrialists agreed that only the state could industrialize India. Even before independence, in 1945, the colonial government of India had announced plans to take over public utilities, railways, and other key industries if their resources were inadequate, and to bring other important industries under its supervision. In 1951, Nehru's administration followed this up with an order for all industrial concerns to obtain government licenses, which among other things specified the quality and limited the quantity of production.

During World War II, limits had been placed on imports of consumer goods, mainly so that India-bound ships had room for matériel needed for the war effort. After 1947, import restrictions were temporarily reimposed several times. Food and raw materials cost more in India than elsewhere, and other countries could not afford Indian exports. As a result, no foreign currency was coming into the country, even as it flowed out to buy nonessential imports. The controls saved foreign exchange for imports that were really needed. During the 1950s, the government instituted steep protective tariffs on imports, and quantitative restrictions that limited or barred outright importation of over 10,000 consumer and agricultural items. At the same time, the right of private citizens to own foreign currency was restricted. All this was intended to force Indian industry to supply all the manufactured goods that the country needed, which would eventually render imports unncessary. "Indian industry" was defined so that foreign investment was also barred. At the same time, economists believed that if Indians could neither buy consumer goods nor hold foreign currency, they would by default invest their savings in the domestic economy.

The most distinctive feature of "Nehruvian" economic policy, however, was central planning. In 1944, the British had established a Department of Planning and Development to discuss India's postwar economic policy. Its proposals ultimately gave rise to the National Planning Commission, created in 1950 to advise the government on questions of economic development. As prime minister, Nehru was chairman of the Commission, which he allowed to make economic policy rather than simply advise. The Commission spelled out its policy in its Five Year Plans, programs to foster economic growth over a period of five years. The main objective of the First Plan, which ran from 1951 to 1956, was to stabilize the economy, and it poured government investment into agriculture, and transportation and communications; only 2.8 percent of investment went to large-scale industry and mining. In the early 1950s, good weather, the cultivation of new land, more intensive use of labor, and improved irrigation increased agricultural production. The result was that although economic growth during the First Plan was not spectacular, it was adequate.

This gave the Commission the heart to move on to industrialization, the real objective, in the Second and Third Plans (1956–1966). These gave a central role to government-owned factories. In 1956, an Industrial Policy Resolution divided Indian industry into three parts. In seventeen strategic industries, including iron and steel production, and most mining and mineral-processing, all new operations would belong to the government, which could nationalize competitors whenever it wished. Another eleven "basic industries," such as machine tool and fertilizer manufacturing, were to be in mixed public and private ownership. Other industries would remain in private hands, subject to the licensing laws. The Second and Third Plans set up state-owned factories that produced everything from cars to chemicals, not to mention the industrial machinery that was supposed to end India's dependence on imported machines.

By the late 1950s, the Nehruvian economy was well-established, with its tight regulation of industry, import controls, planning, and mixed government and private ownership. The tariff barriers and quantitative restrictions protected domestic manufacturing, and those who knew how to work the licensing system could shut out rivals. Many businessmen found all this to their liking, and the output of heavy industry grew rapidly: Between 1951 and 1966, India's industrial output doubled, and the share of manufacturing in the national product grew from 10 percent to 16 percent. India could now produce many goods that had to be imported in 1947, and there is little doubt that none of this would have happened without government direction and state-owned factories. But the Second and Third Plans were less successful than anticipated. Agriculture remained stagnant, so total economic growth was modest. All the while, the population was growing more rapidly than ever before, keeping pace with the creation of industrial jobs.

Moreover, the government was unable to invest the sums called for by the Plans. Much of the reason was the need for imported machinery, which could only be bought with foreign currency. At first, India drew on the Sterling Balances, the debt that Britain had run up during World War II, which it put toward imports from countries that used the pound. But the Sterling Balances were spent in 1956, just as another source of foreign exchange, Indian exports, was rapidly declining due to rising prices and poor promotion. (For example, in 1955 India supplied 46 percent of the world's peanut oil exports. The figure shrank to just 1 percent only five years later.) This left Plan expenditure dependent on budgetary deficits, higher taxation, and—increasingly—foreign aid.

Lack of resources was not the only problem faced by the government-owned firms, which were built in bad locations, overstaffed, and subject to shortages of supplies, mechanical difficulties, and poor labor relations. Most made no profits and relied on government subsidies to meet their expenses. Even private industry was inefficient, shielded as it was from competition by import restrictions. Productivity was further hurt by the limitations of the industrial labor force. The Indian constitution states the desirability of assuring primary schooling to all children. Education, however, is a state responsibility, and most states lacked either the funds or the will to institute universal education. Instead, resources went to higher education for the few. This gave India a pool of well-trained intellectuals, professionals, and technicians (now typically experts in computer software). Most came from the existing educated elite, whose dominance was thus reinforced. The bulk of the population was unable to obtain even the primary education required to take up skilled jobs or further studies. As a result, Indian workers lag behind East Asians, Southeast Asians, and Latin Americans in literacy and skills.

Perhaps the greatest failure of the Second and Third Plans was in agriculture. Rural India was crucial to the Nehruvian economy: The peasants who formed the majority of the country's population were supposed to be the principal buyers of Indian industrial products, the taxpayers who would help finance the Plans, and (with their savings) the investors in private industry. They would also feed the country so that foreign currency would not have to go toward imported food. All this assumed a strong agricultural economy, something India did not have. Population growth outstripped food production, and from 1957, grain had to be imported in large quantities. Most peasants had no money for buying anything beyond necessities or paying taxes, let alone investing.

For many years, Congress had blamed this poverty on zamindars and other rural aristocrats who collected rent from the peasants and forwarded land revenue to the government. In the 1950s, state laws abolished such "intermediaries," so that the only payments required of cultivators were their taxes to the government. Other than eliminating the landlord class, however, this had little effect. Most rural Indians held either no land at all, or farms so small that they could not even feed themselves, let alone produce a surplus (in the 1950s, three quarters of landholdings measured less than five acres). To make ends meet, they often rented additional land from rich peasants or from former landlords who had set themselves up as gentleman farmers. Moreover, zamindari abolition had no effect on the millions of landless laborers who worked the fields of their wealthier neighbors.

The First Five Year Plan attacked these problems by calling for peasants with under five acres of land to merge their plots into cooperative farms. These would be jointly worked by all the smallholders and laborers of the village, and would be large enough to qualify for the subsidized water, fertilizers, and machinery that the Plan provided for farmers with larger holdings. This was ineffective, as most peasants had no desire to pool their resources with neighbors whom they knew only as rivals in the competition for scant resources. The Second Plan did little for agriculture beyond urging the states (which are responsible for agriculture under the constitution) to limit the amount of land one person could own; the excess was to be confiscated and given to laborers and smallholders. This was a direct attack on the wealth of the rich peasants who were Congress stalwarts in the countryside, and most of the time they ensured that land reform did not hurt them. In the early 1970s, 39 percent of India's land was controlled by 6 percent of its households.

The Third Plan all but gave up on state-driven agricultural development. It advocated private investment in fertilizers and irrigation, but beyond that, it left it for the wealth that would supposedly be generated by industrialization to trickle down to the peasantry. Rural India remained poor and was unable to play the part assigned to it in the Nehruvian economy.

FOREIGN POLICY

Nehru and Jinnah hoped for friendship between India and Pakistan, but the events of 1947–1948 guaranteed a rocky relationship. Pakistan is central to India's foreign policy, but has never monopolized it. During the 1950s, Nehru's international travels made him one of the world's best-known statesmen. His foreign policy centered on nonalignment, or neutrality in the Cold War. He urged other countries to follow his example, which he promised would make the world a more peaceful place. He also believed that nonalignment gave India the freedom to devote its resources to development rather than to defense. Certainly it made possible friendly relations with both superpowers, and the United States, the Soviet Union, and their respective allies were generous with their aid to India.

Associated with nonalignment was decolonization, ending European rule in Asia and Africa. Nehru tried to recruit newly independent countries to his nonaligned movement, and to join him in working for development. Peaceful decolonization was the ideal, as when Nehru persuaded France to give him what remained of its holdings in India. This did not always work, though. Portugal refused to cede Goa and other Indian territories that had been under its rule since the sixteenth century. Nehru finally had enough; in 1961 his army invaded the Portuguese settlements, and after some loss of life, incorporated them in India.

THE END OF THE NEHRU AGE

Nehru assumed that once he and the Planning Commission had made policies, they would be implemented, and the modern India of his dreams would swiftly come into being. The problem was that for implementation, he had to rely on the bureaucracy, and Congress's state and local leaders. Before 1947, Nehru had advocated thoroughly reforming the ICS and the rest of the civil service, to root out the conservatism that was natural in a body whose purpose was to maintain stability in British-ruled India.

The aftermath of independence, however, ruled out reforms, which would have antagonized the people whom the government needed to deal with refugees, communal violence, the merger of Indian India, and development. The ICS was renamed the Indian Administrative Service, or IAS, and most of its British members retired. But the IAS recruited its officers with the same competitive examinations that the ICS had used, and drew on the same segment of English-educated Indians. Bureaucrats in New Delhi and the state capitals were often halfhearted in implementing measures dictated by politicians. District collectors, normally from the IAS, kept the authoritarian powers that they had held under the British, and rarely thought it necessary or desirable to enforce reforms that would disturb the people under their control. Perhaps significantly, one change that did take place in local administration was an increase in the power of District Superintendents of Police, who became almost partners of the collectors. A DSP was even less likely than an IAS officer to want to shake up rural society.

The rich peasants among Congress politicians and bosses might eagerly cooperate in the abolition of zamindari rights, which eliminated their principal rivals in the countryside, just as urban professionals supported new university programs for their children. But few Congress leaders were willing to work toward the socialistic society that Nehru wanted, as this would inevitably erode their own standing. Their ability to obstruct change they opposed was highlighted in 1959. Two years earlier, a Communist government had been elected to power in the state of Kerala. It launched reforms in land ownership and education, directly attacking the interests of local Congress strongmen. The latter started an agitation against the Communists. Nehru was very reluctant to use the Center's powers to interfere in state politics, but the Kerala Congress got the support of party bosses in other states. They eventually forced Nehru to dismiss the Communist government, impose President's Rule, and ensure that Congress won the ensuing election to the Kerala legislature. This was a violation of Nehru's federalist principles, as well as flagrant misuse of a constitutional power that had been designed to cope with instability or unrest. It inaugurated a trend that lasted until the 1990s, with the Center using President's Rule to remove state governments that it disliked.

The results of obstructionism can be seen in the fate of a reform to which Nehru attached great importance, raising the status of women and Scheduled Castes or SCs (the former Untouchables). True, women were admitted on the same terms as men to all public services. In 1955–1956 laws enhanced the rights of Hindu women in marriage, divorce, inheritance, and adoption, and in 1961 it was made illegal to demand dowry from a bride. The constitution banned discrimination against SCs and guaranteed them places in legislatures, government jobs, and universities. In 1955, Parliament passed a law to punish violations of the ban, and SC ministers sat in the Central and state governments.

Some women and members of SCs did benefit, particularly if they had the education to know their rights and the opportunity to assert them. But families and village leaders often ignored the new laws, which provided minimal penalties for violators even when state and local officials were willing to enforce them. To this day, young girls are married off by their families, dowry is collected, and women are deprived of inheritances. SCs often remain at the bottom of society. Even the franchise did not help much: Until the mid-1980s, Congress bosses were usually able to ensure that the former Untouchables voted for their party.

In 1958–1959, Nehru tried to overcome obstructionism by introducing elected institutions at the level of government that had the closest contact with the people. His *panchayat* (council) scheme called for elected bodies to run villages, groups of villages, and districts. The power to create panchayats lay with the states, most of which did set up the councils. But they refused to give them the power or the resources to accomplish anything significant. Moreover, and not surprisingly, local elites often gained control of the panchayats, and used them to secure their own interests.

The failure of many of Nehru's domestic policies only became apparent after his death, which was hastened by a humiliation arising from his foreign policy. Nehru believed that China was India's natural friend, as the two Asian giants shared a glorious cultural heritage and (at least after Mao Zedong's breach with the Soviet Union) nonalignment. This, and a natural unwillingness to risk war unless India came under attack, led Nehru to acquiesce in the Chinese occupation of Tibet in 1950. Four years later, he renounced the diplomatic and trading rights that the British had obtained for India in Tibet. When the Chinese crushed the Tibetan revolt of 1959, Nehru granted the Dalai Lama refuge, but refused to criticize China's policy.

For many years, China had claimed territory in both northeastern and northwestern India. The late 1950s saw border skirmishes and unsuccessful talks between the two neighbors, but Nehru refused to heed suggestions that India was in serious danger. Then, without warning, Chinese forces invaded the disputed regions in October 1962, and routed the unprepared Indian army. After a month of fighting, China announced a cease-fire, but it never left the conquered areas.

Nehru realized that he had erred by failing to recognize either the intense nationalism of Mao's government, which wanted to secure every square inch of land that it considered to be Chinese, or China's desire to prove its military strength to its former Soviet ally. The immediate effect of the war was a massive increase in India's defense spending, which ate up 40 percent of the budget in 1963–1964 at the cost of deep cuts to development expenditure. Nehru did not renounce nonalignment. During the war, however, he asked the United States for assistance (Washington agreed to send an aircraft carrier to the Indian Ocean as a show of solidarity), and afterwards he sought military aid from the West.

The war cost Nehru much of his popularity. Opposition politicians stepped up their criticism, and the prime minister's support in Congress, parliament, and the cabinet weakened. Nehru turned to a group of state bosses who became known as the Syndicate and were unimpeachably loyal to him. He began to put them in positions of power in the cabinet and the party organization. At the same time, several important politicians who had questioned Nehru's leadership were sent to work at the lower levels of the party. But in January 1964, Nehru suffered a stroke. Four months later, a second stroke killed him, ending the seventeen-year tenure of independent India's first prime minister.

9

The Rise of the Nehru-Gandhi Dynasty

LAL BAHADUR SHASTRI

Nehru always refused to name a successor. He said that if he died in office, it would be up to the Congress members of parliament to choose a new party leader who (provided Congress retained its majority in the Lok Sabha) would automatically become prime minister. Nehru's dominance prevented the emergence of even an unofficial political heir, and throughout his tenure most of his principal colleagues were men of his generation who had been active in the nationalist movement. The strongest of these was Morarji Desai, who was finance minister until 1963 when he became one of the cabinet ministers to be banished to the lower levels of the party organization by Nehru and the Syndicate.

At Nehru's death, Desai staked his claim to the succession. His plans were, however, blocked by the Syndicate bosses, who knew that the former finance minister would curb their power if he became prime minister. Instead, they used their influence to secure the selection of a man who would rule in cooperation with them. This was Lal Bahadur Shastri, a quiet but respected member of Nehru's cabinet, who became the second prime minister of independent India. One of the junior members of the new government was Nehru's daughter, Indira Gandhi. (Indira, as she was known, was unrelated to Mahatma Gandhi: Her husband had been a Congress politician named Feroze Gandhi.)

Shastri's premiership was dominated by one issue: India's relations with Pakistan. In 1962–1963, the two neighbors held talks to try to resolve their differences, of which Kashmir was the most important. By the time the talks ended in failure, the president of Pakistan, Mohammad Ayub Khan, realized that India planned to keep its portion of Kashmir forever. Then, at the end of 1963, an Islamic relic was stolen from a mosque in the Kashmiri capital, Srinagar. Angry Kashmiri Muslims protested the theft with demonstrations and riots that had anti-Indian overtones. Ayub Khan took this as a sign of Kashmiri support for annexation to Pakistan, which he decided to bring about by military means. In early 1965, Pakistani troops crossed the Indian frontier in the Great Rann of Kutch, a desolate area between Sindh and Gujarat. As Ayub Khan had hoped, Shastri agreed to let an arbitrator determine the exact location of the border. To the Pakistani leader, this meant that India was unwilling to fight.

That summer, infiltrators entered Indian Kashmir from Pakistan to carry out acts of arson and sabotage, with which they hoped to incite a popular uprising. In August, the Indian army attacked the infiltrators' bases inside Pakistan, and on September 1 the second Indo-Pakistani War broke out. The conflict lasted three weeks before it ended with a cease-fire arranged by the United Nations. The government of the Soviet Union invited Shastri and Ayub Khan to meet at the Soviet city of Tashkent and work out a permanent settlement to replace the cease-fire. The meeting was successful. In January 1966, Shastri and Ayub Khan concluded an agreement that provided for all troops to withdraw to the positions they had held before the war, and committed the two leaders to working for friendly relations between their countries. Shastri was worn out by the grueling conference, however, and died in Tashkent just a few hours after signing the document.

THE RISE OF INDIRA GANDHI

The Congress members of parliament therefore had to choose a new prime minister for the second time in less than two years. Morarji Desai was again the leading candidate. The Syndicate, however, arranged the election of Indira Gandhi, who the party bosses thought would be too weak to resist their domination. This was a miscalculation on their part, as Indira had no intention of letting anyone dominate her. For the next six years, Indira, Desai, and the Syndicate struggled for control, until

Indira outmaneuvered her rivals and assumed more power than any previous leader in Indian history.

Elections for the Lok Sabha and the state legislatures were due a year after Indira became prime minister. By this time, the Indian economy was flagging. The industrial expansion fueled by the Second and Third Five Year Plans was coming to an end, partly because the market for replacements for foreign imports could not grow indefinitely. Agriculture was hit by a bad harvest in 1965–1966 and a severe drought in 1966–1967, resulting in famine in the north, scarcity elsewhere, and high prices everywhere. Heavy expenditure on defense since 1962 had drained India's foreign currency reserves, which were further weakened by low sales of the country's few exports. Unable to buy much food abroad, India became increasingly dependent on food aid, but even that was never enough. Indira and her cabinet could not agree on how to handle the economic difficulties. One sign of this was their failure to approve a successor to the Third Five Year Plan, which ended in 1966; for the next three years, the Indian economy was guided by a series of stopgap one year plans. Inevitably, and not without justification, the Congress party was widely blamed for all this.

At the same time, some of Congress's long-standing weaknesses now came to the surface. The party's inclusiveness had become a liability. There were constant factional struggles among bosses and politicians whose interests were incompatible, and Congress was increasingly unwilling to enact policies that would inevitably anger some of its diverse supporters. New sections of the community were becoming active in politics, alongside the upper castes and rich peasants who had hitherto dominated. The new entrants were typically "middle peasants," members of agricultural castes that ranked between rural elites and the Scheduled Castes. Their place in society was largely responsible for their political mobilization: They lacked the jobs, education, and power enjoyed by the higher or "Forward" castes, but—unlike most members of the Scheduled Castes—they had enough resources to be able to raise themselves. They were commonly called Other Backward Classes, or OBCs.

These resources often included numbers, as in much of rural India OBCs formed the largest segment of the population. In some states, they used this advantage to take over control of Congress from the Forward Castes. Where this was impossible, they often formed their own parties, which could count on much of the OBC population as a "vote bank." This created a distinctive feature of Indian state politics between the 1960s and the 1990s: a two-party system that pitted a national party,

Congress, against a party that existed only in the state in question, and drew its support from local OBCs.

The elections were held in February 1967. Congress retained its majority in the Lok Sabha, but with only 54 percent of the seats compared to the 73 percent it had won in 1962. The party lost heavily in the state legislatures, and non-Congress governments—usually from regional parties—assumed office in eight of the seventeen states that India then comprised. In Punjab, which had had a Sikh majority in the population since the separation of Haryana four months earlier, the Sikhs' Akali Dal formed a government for the first time. The Dravida Munnetra Kazhagam (Dravidian Progressive Federation) or DMK took power in Madras, and showed its Tamil regionalist credentials by renaming the state Tamil Nadu or Tamil-land. (The DMK and its offshoot the All-India Anna Dravida Munnetra Kazhagam, AIADMK, named for a leader called C.N. Annadurai, have ruled Tamil Nadu ever since.) The "Communist Party of India (Marxist)," which had broken away from the Communist Party of India in 1964, won control of the legislature of Kerala eight years after Nehru had dismissed the state's last Communist government. In Uttar Pradesh, the peasant leader Chaudhuri Charan Singh took his followers out of Congress and became chief minister. His new Bharatiya Kranti Dal (Indian Revolution Party) joined with other North Indian peasant movements to form the Lok Dal, the People's Party, which supported land ownership by peasants in opposition to both landlords and cooperatives.

The Syndicate blamed Congress's loss of its monopoly of power on the alienation of the party's conservatives, who looked to Morarji Desai as their leader, and forced Indira to bring her rival back into the cabinet as deputy prime minister and finance minister. New Delhi then set about undermining the non-Congress state governments, usually by persuading legislators to withdraw their support so that the chief minister lost his majority and had to resign. In February 1968, for example, this happened to Charan Singh of Uttar Pradesh; the Center put the state under President's Rule for a year, then orchestrated a new election that Congress won.

After the elections, Indira, the Syndicate, and Desai schemed against one another to dominate the government. Then, in May 1969, the president of India, Zakir Husain, died. Under the constitution, the members of parliament and the state legislatures were to choose his successor. The Syndicate selected Congress's candidate, Neelam Sanjiva Reddy, a former president of the party. It was taken for granted that with the backing of the bosses, he would win easily. Indira, however, put up her own candidate, the country's former vice president, Varahagiri Venkata Giri, and made it clear that she regarded the presidential election as a test of strength between herself and the Syndicate. At the same time, she struck against her other rival when she fired Desai as finance minister. He angrily quit his other post, that of deputy prime minister, and aligned himself with the Syndicate.

The presidential election was held in August. Giri won narrowly, showing that Indira had more support among the country's lawmakers than the Syndicate did. The Congress bosses responded by announcing that Indira no longer belonged to their party. They assumed that this would force the Congress members of the Lok Sabha to withdraw their support from her, depriving her of her majority and compelling her to resign as prime minister. Indira, however, called on her followers to accompany her out of the bosses' Congress. The party split in two, as the Congress executive, legislators, and ordinary members joined either Indira's Congress (R) (the R stood for Requisitioned, as Indira had launched her faction with a written order or requisition for her supporters to meet) or the Syndicate's Congress (O) (Organization, because the power of the bosses derived from their control of the party organization).

Congress (R) had fewer than half the seats in the Lok Sabha. To keep her majority and stay on as prime minister, Indira sought the support of members of parliament from the regional and Communist parties. Concessions in Punjab and Tamil Nadu secured the cooperation of the Akali Dal and the DMK. The alliance with the Communists was the natural sequel to leftist policies with which Indira had increasingly come to identify herself. For example, she had ended the friendly relationship that India and the United States enjoyed after the war with China. During the agricultural crisis of 1965–1967, Washington increased what was already substantial food aid to India. The administration of Lyndon Johnson, however, tied the aid to economic reforms: New Delhi was forced to loosen its restrictions on foreign investment and devalue the Indian rupee in relation to other currencies. The latter step made Indian exports more competitive, which brought in foreign currency with which to buy food, but also priced whatever goods India still imported out of reach of most consumers. The Indian left criticized these concessions to foreign interests. In July 1966, mainly to show that she was not a puppet of the United States, Indira condemned American policy in Vietnam. Johnson responded by tightening the conditions under which India received food aid. This forced Indira to adopt an openly anti-American tone.

During her struggle with the Syndicate, Indira made another gesture to the left. Some time earlier, Congress had voted to nationalize India's large private banks so that they could be compelled to serve rural and small-business clients (many of whom were unable to open bank accounts or obtain bank loans). The Syndicate had blocked implementation of the policy, but in July 1969 Indira suddenly used her powers as prime minister to nationalize the banks. This not only won her the support of the Communists in parliament. It was also a play for the support of OBCs and other poorer voters who had become disillusioned with Congress: They could interpret nationalization as a sign that the prime minister had their interests at heart.

Bank nationalization was a dramatic gesture, but one that carried few risks: The only people whose interests it adversely affected were the handful of bank owners, who were already more likely to support the Swatantra Party or Congress (O) than Congress (R). The same was true of Indira's policy toward the princes and chiefs who once governed Indian India. When they gave up their states in 1947–1949, the former rulers were accorded pensions (called privy purses) and certain royal privileges. These were confirmed in the Indian constitution. In 1967, Congress voted to delete the constitutional provisions relating to privy purses and privileges, but (like bank nationalization) the decision was not implemented.

During the 1960s, Indian royalty became increasingly active in politics. In 1967, twenty-four princes were elected to the Lok Sabha, and others entered state legislatures. Many of them belonged to Congress, but not all did. For example, the maharaja of Patna led the Swatantra Party to victory over Congress in Orissa, and became chief minister of his state. When Indira's government attempted to give parliament the power to amend the constitution's Fundamental Rights (mainly to make it easier to nationalize property), the maharaja of Dhrangadhara, a member of the Lok Sabha, floated a plan under which the Fundamental Rights could only be altered with the approval of the voters.

Indira now fixed her sights on the princes, both to punish such political opponents as the maharajas of Patna and Dhrangadhara, and to demonstrate her leftist credentials. In 1970, she tried to secure a constitutional amendment abolishing the privy purses and privileges, but was narrowly defeated in the Rajya Sabha. She then had the president of India withdraw recognition of all former rulers, making them ineligible for their privy purses and privileges. In December 1970, in response to a petition from a group of princes including Dhrangadhara, the Supreme Court ruled that the president had acted illegally.

Indira acted immediately, arranging a Lok Sabha election for March

1971; for the first time since independence, it did not coincide with state legislative elections. Over the previous four years, Indira had traveled all over the country, meeting with the poor and hearing their problems. This had made her the best-known politician in India. During the election campaign, she pointed to her policies toward the banks and the princes as early installments in her campaign to *gharibi hatao* ("drive away poverty"). All this paid off. When the voting took place, Congress (O) and the other opposition parties lost heavily, while Congress (R) won two thirds of the seats in the Lok Sabha. Indira was firmly in control at the Center. She used her position to push through the constitutional amendments that had eluded her before the election, giving parliament the power to amend Fundamental Rights and abolishing the rulers' privy purses and privileges.

There remained only for Indira to secure her power in the states, where legislative elections were scheduled for 1972. Pakistan inadvertently came to her aid. In December 1970, the first parliamentary election in Pakistani history was held. The Awami League (Common People's League) won a majority in parliament, but the country's president (Ayub Khan's successor Agha Mohammad Yahya Khan), army, and political elites all opposed the formation of an Awami government. This was because the Awami League was based in East Pakistan (the former East Bengal), and its victory signaled a shift in power from the Punjabis, Sindhis, and other West Pakistanis who had dominated Pakistan since 1947. Mujibur Rahman, known as Sheikh Mujib, the head of the Awami League, was willing to settle for autonomy for East Pakistan rather than the prime ministership of the whole country, but this too was rejected by Yahya Khan.

When the president tried to crush the Awami League by imposing martial law on East Pakistan in March 1971, Sheikh Mujib declared his province independent under the name of Bangladesh. A crackdown by Pakistani troops sent almost 10 million Bangladeshi refugees, most of them Hindus, across the border into India. Ostensibly to make it possible for the refugees to return home, but in reality to strike a blow against Pakistan, Indira decided to support the struggle for an independent Bangladesh. She provided training and equipment to the Mukti Bahini, the Freedom Army, a force of Bangladeshi guerrillas who fought the Pakistanis. An angry Yahya Khan declared war on India in December 1971. The third war between the two neighbors ended in a total victory for India; Pakistan recognized the independence of Bangladesh, and India was predominant in the subcontinent.

Indira took advantage of the situation in Bangladesh to reorient her

foreign policy. Uncertain relations with India had led the United States
to turn to Pakistan as its principal ally in South Asia. This was reinforced
by the normalization of relations between Washington and Beijing,
which was also friendly to Pakistan. Throughout 1971, the United States
therefore backed Yahya Khan against Sheikh Mujib's demands. To fend
off American criticism of India's support for the Mukti Bahini in the
United Nations, and to obtain the support of a superpower in the event
of trouble with China, Indira turned to the Soviets. In August 1971, India
and the Soviet Union signed a twenty-year pact of peace, friendship, and
cooperation. Indira had abandoned her father's doctrine of nonalignment
in all but name, while strengthening her alliance with Communists in
her own country. In March 1972, the state elections were held. Indira's
defeat of Pakistan, and her wooing of leftist and poor voters, won Congress (R) majorities in every legislature except that of Tamil Nadu.

INDIRA IN POWER

Her battles with the Syndicate and Morarji Desai left Indira obsessed
with the danger of rivals inside her own party. She therefore set about
filling the political and organizational wings of Congress (R) with people
who were unquestionably loyal to her. This often meant displacing
bosses with independent power bases in favor of men whose only asset
was their obsequiousness to her. They could not challenge her, as their
careers depended on her favor. They were also unlikely to block policies
set out in New Delhi, because unlike their predecessors, they could not
afford to place their interests or those of their dependents above the
goodwill of the Center.

In the long run, however, this destroyed the grassroots base on which
Congress had drawn since the 1930s. In much of India, lower-level Congress committees disappeared altogether. Where they did survive, their
power was greatly reduced. Whereas the old-style bosses had been local
strongmen who could be counted on to bring out voters in return for
the party's patronage, the new ones were often little more than representatives of a prime minister whose electoral success depended on her
personal popularity. This meant that Congress (R) faced electoral disaster
if anything happened to diminish Indira's popularity, as there was no
longer any effective party organization to prevent voters from turning
to other parties.

Loyalty to Indira also became the route to seats in parliament and the
cabinet, which both consequently declined in importance. The prime
minister did not expect Congress backbenchers in the Lok Sabha to take

an active part in debates; their function was to vote in favor of the government's policies. Indira's insistence on blind obedience from her ministers produced a decline in the quality of the members of the cabinet, until she could no longer rely on them for advice. The prime minister increasingly set policy in consultation with her secretariat, comprising senior bureaucrats chosen by her, or with her circle of friends and relatives.

To ensure the loyalty of state governments, Indira personally chose chief ministers and their cabinets. If she wanted to replace a chief minister, she first won over the support of enough state legislators for her opponent to lose his majority, and then threw her new allies behind her candidate. More and more often, the Center used dubious pretexts to place a state under President's Rule in order to remove a suspect chief minister from office. All this eroded the constitution's division of authority between the states and the Center. Opposition parties increasingly demanded the restoration of a genuine federal system in which the Center respected the autonomy of the states. Indira denounced all such protests as subversive. This was a dangerous course to take, as it could easily turn frustrated exponents of states' rights into secessionists.

Indira's method of dominating Congress and the states was ultimately counterproductive. Dismissed bosses and chief ministers turned against the prime minister, taking their power bases with them. Denied access to power through Congress, trade unions, religious organizations, caste societies, and other nonpolitical bodies became increasingly vocal in pursuit of their interests. This created new foci for the political aspirations of many Indians. In some states, Indira's replacement of independent-minded upper-caste chief ministers with loyal OBCs provoked caste conflict.

Perhaps paradoxically, Indira found that by centralizing power in her own hands, she had reduced her ability to implement her own policies. In the early 1970s, she nationalized the coal and insurance industries, as further symbols of her war on poverty. Nationalization accomplished little, but more importantly it met with no significant opposition because—like the attack on the princes—it hurt so few people. The story was different with programs to provide the poor with tools, skills, and temporary jobs, and to break up large landholdings for the benefit of poor peasants. By undermining the Congress organization and the state governments, Indira had destroyed the only bodies that could have made her plans work over the objections of rich peasants and other vested interests, and she was no more successful at driving away poverty than her father had been.

In economic policy, Indira abandoned Nehru's dream of transforming India with central planning. After the "plan holiday" that followed the end of the Third Five Year Plan in 1966, the Fourth and Fifth Plans (1969–1979) focused on specific problems rather than grandiose visions. For example, the population of India was now increasing so fast (there were almost 600 million people) that it ate up any economic growth that occurred. The Fifth Plan addressed this with heavy government spending on birth control. The plans of the 1970s also restored the emphasis on agriculture that had characterized the First Plan.

In part, this reflected developments that had taken place during the previous decade. Scientists in Mexico and the Philippines had developed new strains of wheat and rice that produced much more grain per acre than traditional varieties. In 1965, one of their creations, a kind of wheat, was introduced on farms in Punjab, Haryana, and western Uttar Pradesh. This region, India's "wheat belt," was characterized by consolidated landholdings, mostly owned by rich peasants who could afford to experiment with their crops. Over the next four years, the government used a loan from the International Monetary Fund and aid from the United States to provide the irrigation facilities and chemical fertilizers that the new high-yield variety required. This launched the "Green Revolution." By 1970, India grew five times as much wheat as it had ten years earlier. Thanks to continued population growth, this translated into only a slight increase in the amount of food available per person. Nevertheless, it was enough that the country normally no longer needed to import food, and in fact became a net agricultural exporter.

In the early 1970s, however, the impact of the Green Revolution was limited. The tiny holdings and poverty of most Indian peasants precluded the introduction of the new wheat on their farms, as did the impossibility of year-round irrigation in many areas. Moreover, outside of the wheat belt, the principal crop in much of India was rice. It was only in the 1980s that high-yield rices were found that suited the Indian environment, and they merely doubled rather than quintupled production. The Green Revolution made Punjab the richest state in India, but most of the gains went to the successful wheat farmers. It also cemented the social and economic dominance of rich peasants in the northwest, while leaving the lives of poor and landless cultivators unchanged. Nor was the new wealth as secure as it seemed, as the high-yield crops proved far more susceptible to drought and disease than ordinary Indian wheats and rices.

As the Green Revolution got underway, the concentration on high-yield wheat led to a decline in the production of other grains. In 1972–

1973, this contributed to a steep increase in the price of food, and short-ages in some areas. Then, after the Arab-Israeli War of 1973, oil produc-ers cut their exports sharply, and the cost of petroleum-based fuel skyrocketed. Indira was powerless to halt the inflation that the agricul-tural and oil crises unleashed, and her popularity plummeted. She tried to recover the lost ground by trying out the nuclear explosives that In-dian scientists had secretly developed. Indira asserted that her country intended to use the technology for peaceful purposes, but the successful tests in 1974 signaled that India was capable of making nuclear weapons.

Despite the surge in Indian patriotism that followed the tests, discon-tent mounted, thanks not only to the economic situation but also to the incompetence and corruption of many of Indira's handpicked colleagues and chief ministers. One symptom was increasing industrial unrest, cul-minating in paralyzing strikes. Another was a surge in the kind of ex-traparliamentary protest movements that India had known since the campaigns against the partition of Bengal. During the 1950s, agitation had typically centered on linguistic and religious questions and on the demands of peasants for higher agricultural prices. By the 1960s, some protests had turned to violence, notably the various Communist terrorist cells collectively called Naxalites (from the Naxalbari area of West Ben-gal, where they first struck). The 1970s saw violent and nonviolent pro-tests against Indira and Congress state governments in many parts of India.

One of the most unpopular governments was that of Bihar, where a nonviolent movement was launched to force the resignation of an inept administration. This set the stage for the return to politics of Jayaprakash Narayan. J.P., as he was called, had risen to prominence in 1921, during Gandhi's first great satyagraha campaign. A friend of Nehru, he was leader of the socialists within Congress in the 1930s and 1940s, until he was driven out of the party by Sardar Patel. In the 1950s, J.P. left politics to devote himself to improving the lives of villagers. He was revered by many as a true successor to the Mahatma. In March 1974, he accepted leadership of the agitation in Bihar. Meanwhile, Indira's old rival Morarji Desai organized protests against the Gujarat state government. Later in the year, J.P. and Desai joined forces and established the Janata Morcha or People's Front. They increasingly directed their ire at Indira, whom they saw as the ultimate cause of India's problems.

On June 12, 1975, the state High Court of Uttar Pradesh rendered its decision on a complaint that had been lodged after the 1971 election. An opposition candidate in Indira's Lok Sabha constituency had charged that the prime minister's use of government facilities during her campaign gave her an unfair electoral advantage. The court upheld the complaint, and imposed the penalty of barring Indira from elective office for six years. The next day, the Janata Morcha won a majority in elections for the Gujarat legislature, which had been dissolved as a result of Desai's agitation. By now, J.P. and Desai had garnered support across the political spectrum, from the remnants of the now-fragmented Socialist party; Charan Singh and his Bharatiya Lok Dal (Indian People's Party), formed in 1974 through the merger of the Lok Dal with a radical socialist group; and the Swatantra Party. On June 25, the two Janata Morcha leaders organized a huge rally in New Delhi. They called for a nationwide satyagraha to force Indira to abide by the court's ruling, and resign as prime minister.

The next day, on Indira's instructions, the president of India declared a state of emergency. This activated the constitutional provisions that allowed the Center to suspend basic rights. Indira's main opponents were immediately arrested, and the government took control of the press. According to Indira, the Emergency was necessitated by the breakdown of order, by which she meant the strikes and protests of recent months. She attacked the economic causes of discontent with a twenty-point program that included controls on wage and price increases (these quickly brought inflation under control) and further promises of land reform. Indira also enforced workplace discipline, compelling bureaucrats to work harder than many had ever done before and banning strikes. Partly for these reasons, industrial production rose. This, and good harvests in 1975, seemed to support the prime minister's claim that her policies would create the prosperity that had hitherto eluded India.

Indira said that the Emergency would be withdrawn once order was restored, but many of her actions suggested that she was creating a permanent dictatorship. She had parliament erase the laws under which the Uttar Pradesh court had convicted her, and oversaw constitutional amendments that further restricted rights and increased the power of the prime minister. In 1976, she imposed President's Rule on Tamil Nadu and Gujarat, the two states with non-Congress (R) governments, and postponed the Lok Sabha elections due the same year.

By now, Indira relied heavily for advice on the younger of her two sons, Sanjay Gandhi. Sanjay had little use for the democratic forms that his grandfather had so carefully fostered, and transformed the Youth Congress into a private army to turn against his opponents. His rise to power was a sign of a growing belief in a "Nehru-Gandhi dynasty." For all but two years since independence, the country had been ruled by Nehru and Indira, and many now felt that their family was uniquely qualified to govern. Sanjay was increasingly seen as Indira's political heir, in a way that his mother had never been regarded during Nehru's lifetime.

Two of Indira and Sanjay's policies were particularly hated. One was slum clearance in the Mughal city of old Delhi. Thousands of poor people, mostly Muslims, saw their homes bulldozed and were forcibly removed to new residences miles from their places of work. Their discontent spread among the Muslims of north India, who had faithfully supported Congress since 1947. The other was sterilization, which Sanjay saw as the only way of bringing population growth under control. All male government employees with three children or more were required to have vasectomies, and other men were encouraged to undergo the operation. In some areas, local officials were given vasectomy quotas, which they inevitably met by forcibly sterilizing unwilling patients. A wave of fear swept the country, especially among peasants.

As a result, anger against Indira grew rather than receded during the Emergency. The prime minister was oblivious to all this, though, as Sanjay and the rest of her circle carefully shielded her from knowledge of the public's resentment. In January 1977, convinced that she was as popular as she had been five years earlier in the wake of the Bangladesh war, Indira ended the Emergency, freed political prisoners, and scheduled a Lok Sabha election for March. All the principal non-Congress parties except the Communists joined with J.P. and Desai's Janata Morcha in an alliance called the Janata Party, People's Party. For many voters, the sole issue was the experiences of the Emergency.

Just before polling day, the Janata Party acquired a new ally when Jagjivan Ram, the country's most important Scheduled Caste leader, resigned from Indira's cabinet to support J.P. and Desai. Many Scheduled Caste voters followed his lead. When the votes were counted, Janata and its allies held two thirds of the seats in the Lok Sabha, and Congress (R) was reduced to little more than a quarter. The new party also won many of the state legislative elections that followed in 1977–1978.

THE JANATA GOVERNMENT

The Janata government started off badly, with a disagreement between Jagjivan Ram and Morarji Desai as to which of them should be prime minister. With J.P.'s support, the eighty-one-year-old Desai won, but he had to share power with Chaudhuri Charan Singh, aged seventy-four, who assumed Sardar Patel's old posts of deputy prime minister and home minister. The new parliament rescinded the more authoritarian of

Indira's constitutional amendments, and passed laws to make a future declaration of Emergency more difficult. Desai left foreign policy in the hands of Atal Bihari Vajpayee of the Jan Sangh, who dropped Indira's tilt toward the Soviet Union in favor of genuine nonalignment. Charan Singh presided over an economic policy that centered on peasant agriculture and small-scale industry, and underlay the Sixth Five Year Plan from 1980 to 1985.

Some aspects of the Emergency had found favor with many Indians. Among these were the taming of inflation and the ban on strikes. The lifting of repression led to a recrudescence of both, and the economy slowed down sharply. Perhaps inevitably, the heterogeneity of the Janata coalition frequently paralyzed the government. If the cabinet went so far as to implement policies, it would almost certainly lose the support of one or another of its members. At the same time, most ministers were as concerned with preserving the identities of their original parties as they were with governing India. Whatever the intentions of J.P. and Desai, it was clear that many members regarded the Janata Party as a temporary alliance, which they could leave just as easily as they had joined it.

Relations between Desai and Charan Singh were especially acrimonious. After one bad quarrel, Desai dismissed his deputy prime minister, losing Janata the support of the Bharatiya Lok Dal. In July 1979, the coalition's leftists grew concerned that Desai was leaning toward the Hindu nationalists of the Jan Sangh. First the socialists and then the followers of J.P. withdrew their support, depriving the prime minister of his majority in the Lok Sabha. On July 19, Desai resigned. He was succeeded by Charan Singh, who was unable to cobble together a majority and in turn resigned after only three weeks. It was clear that the Lok Sabha was so divided that no one could get the support of a majority of its members. The president saw no alternative but to hold a new election. Charan Singh remained as caretaker prime minister till the voting took place in January 1980.

In 1977, many leaders of Congress (R) had turned against Indira, whom they blamed for the victory of the Janata Party. Indira and her followers responded by forming a new party, called Congress (I). The "I" stood for Indira, making it clear that this was even more her vehicle than Congress (R) had been. Between then and 1980, Indira rebuilt her power base. She was particularly eager to win back the support of Muslims and Scheduled Castes, whose desertion had been crucial to her loss in 1977. Two and a half years of Janata rule had persuaded many disadvantaged groups that whatever her faults, Indira was better than any alternative. The lethargy of Desai's government contrasted sharply with Indira's decisiveness. During the runup to the 1980 election, it became increasingly likely that Indira would win. Her support grew as people scrambled to get on the winning side. By the time the voting took place, the Janata Party was on the verge of breaking up into its component parts. Congress (I) won two thirds of the seats in the Lok Sabha, and Indira Gandhi was once again prime minister of India.

10

The Fall of the Nehru-Gandhi Dynasty

THE DYNASTY

After leading her new Congress (I) to victory in the Lok Sabha election of 1980, Indira Gandhi was prime minister of India until her death in 1984. Soon after her return to power, the pervasiveness of belief in the "Nehru-Gandhi dynasty" was illustrated when her son Sanjay, her right-hand man and heir apparent, was killed in a flying accident. Indira immediately turned to her other son, Rajiv. He was an airline pilot who had shown no interest in politics, but he was quickly brought into parliament and installed as the new heir. His sole qualification was that he was Indira's son. The 1980s and 1990s saw the spread of this kind of dynasticism to some states, as the offices of chief minister or party leader became the patrimony of particular families.

More even than during the 1970s, in the 1980s the Center devoted considerable effort to maintaining the power of the dynasty. The Congress (I) organization, parliament, and the cabinet often seemed to have little purpose beyond glorifying Indira and Rajiv. The erosion of federalism continued, as Indira used intrigue and President's Rule to make and unmake chief ministers. In 1984, she had her governor of Andhra Pradesh announce that the state's chief minister had lost his legislative majority and dismiss him, without even allowing a meeting of lawmakers to prove the claim. A handpicked successor was installed, but the governor ensured that the legislature did not convene until the new chief minister had won over enough members to have a majority. This practice thereafter became common.

State governors were one agency that Indira and Rajiv used as instruments of Congress (I). Others were the bureaucracy and the police. In 1980, Indira purged the administration of senior civil servants who had been appointed by the Janata government. The bureaucracy was politicized as Indira and her chief ministers made loyalty the test for appointments and promotions. Bureaucrats and politicians became interdependent, with administrators upholding the interests of their political masters in return for rewards. These rewards often included the right to corruption. During the 1980s, bureaucrats at all levels (except perhaps the IAS) demanded bribes from the public simply for carrying out their assigned duties. This might be a way of recovering their own losses, as government ministers sometimes exacted payments in exchange for plum bureaucratic appointments.

Indira continued the practice that she had begun in the 1970s of relying on the upper bureaucracy rather than the cabinet for advice in policymaking. This allowed administrators to institute measures that furthered their interests, or at least to ensure that the government did nothing to harm them. All the while, the civil service was undergoing the rapid expansion that had begun with the creation of the Nehruvian economy: Between 1953 and 1988, the number of bureaucrats rose from 4 million to 18.5 million. It has been suggested that the burden of bureaucrats' salaries was part of the reason the Indian government was never able to invest adequately in development projects.

The Center and the states also appointed senior police officers on the basis of political loyalty, or in return for payments, rather than for competence. This contributed to demoralization in the lower ranks of the police, symptomized by increasing police brutality. The demoralization was worsened as criminals went into politics, particularly in northern and western India. Drug lords and extortionists had the wealth and power to coerce or buy votes, and Congress (I) was only one of several political parties that welcomed such men into parliament and state legislatures in return for their support. The criminals then expected to be shielded from the law. In some areas, bureaucrats and police cooperated with gangsters, demarcating interests and refraining from causing any trouble to one another.

This fed rising political violence, as politicians used criminal allies to intimidate or eliminate rivals. The pattern set by Sanjay Gandhi's Youth Congress during the Emergency became normal: Most parties now recruited toughs from gangs, slums, and universities and set them against their enemies. (Students were susceptible to recruitment because the proliferation of poorly funded regional universities had created a pool of young people stuck in mediocre schools, living in abysmal "hostels" or dormitories, with few prospects after graduation.) Peaceful extraparliamentary politics gave way to violent demonstrations to secure political ends. More and more politicians needed bodyguards, and even those who were not in danger demanded protection as a status symbol. The unreliability of the police, and the scale of the violence, led the Center to rely on troops to control political disturbances.

The destruction of the federal system and the spread of political violence were symptoms of the weakness of the Nehru-Gandhi dynasty rather than its strength. The Center and states often virtually lost control of local administration. Criminals and corrupt bureaucrats or police officers simply ignored the government as they pursued their own interests. After 1977, non-Congress state administrations had revived the panchayat system of local councils to secure some power for themselves even if Congress returned to power. As in the 1950s and 1960s, the panchayats were often dominated by rural elites.

PUNJAB

Indira's meddling in state politics and her toleration of political violence led to her death at the hands of two Sikh bodyguards. Although a small community, the Sikhs formed a prominent one. Sikh farmers were among the principal beneficiaries of the Green Revolution. In the 1960s, many Sikhs migrated from Punjab to other parts of India, where they were heavily represented in fields ranging from the army officer corps to the taxi service in Delhi.

After the separation of Haryana in 1966, Punjab had a population that was three fifths Sikh. Many Sikhs were still not satisfied, however. They wanted "their" Punjab to enjoy the same autonomy as India's only Muslim-majority state, Kashmir. They were angry over what they believed to be unfairness in the division of both irrigation river waters and territory between Punjab and Haryana. The symbol of Sikh disgruntlement was Chandigarh, a city designed by the modernist architect Le Corbusier in the 1950s to serve as the capital of Punjab. In 1966, Punjab and Haryana each claimed Chandigarh. The Center compromised by making the city the capital of both new states. It was placed on the border between them but did not belong to either, being administered directly by New Delhi. Most Sikhs wanted exclusive possession of Chandigarh for Punjab.

The main political parties in Punjab were Congress and the Sikhs' Shiromani Akali Dal. After the split of Congress in 1969, Indira needed the support of the Akali Dal to keep her majority in the Lok Sabha, and she promised that Chandigarh would become part of Punjab in 1975. But her election victory in 1971 eliminated the need to court other parties, and Indira ignored her promise. Thereafter, relations between Indira and the Akali Dal deteriorated. In 1973, the Sikh party passed the Anandpur Sahib Resolution, calling for an enlarged and autonomous Sikh state; in 1975, it was prominent in opposing the Emergency; in 1977, it demanded that the Center respect federalism, and hand over Chandigarh. During the 1970s, many Sikhs transferred their loyalty from Congress to the Akali Dal.

Not surprisingly, after she regained power in 1980, Indira dismissed the Akali Dal government that had won the Punjab legislative election in 1977. A fresh state election brought Congress (I) to power. Soon afterwards, the prime minister approved construction of a massive new canal that would divert water from Punjab to Haryana. In 1982, Sant Harchand Singh Longowal, the leader of the Akali Dal, inaugurated a satyagraha to stop the canal project, and to force New Delhi to accept the Anandpur Sahib Resolution.

To Indira, the solution was to wean the Sikhs away from the Akali Dal. She thought she had a means of doing just that. During the nineteenth and twentieth centuries, the great majority of Sikhs came to accept the reforms of Guru Gobind Singh, the creator of the Khalsa. Among the few remaining non-Khalsa Sikhs were the Sant Nirankaris, who had their own guru. There was considerable hostility between Khalsa and Sant Nirankari Sikhs, each of whom considered the other to be heretical. In 1977, a holy man named Sant Jarnail Singh Bhindranwale became head of the Damdami Taksal, an organization dedicated to upholding the Khalsa as the only authentic embodiment of Sikhism. The following year, the Sant Nirankaris met in the Sikh holy city of Amritsar. Seeing this as an affront, Bhindranwale's followers attacked the meeting with swords. Unfortunately, the Sant Nirankaris had firearms and won the resulting battle.

This increased the enmity between the Khalsa and the Sant Nirankaris. In 1980, the Sant Nirankari guru was assassinated. This was followed by a wave of murders of Sant Nirankaris, almost certainly instigated by Bhindranwale, whose disciples also attacked Punjab state police, officials, and government buildings. By 1983, ordinary Hindu Punjabis as well as Sant Nirankaris were being killed. Hindus in Punjab and elsewhere took revenge by murdering innocent Sikhs. Violence between Hindus and Sikhs became so common that it seemed almost inevitable. Many took it for granted that the two faiths could not get along, overlooking the fact that they had lived together peacefully for centuries. (In the same way, in the 1990s, Hindu-Muslim violence on a scale not seen for forty years convinced many that the two largest religious communities of South Asia were natural enemies.)

Bhindranwale wanted a Punjab that was inhabited exclusively by Khalsa Sikhs. It is not clear just what place he saw for his purified Punjab. He certainly supported the autonomy demanded in the Anandpur Sahib Resolution, but many believed that his real goal was Khalistan, the "land of the Khalsa" or "Pure Land," an independent Sikh state. The idea of Khalistan had been discussed throughout the 1970s. It initially found little support, but during the 1980s it attracted increasing numbers of Sikhs who became convinced that their community's interests would be ignored as long as Punjab remained part of India.

Indira saw Bhindranwale as an instrument in the struggle to uphold her dynasty. She both prohibited action against him and refused to make even token concessions to Longowal's demands. This was intended to undermine the Akali Dal, by suggesting to Sikhs that—however questionable his methods—Bhindranwale fought for their interests far more effectively than Longowal. The prime minister also hoped to use Bhindranwale to control the Congress (I) state government in Punjab: Chronic violence would ensure that the chief minister remained dependent on the Center. It would also foster disagreements over strategy within his government, creating factions that Indira could play off against each other. In October 1983, however, a bloody massacre of Hindus by Bhindranwale's followers generated enough political pressure that Indira had to do something: Blaming the chief minister of Punjab for allowing the killings, she put the state under President's Rule.

This did not stop either the slaughter of Hindus or tit-for-tat murders of Sikhs. By December 1983, Indira realized that the situation in Punjab was spiraling out of control, and she ordered Bhindranwale's arrest. The holy man, however, evaded capture by moving into the Akal Takht, the headquarters of the Sikh priesthood in the Golden Temple complex at Amritsar, from where he apparently orchestrated attacks by "militants" in Punjab and beyond.

A Lok Sabha election was due in 1985. For Indira, this transformed the violence in Punjab into a political liability: If the Hindus who formed four fifths of India's population felt that a Congress (I) government could not protect them from Sikh attacks, they might give their votes to other parties, particularly the new Hindu nationalist Bharatiya Janata Party. The prime minister decided to crush Bhindranwale. On June 4, 1984, the Indian army attacked the Golden Temple complex. Three days of hard fighting ended with the Akal Takht in ruins and almost 6,000 dead. Bhindranwale had perished. So had priests and pilgrims in the Golden Temple complex, and villagers who had tried to go to Amritsar to defend their holy places.

Even Sikhs who opposed Bhindranwale and Khalistan were outraged by the desecration of the center of their religion. Their protests were broken up by the police, and many demonstrators were killed. The discontent extended to Sikh soldiers. Many deserted; others mutinied, and were often shot. Sikh anger focused on Indira, but the prime minister insisted that only a small faction of unpatriotic Sikhs opposed her. Whether out of bravery or out of naïveté, she showed her faith in India's Sikhs by using them as guards. Her trust was misplaced. On October 31, 1984, her bodyguards shot her dead. Sikhs around the world celebrated. In several Indian cities, particularly Delhi, Hindus responded by massacring thousands of Sikhs, indiscriminately blaming them for the assassination. The police stood by, and in some neighborhoods, Congress (I) leaders directed the killings.

RAJIV

The Congress (I) members of parliament immediately chose Rajiv Gandhi to be party leader and prime minister. Rajiv had been in politics for only four years, but as Indira's son, he was taken to be the best person to rule India. It was also assumed that his lineage would draw votes to his party. Rajiv called a Lok Sabha election for December 1984. He campaigned on the Nehru-Gandhi dynastic record and his mother's memory. He urged all patriotic Indians to vote for him as the only person who could protect the country against its enemies, external (the United States and Pakistan) and internal (the Sikhs). Ironically for a grandson of the secularist Nehru, he stressed his commitment to defending Hindus and Hinduism. All this paid off. Congress (I) did better than ever before or since, garnering just under half of all the votes cast, and 77 percent of the seats in the Lok Sabha.

India had high expectations of the young and handsome Rajiv. For a time, it looked as if the new prime minister was replacing the government-directed economy with the free market, as he loosened licensing laws, import controls, and restrictions on joint business ventures between Indians and foreigners. His Seventh Five Year Plan (1985–1990) made the private sector responsible for funding economic development. Then, Rajiv lost interest in economic reform. It has been suggested that he wanted nothing more than to open India to the high-technology imports (such as computers or videocasette recorders) that were desired by the urban middle class; Rajiv claimed that these goods would help fight poverty, but he never properly explained how. He probably could have done little under any circumstances: Too many people benefited from the planned economy, from the bureaucrats who oversaw it to the politicians who sold licenses.

Nevertheless, the Indian economy grew rapidly throughout the 1980s. The reasons are uncertain, although they probably had little to do with Rajiv's reforms. It has been suggested that Nehruvian economics was finally paying off: Investment in roads, electricity, and so on had created a modern infrastructure that, although by no means complete, made growth inevitable. Others point to the huge middle class that had come into being since the 1950s, again partly as a result of Nehru's policies; educated, well-off professionals, businessmen, civil servants, and service employees wanted consumer goods, and had the money to buy them. Or perhaps it was heavy government spending that stimulated the economy. Whatever the cause, from the late 1980s it was joined by a boom in Indian exports of everything from trucks to chemicals, which were sold in East Asia, the Middle East, Europe, and North America. Meanwhile, the proportion of the population unable to afford basic needs declined steadily from the mid-1970s to the late 1980s. This was partly because the Green Revolution lowered the cost of food. Another cause was the growth of alternative employment for the rural poor, who could work in construction or services in the expanding cities, or as laborers and servants in the Persian Gulf states.

Like Indira, Rajiv dominated a weak cabinet. For advice, he relied on his "cronies," many of them old friends from his boarding school. He continued his mother's policy of dismissing chief ministers and imposing President's Rule to make sure that state governments were loyal to him. His interventions in state politics could be dramatic. In the 1960s, the Mizo Tribals rebelled against the state government of Assam, which they felt had ignored them during a famine. In 1972, Indira pacified the Mizo moderates by forming their homeland into the Union Territory of Mizoram; as a territory, it had its own legislature and chief minister, but was more tightly controlled by the Center than states were. The hardliners continued the rebellion. In 1986, however, Rajiv met the leader of the rebels, and bought him off by making him chief minister in place of the Congress (I) incumbent. Shortly afterwards, Mizoram was made a full-fledged state.

Just as Rajiv was ending the revolt in Mizoram, he was helping to provoke one in Kashmir. From the 1930s, the most important politician in Kashmir was Sheikh Mohammad Abdullah, who led a party called the National Conference. The Sheikh died in 1982, when his son Farooq Abdullah succeeded him as head of the National Conference and chief minister. Farooq ran afoul of Indira, who replaced him with one of his rivals in the National Conference. The new chief minister was dismissed in 1986. Soon afterwards, Rajiv reinstated Farooq, and ordered elections for the Kashmir legislature for March 1987. Knowing that their parties had become unpopular in the state, Rajiv and Farooq rigged the voting so that Congress (I) and the National Conference won 66 of the 76 legislative seats. Such blatant electoral fraud provoked great anger, especially among educated young Kashmiri Muslims. They were already suffering from high unemployment and a lack of opportunities, and saw the election as the last straw. Many traced all their problems to the fact that Kashmir was part of India, and now called for independence or merger with Pakistan.

Rajiv's principal concern was, of course, Punjab. He started out well, meeting the Akali Dal leader Longowal and promising to compensate the families of victims of the Delhi massacres, to reinstate Sikh soldiers who had been dismissed after the attack at Amritsar, to give Chandigarh to Punjab, and to review the division of water between Punjab and Haryana. The promises did not stop the violence, however. Its victims included Longowal, who was assassinated by hard-line Sikhs soon after his accord with Rajiv. Leadership of the Akali Dal passed to Surjit Singh Barnala, who became chief minister of Punjab when President's Rule ended in September 1985.

The massacres had left many Sikhs unable to trust Hindus, Congress (I), or the Center. Their attitude hardened when Rajiv did not honor his undertakings. Barnala was discredited by his association with the prime minister; his legislative majority collapsed; and Punjab was again put under President's Rule. More and more Sikhs were drawn to the idea of Khalistan. All the while, Punjab was suffering from economic problems. Agricultural profits declined with the end of the growth generated by the Green Revolution, and political unrest helped raise unemployment. Discontented young men were drawn into militant groups, who called their terrorist strikes a war of independence for Khalistan. The police and army retaliated with unprovoked attacks on Sikh villagers. During 1987, Punjab slipped into a full-scale civil war.

Probably with justification, India accused Pakistan of helping the militants in Punjab. Pakistan also indirectly affected India's relations with the superpowers. In 1979, the Soviets invaded Afghanistan to bolster Communist rule there. They were met by Afghan guerrillas, who obtained the backing of the United States. Washington funneled its support through Pakistan, which from 1981 received heavy American economic aid and military assistance. A worried Indira turned to Moscow, which agreed to give India the same volume of aid as Pakistan received from the United States. In return, Indira and then Rajiv refrained from criticizing the Afghan war, and in the 1980s, India was even closer to the Soviet Union than it had been in the 1970s.

India was not a superpower, but Rajiv saw it as a regional power in South Asia. In 1987, he intervened in the war between the government of Sri Lanka and the Liberation Tigers of Tamil Eelam or LTTE, who wanted self-rule for the Tamil-speaking parts of Sri Lanka. Rajiv brokered an agreement between the two sides, then sent Indian troops to Sri Lanka to oversee its implementation. The LTTE refused to keep their promise to disarm, however; fighting resumed, and the Indian peacekeepers soon found themselves at war with the Tamil rebels. They suffered heavy losses until their withdrawal in 1991.

THE ELECTION OF 1989

By the late 1980s, the patent failure of Rajiv's policy in Punjab and Sri Lanka was eating away at his popularity. So was the arrogance of many of his cronies, who were widely suspected of using their friendship with the prime minister for personal gain. One of the members of Rajiv's team with a reputation for honesty was Vishwanath Pratap Singh, called V.P. V.P. was a Rajput landlord from Uttar Pradesh, who served as minister of finance and then of defense. In 1987, he found indications that some of the cronies had received money from Bofors, a Swedish armaments manufacturer, in return for a lucrative contract to supply the Indian army with artillery. The prime minister's role in the Bofors scandal is still unclear, but at the very least he shielded his friends from investigation. V.P. angrily resigned from the cabinet. A few months later, Rajiv's cronies orchestrated his expulsion from Congress (I).

V.P. was widely seen as a new J.P. Narayan, a crusader against a corrupt Congress government. He reestablished J.P. and Desai's Janata

Morcha (People's Front) and with a Lok Sabha election due in 1989 pursued alliances with other parties. The most important of these were two offshoots of the old Janata Party, which had broken up in 1980. One, which kept the Janata Party name, was led by Chandra Shekhar, a former member of Congress with leftist leanings. The other was the Lok Dal, the resuscitated party of Chaudhuri Charan Singh (who had died in 1987). At the end of 1988, V.P.'s Janata Morcha, the Janata Party, the Lok Dal, and various defectors from Congress (I) united to form the Janata Dal (People's Party), under V.P.'s leadership.

Other parties were also readying themselves for the election. Regional parties had proliferated since the 1970s. Besides the National Conference in Kashmir, the Akali Dal in Punjab, and the DMK in Tamil Nadu, they included the Telugu Desam Party of Andhra Pradesh, the Asom Gana Parishad (Assam Community Council) of Assam, and the Shiv Sena (Army of Shiva or of Shivaji) of Maharashtra. These were devoted to upholding the language and culture of their own states and the interests of their native-born inhabitants. India also had a new national party in the BJP, the Bharatiya Janata Party or Indian People's Party.

The BJP was founded in 1980 by people who had belonged to the Jan Sangh until its merger into the Janata Party in 1977. The BJP's Hindu nationalist principles are summed up by the word *Hindutva*, or Hinduness. The party's goal is to transform India into a world power, industrialized, and militarily strong. This requires national unity, which according to the BJP can only come from India's shared Hindu culture. In the interests of unity, the minority of Indians who are not Hindus must accommodate themselves to that culture. This necessitates the abandonment of Congress's version of "secularism," which by giving official recognition to the special interests of non-Hindus undermines India.

The BJP was particularly concerned over what it saw as pampering of Muslims: Their Aligarh Muslim University was subsidized by the government; their state of Kashmir enjoyed special autonomy; they were exempt from the family law that applied to other Indians. This had recently been illustrated after a court awarded alimony to Shah Bano, a divorced Muslim woman. Muslim theologians protested that the award violated the teachings of Islam. To pacify them, Rajiv had parliament reiterate that Muslim divorces were governed by Islamic law, as interpreted by the theologians, who could thus ensure that women like Shah Bano did not receive alimony.

The BJP has wrongly been called conservative or Hindu fundamentalist. The party's vision of a modern India is emphatically not conservative; and the BJP upholds Hindu culture and symbols, but not religious and social practices. For example, it rejects the traditional caste system as a barrier to national unity. The party is associated with several like-minded groups in what is called the Sangh Parivar or Family of Organizations. The oldest is the Rashtriya Swyamsevak Sangh (RSS), founded in 1925, which calls itself a cultural organization. Then there are the Bajrang Dal or Strong Party, an armed force that ostensibly protects Hindus during communal disturbances; the Bharatiya Mazdoor Sangh (Indian Laborers' Organization), a federation of Hindu nationalist trade unions; and the Vishwa Hindu Parishad (VHP, World Council of Hindus).

From the late 1940s until the early 1980s, Hindutva found solid but limited support. The creation of Pakistan, Hindu-Muslim violence, and the assassination of Mahatma Gandhi helped discredit religious-based nationalism in the eyes of many Indians. Rajiv's tenure as prime minister, however, saw an explosion of support for the BJP, especially in the urban middle class of the Hindi-speaking states of the north. The party attracted people who disliked the corruption of Congress (I) and its fixation on the Nehru-Gandhi dynasty, and of course Hindus who felt that their interests were being overridden to placate religious minorities.

Much of the BJP's strength was drawn from the Rama temple movement. Rama, the hero of the *Ramayana*, is regarded as an earthly incarnation of Vishnu and in north India is one of the most popular Hindu deities. He is said to have been born at Ayodhya in Uttar Pradesh. In the sixteenth century, a general of the Mughal emperor Babur built a mosque at Ayodhya, called the Babri Masjid or Babur Mosque. According to devotees of Rama, the mosque was built on the site of a demolished temple to their deity, and from at least the nineteenth century, Hindus and Muslims disputed control of the site. After independence, the Ayodhya district administration sealed the mosque and prevented members of either community from worshipping there.

In 1986, the VHP started a campaign to tear down the Babri Masjid and build a new temple to Rama. The drive was supported by the other organizations of the Sangh Parivar, including the BJP. The Rama temple movement became a symbol of the dispute between Hindutva and secularism and hence of the differences between the BJP and Congress (I). Building the temple would affirm India's essentially Hindu character; preserving the mosque would prove that India heeded the wishes of Muslims and other minority communities, even if this meant ignoring the sensibilities of the majority.

V.P. SINGH AND CHANDRA SHEKHAR

Early in 1989, V.P. Singh's Janata Dal, the Telugu Desam Party, the Asom Gana Parishad, and the DMK formed the National Front, an alliance to fight Congress (I) in the election at the end of the year. The BJP and the National Front later agreed not to run candidates in the same constituency, which reduced the chance of splitting the anti-Congress (I) vote. The election left Congress (I) the largest party in the Lok Sabha, but for the first time ever no party won a majority: Rajiv's party was reduced to 37 percent of the seats; the Janata Dal followed with 27 percent, and the BJP got 16 percent. Rather than see Rajiv retain power, the BJP and the Communist Party of India (Marxist) agreed to support a National Front government. This gave V.P. just enough backing to become prime minister.

V.P.'s short term seemed dominated by war against secessionists. His efforts to resolve the conflict in Punjab came to nothing, as the need to keep his parliamentary allies happy forced him to renege on promises to end President's Rule, try the ringleaders of the Delhi massacres, and reinstate Sikhs in the army. Just as V.P. was taking over the prime minister's office in December 1989, the simmering anger of many young Kashmiris boiled over into a violent revolt. Pakistan gave moral and probably financial support to the militants, and India accused its neighbor of organizing the uprising. The Indian army planned an attack on what it said were rebel bases in Pakistan. Pakistan responded by readying the nuclear weapons it had developed after Indira Gandhi tested her country's in 1974, and for several days there was a danger of nuclear war in South Asia. It passed, but during 1990 the rising in Kashmir developed into a civil war far deadlier than that in Punjab.

At the same time, fighting broke out in Assam. Thanks to its low population density, the northeastern state saw heavy immigration throughout the twentieth century. After the Bangladesh War of 1971, Hindus and Muslims from Bangladesh illegally settled in Assam in such numbers that the Assamese were afraid of being overwhelmed. The United Liberation Front of Assam (ULFA), which was established in 1980, organized a civil disobedience campaign to force the Center to deport the immigrants. In 1985, Rajiv promised to deprive illegal immigrants of the right to vote and deport those who had come from Bangladesh since 1971. Nothing was done, however, and in 1990 the ULFA launched a war of independence in Assam, arguing that the immigrants would not leave as long as the state was part of India.

It has been suggested that V.P. should have remained a purely moral leader, as Mahatma Gandhi and J.P. Narayan had done. By accepting political power, he set himself up to fail. It is unlikely that any prime minister could have met the expectations that V.P.'s campaign against Rajiv had generated. The need to hold together the Janata Dal and the National Front, and retain the parliamentary support of both the BJP and the Marxists, made V.P.'s administration particularly ineffective. During 1990, his popularity fell rapidly. When Devi Lal, the deputy prime minister and leader of the Lok Dal, was dismissed from the cabinet in August 1990, it was obvious that the days of the Janata Dal government were numbered. Its collapse might require a new election, and V.P. decided to shore himself up with a dramatic gesture.

Twelve years earlier, Morarji Desai's government had appointed the Mandal Commission to study the position of the Other Backward Classes (OBCs), the Hindu communities that were neither upper castes nor Scheduled Castes and Scheduled Tribes. OBCs were not guaranteed seats in legislatures, government jobs, or universities, even though many of them were almost as disadvantaged as the SCs and STs that did enjoy reservations. The Mandal Commission advocated the extension of reservations to OBCs and provided a long list of communities that it claimed fell into that category. New Delhi refused to implement the recommendations. This was partly because the Mandal list included many groups that had no need of help—for example, castes composed of rich peasants.

On August 7, 1990, V.P. announced that, in accordance with the ten-year-old report, 27 percent of all employment under the Center would be reserved for OBC communities named in the Mandal list. This included jobs in both the bureaucracy and state-owned firms, although the reservations would not apply to seats in the legislatures or to education. With the 22.5 percent of posts already guaranteed to SCs and STs, this closed half of the Center's positions to the higher castes, who protested with demonstrations and even public suicides. Groups not in the Mandal Report began fighting for recognition as OBCs, and caste conflict reached new heights.

Earlier in the year, the BJP had formed its first state governments after winning legislative elections in Himachal Pradesh, Madhya Pradesh, and Rajasthan. As V.P.'s popularity fell, that of the party of Hindutva soared. The discord evoked by the Mandal Report posed a serious threat to the BJP, which was devoted to Hindu unity both as a matter of principle and to maximize its support among voters. Lal Krishna Advani, the leader of the party, resolved on a gesture of his own to unite Hindus behind the BJP. In September 1990, he set off on a great *rath yatra*. This

term, literally "chariot procession," is normally used in connection with
a parade of the image of Vishnu. Advani's rath yatra was a motorized
journey across north India, from Somnath in Gujarat to Ayodhya. The
significance of its starting point was unmistakable. A thousand years
earlier, the Muslim raider Mahmud the Ghaznawid had destroyed a
great temple of Shiva at Somnath. In 1950, devotees had begun to rebuild
it. Now, the BJP chief was calling for Hindus to follow this example at
Ayodhya, by tearing down the Babri Masjid and restoring the Rama
temple.

Advani was enthusiastically welcomed by Hindus all along his route.
His stops were often followed by attacks on Muslims. A month into the
rath yatra, however, he was arrested by the Janata Dal chief minister of
Bihar on the plea that he was stirring up communal violence. Not surprisingly, the BJP refused to continue to back a Janata Dal government
in New Delhi. It withdrew its parliamentary support from V.P. Singh,
who thereby lost his majority and resigned as prime minister. The president offered the job back to Rajiv Gandhi, whose Congress (I) was still
the largest party in the Lok Sabha. Rajiv refused the invitation. He knew
that if he became prime minister now, he would need the support of
other parties. This would leave him just as weak as V.P. had been. He
preferred to wait for a new election, which he hoped would restore Congress (I)'s majority, and threw his party's support behind Chandra Shekhar, the one-time leader of the Janata Party. By combining his faction of
the Janata Dal with Congress (I), Chandra Shekhar secured a majority in
the Lok Sabha and became prime minister.

But Rajiv was merely waiting till he felt ready to face the voters. The
time came in March 1991. Using the excuse that the government had put
him under police surveillance, he withdrew Congress (I)'s support from
Chandra Shekhar. No one else could assemble a majority in the Lok
Sabha, and an election was scheduled for late May. Rajiv again campaigned on his dynasty's name, although he abandoned the overt appeals to Hinduism that he had made in 1984 and reasserted the old
Congress commitment to "secularism." V.P. Singh aimed for the OBC
vote; and Advani drummed up Hindu nationalist support with refer-
ences to his rath yatra, the Babri Masjid, and communal violence.

Voting began on May 20, 1991. The next day, Rajiv was assassinated
by supporters of the Sri Lankan LTTE, and the remainder of the election
was postponed till mid-June. Rajiv's cronies turned to the only adult
member of the Nehru-Gandhi dynasty, the murdered man's Italian
widow Sonia Gandhi. (Sanjay Gandhi's widow Maneka was an active
politician, but bad relations with her in-laws had taken her into the Jan-

ata Dal.) Sonia declared that she was not interested in politics and declined the leadership of her husband's party. This provoked a power struggle within Congress (I). It was won by Pamulaparti Venkata Narasimha Rao, a former chief minister of Andhra Pradesh and cabinet minister under Indira and Rajiv. For the first time since 1947, barring the nineteen-month tenure of Lal Bahadur Shastri, Congress had a leader drawn from outside the dynasty.

11

India Today

LIBERALIZATION

In the 1991 election to the Lok Sabha, Congress (I) retained its place as India's most popular political party, although it received fewer votes than in 1989. The striking feature of the election was a breakthrough on the part of the Bharatiya Janata Party, which doubled its share of the vote to 20 percent and replaced the Janata Dal as the second largest party in parliament. The rest of the seats in the lower house were divided among a much-reduced Janata Dal, and leftist and regional parties.

There were several reasons for the BJP's success. The party was the natural beneficiary of the continuing spread of Hindu nationalism and (in some quarters) of anti-Muslim sentiment. Both were fueled by the Rama temple movement and communal violence, which were linked to the BJP through Advani's rath yatra. Upper-caste Hindus who were angry over V.P. Singh's decision to implement the Mandal Report and unwilling to support the "secular" Congress (I), turned towards the BJP. More broadly, many Indians who regarded the Congress (I) and Janata Dal governments as failures transferred their votes to the BJP, the only other national party.

As Congress (I) was the largest party in parliament, its leader Pamu-

laparti Venkata Narasimha Rao was installed as prime minister. Narasimha Rao's followers occupied only 42 percent of the seats in the Lok
Sabha, but he managed to secure guarantees of support from enough
small parties to cobble together a majority. Over the next few years,
Congress (I) won several by-elections to fill vacant seats, including (for
reasons that will be explained) twelve of Punjab's thirteen Lok Sabha
seats. In 1994, the prime minister acquired a parliamentary majority in
his own right when a dissident faction that had broken away from the
Janata Dal joined Congress (I).

When Narasimha Rao became the leader of his party, he was ap-
proaching his seventieth birthday and in poor health. He was widely
regarded as an interim chief, and without the authority of the Nehru-
Gandhi dynasty, he lacked the full support of his colleagues in Congress
(I). To secure his position against them, he turned to the party organization. In some states, he called elections to local and state Congress
committees for the first time since the early 1970s. No one could deny
that the new committees represented the party members, and the fact
that they gave their support to Narasimha Rao strengthened the prime
minister against his rivals. In 1992, the All-India Congress Committee,
chosen by the state committees, met to elect the Congress Working Committee (the party executive). Narasimha Rao stood for election as party
president, something that Rajiv had never done. He won, confirming that
he was the chosen leader of Congress (I) and making his position unassailable.

As soon as he became prime minister, Narasimha Rao began to reform
India's economic policy. It has been seen that there is a debate as to
whether British rule enriched or impoverished India. The same is true
of the effects of Nehru's planned economic development. It unquestionably made India a major industrial manufacturer, but there is no way of
knowing how the economy would have fared without it. Many economists believe that when India became independent, planned development offered the only possible route to economic growth, but that it was
kept in place for too long until it became a hindrance rather than a help.
The planners, licensers, and managers of state-owned firms (called
public-sector undertakings) became a massive bureaucracy. Not only
were they expensive; many were also corrupt and determined to prevent
any changes that interfered with their interests. Most public-sector undertakings were grossly inefficient: As late as 2000, after nine years of
economic reforms, only 134 of India's 240 state-owned firms made profits. The rest relied on subsidies from taxation to keep afloat.

All this aside, by 1991 the Nehruvian economy was politically unpopular in many circles. The urban middle class wanted to buy consumer goods, but these were often simply unavailable: Production in India was held back by the licensing laws and limits on foreign investment, while quantitative restrictions and tariff barriers kept out imports. The old arguments in favor of these policies had evaporated. Forty years' experience had proved incorrect the theory that a lack of consumer goods would force Indians to invest their savings in domestic development projects. Few still believed that foreign investment and imports threatened the country's political independence. This was not merely because memories of colonial rule had faded: The nature of the modern global economy meant that if India did open its doors to foreign business, it would attract firms from so many countries that no one of them could acquire control as the British East India Company had done. Finally, the economic collapse of the Soviet bloc had discredited the idea of a planned economy.

During the first half of 1991, India drifted into a severe economic crisis. In 1989, the Soviet satellites in central and eastern Europe had asserted their independence, and now the Soviet Union itself was about to break up. This not only disrupted India's trade with the Eastern Bloc, which had both bought Indian exports and supplied machinery and military matériel, it also cut off most of India's aid from the Soviets. Then came the Gulf War in 1991, which drove up the price of petroleum products and contributed to runaway inflation in India. The war also led to the repatriation of 130,000 Indians who had been working in Persian Gulf states, and whose wages had been one of India's major sources of foreign currency.

In recent years, the Indian government had borrowed heavily to finance its budget deficits. Several big loans from multilateral banks were due for repayment (in dollars) in mid-1991. Unfortunately, despite the restrictions on foreign goods, India was spending more on imports than she was earning from exports. This drained the reserves of foreign exchange, which had shrunk to just $600 million. As a result, India could not repay its loans. One of the last acts of Chandra Shekhar's government was to raise funds by selling $200 million worth of gold. This was only a stopgap measure, though, and full repayment required help from the International Monetary Fund. This body would not issue credits unless India loosened its licensing laws, admitted foreign firms, and reduced government spending.

The economy was therefore Narasimha Rao's first priority. He chose a well-known economist named Manmohan Singh to be his finance minister. Manmohan Singh promptly devalued the rupee, which increased the competitiveness of Indian exports, boosted sales, and thus brought in foreign exchange. He and Narasimha Rao then launched the program of economic reforms, called liberalization. Over the next ten years, India was governed by four prime ministers, from three political parties. All continued the policy of liberalization, which dismantled the central elements of the Nehruvian economy.

One of the first things that Manmohan Singh did was to abolish licensing for all but eighteen industries. Two years later, limits on production were removed from cars and domestic appliances, two lines of consumer goods that had remained licensed. Import duties were also slashed, with the average falling from 71 percent in 1993 to 35 percent in 1998. Between 1996 and 2001, the quantitative restrictions that had curtailed or barred imports were almost entirely phased out. All this resulted in a huge increase in the quantities of goods available to consumers and of equipment available to manufacturers.

During the five years after 1991, new regulations allowed foreigners to own up to 51 percent of businesses in India. One of the most dramatic results of this was in the field of automobile production. In 1991, there were three car manufacturers in India, turning out 190,000 vehicles a year. A decade later, there were ten, producing 500,000 cars. Most of the new entrants were joint ventures between Indian investors and firms based in the United States, Japan, and South Korea.

These reforms were what the International Monetary Fund had wanted, and with the World Bank it lent India enough money to repay the immediate debts. Over the next few years, India's exports increased rapidly, at a rate of growth that reached 27 percent a year in the mid-1990s. The foreign exchange reserves swelled to $18.8 billion in September 1994, and India repaid the International Monetary Fund loans ahead of schedule.

In the long term, Narasimha Rao and Manmohan Singh hoped to bring about economic growth through increased competition, modernization, and foreign investment. This would allow the integration of India into the world economy, boosting trade and investment, and leading to still further growth. In 1994, India signed the final act of the Uruguay round of the General Agreement on Tariffs and Trade, committing itself to an open economy of a sort unimaginable only a few years earlier.

Throughout the first decade of liberalization, almost all public-sector undertakings remained under government control (although in 1994, shares in several state-owned firms were sold to private investors, who from 1998 were allowed to own up to 74 percent of nonstrategic concerns). However, private enterprise was allowed to compete with the public-sector undertakings—for example, in domestic airline service from 1991, steel production from 1992, and coal-mining and processing from 1997. This ended the government monopolies that had been created by the Industrial Policy Resolution of 1956 and Indira Gandhi's nationalizations. The new theory was that increased competition would improve the efficiency of both state and private enterprise.

Liberalization was followed by rapid economic growth, which reached its peak with a 7.5 percent annual increase in India's gross domestic product between 1994/1995 and 1996/1997. After a slowdown, the figure picked up again to 5.8 percent in 1998/1999. The improvement at the end of the decade was partly due to the development of a huge computer software industry: India sold no software abroad in 1991, but $8.3 billion worth in 2000—15 percent of the total value of its exports. This was one of the reasons why between 1996 and 1998, according to the World Bank, the Indian economy replaced the German as the fourth largest in the world (only the American, Chinese, and Japanese were bigger).

Still, many felt that liberalization did not go far enough. Indian industry has not grown as quickly as was predicted in 1991, and foreign investment remains low at $2.2 billion a year (whereas China receives $40 billion a year). Supporters of economic reform say that the process is not yet finished, and that once it is, growth will be much faster. Free market economists who oppose all public-sector undertakings demand privatization, the transfer of state firms to private ownership. Soon after becoming finance minister, Manmohan Singh said that several concerns would be privatized. The process did not really begin until 2000, when the Indian branch of a European multinational bought a government-owned bakery. The following year, the Center promised to privatize twenty-seven firms.

The main obstacle to privatization has been political: The public-sector undertakings have 2 million employees and are administered by another 4 million bureaucrats. India's labor laws prevent firms from laying off or firing workers. Given private business's emphasis on efficiency, this discourages interest in public-sector undertakings, even if the government were willing to sell off its concerns. In 2001, plans to change labor laws were unveiled, but it is unclear whether any prime minister would want to antagonize the millions of public employees who would lose their jobs after privatization.

There have been complaints that the effects of the economic reforms will remain limited unless India's infrastructure is improved. Poor roads and port facilities often hinder trade. The greatest problem is electricity: The power supply is uncertain, with frequent blackouts, and very expensive. One reason is that as much as 40 percent of the electricity generated in India is siphoned off by people who do not pay for it. Another is that to get votes, politicians have given electricity to some groups at virtually no cost, which raises the rates for other consumers. For example, in many states, farmers pay a low flat rate for power, however much they use.

Efforts to reform the electricity system in the early 1990s failed. To a large extent, this was because electricity is controlled by state governments, which for political reasons may not want to see changes. In 2001, the Center launched fresh plans for electricity that include metering all consumption. It is still too early to know whether this will solve the problem.

For several years, the Center fulfilled the International Monetary Fund's demand that it lower the budget deficit. From 1998, however, the deficit rose once more. There were many reasons: bureaucratic salaries; heavy defense expenditure; and the subsidies that keep down the prices of such essentials as petroleum products, food, and fertilizers. The subsidies were reduced in the early years of liberalization, but this did not last in a country where many people simply could not afford to pay world prices. The deficit has snowballed, because the Center's debt is now so high that just under half of its total revenues go to interest payments. This in turn limits spending on infrastructure or development (under 5 percent of revenues go to education, housing, and health care). Moreover, many state governments never stopped running up huge debts, and their finances are in worse shape than those of the Center.

The Center's efforts to balance the budget have also affected liberalization. In the early 1990s, income, corporate, and excise taxes were slashed, on the theory that this would give consumers more money to spend and so stimulate the economy. (The excise is a tax on domestic production.) At the same time, import and export duties were lowered. All this cut into revenues to such an extent that in 1999, most taxes were raised again. In any case, some taxes had never been lowered—for example, the tariff on imported alcohol: Spirits still pay a duty of 222.4 percent, and beer and wine 108 percent.

Successive finance ministers have expressed a desire to rely more heavily on the income tax as a source of revenue, as developed countries do. This is currently impossible. The poor do not earn enough to have to pay income tax. For political reasons, agricultural incomes are not taxed, however high. Moreover, many people who should pay income tax manage to evade it. As a result, only 12 million Indians paid anything in 1997, and attempts to increase collection have failed.

PUNJAB, KASHMIR, AND AYODHYA

Beside economic reforms, Narasimha Rao's term as prime minister saw continuing secessionist and communal violence. To head the Punjab police, the National Front government had appointed K.P.S. Gill, a Sikh but a fierce opponent of the pro-Khalistan militants. Gill led his men in an all-out campaign, fighting terror with terror. Suspected militants, and many innocent Punjabis, were tortured or summarily executed. Some of Gill's officers took advantage of the violence and the resulting climate of fear to commit rape or robbery on the side.

The Akali Dal, which was becoming increasingly friendly toward the militants, was outraged when Narasimha Rao left Gill at his job. When elections for the Punjab seats in the Lok Sabha and for the state legislature were held in February 1992, the party showed its anger by calling on its supporters to boycott the polls. Fewer than one in four Punjabi voters cast ballots. Most of those who did vote were supporters of Congress (I), which won all but one Lok Sabha seat, and a majority in the state legislature.

Whatever else might be said about it, Gill's policy worked. Once enough militant leaders had been killed, their surviving colleagues not only found themselves unable to recruit new members, but lost interest in attacking civilian and government targets. By mid-1993, Punjab was calm, after nine years of virtual civil war that had left 16,000 people dead. The Center had finally begun to heed Sikh grievances, and this eroded support for Khalistan. Chandigarh has not become part of Punjab; but in 1995–1996, the courts convicted and imprisoned many people for their role in the massacres of Sikhs that took place in Delhi in 1984, and a former government minister belonging to Congress (I) was put on trial for instigating the violence. Since 1996, too, governments in New Delhi have seemed to respect the federal system.

In 1992, the state government of Assam won over the moderates of the United Liberation Front of Assam and crushed the extremists. This ended the Front's secessionist campaign. Meanwhile, Bodo tribesmen in the same state, afraid of losing their land and angry over their exclusion from public sector jobs, started a struggle for autonomy in 1988. The conflict became especially violent in the mid-1990s. It is unclear whether the Bodo revolt can be defused. The Bodos form a minority of the population in their traditional home districts, which means that even an autonomous government would be unable to devote itself to their interests.

During the 1990s, Hindu-Muslim relations in India were worse than at any time since the 1940s. Part of the reason was the war in Kashmir between Muslim militants and the Indian government. Pakistan's role in the outbreak of the revolt in 1989 remains unclear. By the mid-1990s, however, Pakistan was intimately involved in the fighting. Guerrillas were trained at camps in Pakistan and probably were funded by the Pakistani government. Many, perhaps most, of them were not Kashmiris, but Muslims from Pakistan and other countries. The guerrillas massacred Hindu, Sikh, and Muslim civilians in Kashmir; dueled with Indian soldiers and police; and bombed government and military installations. Pakistani troops gave them cover by shelling Indian positions, and the Indians shelled Pakistani positions and training camps in return. Over 30,000 civilians have died at the hands of the militants in Kashmir since the 1980s.

One of the few things that most Pakistanis agree on is that none of Kashmir should remain part of India (some want it annexed to their country, others are prepared to let Kashmiris become independent if they wish). As a result, successive Pakistani regimes—whether democratic or authoritarian—have been either unwilling, or politically unable, to stop supporting the militants' campaign against India. The Indian government in turn sees the attacks in Kashmir as terrorism, conducted by proxies of Pakistan. Many non-Muslim Indians, however, knowing that a large number of Muslim Kashmiris support the aims (and sometimes the methods) of the guerrillas who want to take Kashmir out of India, regard the situation in Kashmir as proof of the disloyalty of Muslim citizens of India in general. Their interpretation seems to receive further credence from the fact that a few Muslim groups in other parts of India have declared their support for the militants in Kashmir. This has contributed to increased suspicion and hostility toward Indian Muslims on the part of non-Muslims. Muslims have responded in kind.

At the beginning of the 1990s, the great symbol of Hindu-Muslim conflict was the Babri Masjid at Ayodhya. In Uttar Pradesh, the state where Ayodhya lies, a legislative election was held at the same time as the Lok Sabha polls that brought Narasimha Rao to power. It was won by the BJP, whose leader Kalyan Singh became chief minister. The new administration transferred the land surrounding the Babri Masjid to the Vishwa Hindu Parishad, the organization that had started the temple movement. Then, volunteers from the Parishad and its ally the Bajrang Dal cleared all the buildings around the mosque. The Supreme Court of India banned any construction in the area, but the volunteers ignored it and laid the foundations for their temple.

The central government sent security forces to protect the Babri Masjid, but Kalyan Singh's government barred them from the area, and on December 6, 1992, the volunteers demolished the mosque. Because the Babri Masjid had become such a powerful symbol for many Hindus and Muslims, this immediately raised communal tensions all over India. Riots in Bombay, Ahmedabad, Kanpur, and Jaipur left 1,150 dead within six days. On January 6, 1993, one month after the demolition, fresh Hindu-Muslim clashes broke out in Bombay, killing 557 in a week.

Narasimha Rao responded with a combination of repression and concessions. He dismissed India's four BJP state governments (in Uttar Pradesh, Himachal Pradesh, Madhya Pradesh, and Rajasthan) and temporarily banned militant Hindu and Muslim organizations, including the Vishwa Hindu Parishad, the Bajrang Dal, and the RSS. Two days after the demolition, the prime minister ordered the arrest of Lal Krishna Advani and other BJP leaders (they were freed the next month). Finally, the Center set up a trust to rebuild the Babri Masjid *and* to build a Rama temple beside it, although neither project has yet been started. Since the destruction of the Babri Masjid, India has seen periodic recrudescences of communal violence. The latest began in February 2002, following a mob attack on a trainload of Vishwa Hindu Parishad volunteers from Gujarat who had demonstrated in support of the construction of a Rama temple at Ayodhya.

CASTE POLITICS

In September 1991, Narasimha Rao confirmed that V.P. Singh's promise to implement the Mandal Report would go ahead. To meet complaints that this was unfair to groups that were upper caste but disadvantaged, another 10 percent of jobs were promised to economically backward communities of any caste. The following year, the Supreme Court rejected the guarantee of an additional 10 percent as unconstitutional, and the 27 percent reservations for OBCs alone went into effect in 1993. Many state governments imitated the Mandal Report by restricting jobs at their disposal to OBCs. Ruling parties might recognize communities that supported them as OBCs, even if there was no real social or economic justification for calling them "backward." The situation might verge on the ridiculous: In 1994, Tamil Nadu reserved 69 percent of state posts to SCs and what it defined as OBCs, and Karnataka 73 percent.

To outsiders, it may look as if India is still controlled by the higher Hindu castes. In support of this, it is sometimes pointed out that every prime minister who has held office for at least two years has been a

Brahmin (Nehru, Indira, Desai, Rajiv, Narasimha Rao, and the current incumbent Vajpayee), even though their community forms only one twentieth of India's population. Actually, Rajiv was a Brahmin only on his mother's side, and the role of caste in Indian politics is complicated. A prime minister or chief minister must balance major castes when appointing his cabinet, and state chief ministers are often chosen on account of their caste.

This is particularly true in the two big states of North India, Uttar Pradesh and Bihar. The local Congress organizations in both states were founded by Brahmins, including the Nehrus of Uttar Pradesh. In the 1930s, they were joined by rural elites from the Rajput and Bhumihar castes. After independence, these "forward castes" ensured that their OBC and SC dependents supported Congress as well. During the 1960s, rising political awareness took the OBCs into other parties, first the various incarnations of the Lok Dal, and then V.P. Singh's Janata Dal. Except in the 1977 election, however, the SCs of Uttar Pradesh and Bihar continued to support Congress, which was thus able to retain control of both states. Then, in 1989, many SCs transferred their votes to Janata Dal.

During the 1990s, the Janata Dal fragmented. In Bihar, both OBCs and SCs gave their backing to the Rashtriya Janata Dal (National People's Party), which has been able to keep both Congress (I) and the BJP out of power. In Uttar Pradesh, on the other hand, the two low-caste groupings formed separate parties, the OBCs' Samajwadi (Socialist) Party and the SCs' Bahujan Samaj Party (Party of the Majority Community). The Rama temple movement helped take most members of Uttar Pradesh's upper castes, and some OBCs and SCs, into the BJP. Since 1989, the government of Uttar Pradesh has rotated among the Samajwadi Party, the Bahujan Samaj Party, and the BJP. Another manifestation of the politicization of caste has been an increase in caste violence since the 1990s. The most notorious examples have occurred in parts of Bihar, where higher caste landowners and SC landless laborers are virtually at war.

THE UNITED FRONT

There were frequent accusations of corruption against Narasimha Rao's government. In 1992, a huge stock market swindle came to light. The ringleader of the scheme claimed to have given bribes to Narasimha Rao, but the prime minister denied the charge. Two years later, Arjun Singh, Narasimha Rao's main rival in Congress (I), resigned from the cabinet, alleging that several of his colleagues were blatantly corrupt.

During 1996, corruption became a major political issue. One business-man said that many top-ranking politicians were on his bribe payroll, and another claimed to have given $100,000 to a Hindu holy man who was apparently the prime minister's personal guru. Then, allegations emerged that in 1993 Narasimha Rao had bribed four members of the Lok Sabha from a small party to vote with his government so that he could keep his parliamentary majority.

The rising distrust of Congress (I) was one reason that the party won only three of the nine state legislative elections held in 1994 and 1995. A fresh Lok Sabha election was due in 1996, just as evidence of corruption was piling up. When polling took place, Congress (I)'s share of the vote fell sharply, from 42 percent in 1991 to 30 percent; the BJP's rose from 20 to 24 percent; and support for the Janata Dal continued its freefall. Because the BJP's support was more evenly spread across the country, the Hindu nationalist party won more seats in the Lok Sabha than Con-gress (I). For only the second time in the history of independent India, Congress was not the largest party in parliament.

A trend that had been emerging in 1989 and 1991 was now clear: the division of the Lok Sabha into several blocs, each consisting of a national party and its allies from regional parties. All were modeled on V.P. Singh's National Front (the Janata Dal and its allies): The member parties agreed not to run candidates against each other, and to form a coalition government if they obtained a majority in Lok Sabha. Besides the Na-tional Front, the Lok Sabha contained the BJP and Congress (I) blocs, and the Left Front, which was dominated by the Communist Party of India (Marxist).

In 1993, Atal Bihari Vajpayee had replaced Lal Krishna Advani as the political head of the BJP. Many said that the party had picked Vajpayee, who had been minister of external affairs under Morarji Desai, because he seemed less of an extremist than Advani. Thanks to his party's tri-umph in the 1996 election, Vajpayee took office as prime minister. He became the country's first leader since 1947 who had never belonged to Congress (where Morarji Desai, Chaudhuri Charan Singh, V.P. Singh, and Chandra Shekhar had all spent part of their political careers).

Nevertheless, even with its allies, the BJP controlled only a third of the seats in the Lok Sabha. Vajpayee was unable to persuade other parties to join his bloc, and he resigned after only twelve days. The National Front, the Left Front, and several unaffiliated small parties hastily joined together in a United Front. Congress (I) agreed to support a United Front

government, assuring it a majority in the Lok Sabha. After some infighting, the Janata Dal chief minister of Karnataka, Haradanahalli Doddegowda Deve Gowda, was selected as prime minister.

The United Front spelled out its policy in a Common Minimum Program. To keep the support of Congress (I), the new government undertook to maintain "secularism" and to continue the economic reforms. As
a sop to the regional parties of the National Front, it promised to increase
the autonomy of the states. It met the wishes of peasant parties and the
Left Front with a commitment to increase government assistance to farmers and workers. All this was topped off with plans to guarantee representation in parliament and the state legislatures to women.

Little of this was actually done, however. The main reason was that if
he wanted to retain his majority, Deve Gowda could not alienate either
Congress (I) or any of the members of the United Front. Thus, a bill to
reserve one third of the country's legislative seats for women failed,
largely due to opposition from OBC parties: Their leaders feared that
women's seats would go to upper-caste women, which would reduce
OBC representation. (Although the Mandal Report guaranteed OBCs
government jobs, it did not touch the legislatures.)

Like Chandra Shekhar's administration in 1990–1991, the United Front
government could only last as long as it had the approval of Congress
(I), which after just ten months turned against Deve Gowda. Allegedly
because of his failure to consult it regarding his policies, Congress (I)
withdrew support from the prime minister, though not the rest of the
government. Deve Gowda was replaced with his minister of external
affairs, Inder Kumar Gujral. Then, in late 1997, the report of the official
inquiry into the assassination of Rajiv Gandhi was released. It said that
the DMK, one of the two main parties in Tamil Nadu, had played a role
in the killing. The DMK was now a member of the United Front, and
Congress (I) demanded its expulsion from the ruling coalition. Gujral
refused to dump his ally, lost Congress (I)'s support, and resigned. As
no one else could get a majority in the Lok Sabha, a new election was
called for February and March 1998.

ATAL BIHARI VAJPAYEE

In the election, the Janata Dal was almost wiped out. The BJP rose to
a third of the seats in the Lok Sabha, and Congress (I) held steady at just
over a fourth. Vajpayee was reappointed prime minister in March 1998.
It looked as if there might be a replay of the events of 1996, but there
was an important difference: The destruction of the Janata Dal had so

weakened the United Front that it was unlikely to be able to form a government. On the other hand, the BJP and its allies needed only a few more seats to have a majority. Several United Front parties deserted their sinking ship and joined the BJP bloc in return for places in the government. With this and a few independent members of the Lok Sabha, Vajpayee obtained a bare majority.

The BJP and its allies called themselves the National Democratic Alliance. The new government comprised eighteen parties, five more than the United Front. To maintain unity, Vajpayee agreed not to push Hindu nationalist issues. Instead, his alliance issued a National Agenda for Governance—promising to reconsider nuclear policy; divide the huge states of Bihar, Madhya Pradesh, and Uttar Pradesh; guarantee legislative seats for women; and review the constitution. These were among the few points that all the member parties could agree on.

The National Agenda immediately had dramatic results in one area. Indira Gandhi had successfully tested nuclear explosives in 1974, and India had functional nuclear weapons by the late 1980s. Officially, only the United States, Russia, China, Britain, and France were members of the "nuclear club" although it was general knowledge that India, Pakistan, Israel, and North Korea also belonged. During most of the 1990s, American policy in South Asia centered on nuclear "nonproliferation," which meant putting pressure on India and Pakistan to get rid of their nuclear weapons. This was widely resented in India as hypocrisy: The United States had no plans either to give up its own weapons or to ask the other members of "nuclear club" or Israel and North Korea to do so. (This was because Britain, France, and Israel were Washington's friends, while it was a foregone conclusion that any pressure on Russia, China, and North Korea would be futile.)

Indeed, many Indians wanted their country to test its weapons and become a full member of the club. This was partly for security, especially against India's nuclear neighbors China and Pakistan, but it was also for symbolic reasons: It would make it clear that India was both a major power and a modern country with some of the best scientists in the world. This view was shared by most Indian political parties; Narasimha Rao and Gujral both refused to sign the Nuclear Non-Proliferation Treaty, and in 1996 India voted against the Comprehensive Test Ban Treaty in the General Assembly of the United Nations. The review of nuclear policy promised in the National Agenda for Governance resulted in successful tests of the weapons on May 11 and 13, 1998. Pakistan followed with its own tests two weeks later.

Western countries were furious at this South Asian intrusion into the

nuclear club, and the United States banned both technological cooperation with India and American investment in Indian industries. Most Indians were pleased, however. Progress was rather slower with the other
items on the National Agenda. As under the United Front, political cal-
culation stalled plans to reserve seats for women. In 2000, though, the
three big states were divided, creating Jharkhand, Chhattisgarh, and Uttaranchal. The first two are inhabited largely by Tribals. Most of the
people of Uttaranchal are considered high caste (60 percent of them are
Rajputs, who in the rest of India are a small elite community). In Uttar
Pradesh as a whole, however, OBCs and SCs formed half the population,
and the Uttaranchalis—often as disadvantaged as low-caste Hindus elsewhere—demanded their own state to end "reverse discrimination" at the
hands of the OBCs and SCs who dominated the Uttar Pradesh government in the 1990s.

Also in 2000, a commission was appointed to study possible constitutional reforms. If reforms are carried out, they may well enshrine several tendencies that have been developing over the last decade. With the
exception of Narasimha Rao in 1994–1996, the prime ministers since 1989
have lacked majorities in the Lok Sabha (with his bloc allies, Vajpayee
has a majority, but on its own the BJP does not). If they want to keep
their blocs or supporters, they cannot ignore parliament as Indira and
Rajiv did. As a result, parliament has regained some power. Moreover,
the governments since 1996 have been coalitions, presided over by cabinets that include representatives of not only the main party but also its
allies. To keep those allies, the prime minister must listen to his ministers,
whose power has accordingly increased.

Many Indians say that the need for the prime minister to pay attention
to parliament and the cabinet makes the government less efficient. They
either call for a presidential system such as they believe exists in the
United States (they are unaware that a hostile Congress can curtail the
authority of the president of the United States) or look back nostalgically
to the strong prime ministership of Indira Gandhi.

Federalism is also being revived. In 1994, the Supreme Court limited
the circumstances under which the Center can impose President's Rule.
The United Front and National Democratic Alliance governments have
both included regional parties, so Deve Gowda, Gujral, and Vajpayee
have been sensitive to state concerns. Vajpayee has promised not to impose President's Rule except where it is legitimately needed, a commitment that may find its way into the constitution.

INTO THE TWENTY-FIRST CENTURY

Narasimha Rao had resigned as head of Congress (I) a few months after losing the prime ministership in 1996. He was replaced with Sitaram Kesri, who during the 1998 election campaign was overshadowed by Rajiv Gandhi's Italian-born widow Sonia. Some credited Sonia with saving Congress (I) from oblivion by appealing to voters who believed in the Nehru-Gandhi dynasty. After the election, Sonia took Kesri's place as leader of the party. The new chief's lack of political skills was made painfully clear in April 1999. Sonia became persuaded that if the Tamil regional party the AIADMK pulled out of the National Democratic Alliance and joined the Congress (I) bloc, she would have a majority in the Lok Sabha. She got the AIADMK to withdraw its support from Vajpayee, depriving him of his majority and forcing him to resign.

Sonia thereupon asked the president to appoint her as prime minister. She had miscounted, however. When the numbers were tallied, Sonia did not have a majority either. As no bloc could now control the Lok Sabha, a new election had to be held. It was set for September-October, after the rainy season, and only nineteen months after the last election. Vajpayee remained in office as caretaker prime minister. Foreign affairs were to assure him an electoral victory.

Nehru had based his foreign policy on nonalignment and decolonization, to which Indira added friendship with the Soviet Union. In the 1990s, however, all these became unviable. The close of the Cold War made nonalignment meaningless. With the end of the European colonial empires, India had transformed "decolonization" into opposition to white rule in South Africa, but this too ended in 1993. And after the collapse of the Soviet Union in 1991, Russia was unable and unwilling to maintain a close relationship with India.

By way of compensation, India pursued friendly relations with the United States. In 1992, the two countries conducted joint military exercises. Indo-American relations worsened after the nuclear tests in 1998, but thereafter improved, especially when President Bill Clinton visited India for five days in 2000. Clinton was only the fourth U.S. president to go to India. His visit was very successful, and later the same year Vajpayee made a return visit to Washington, during which the United States agreed to resume the economic assistance that had been stopped in 1998. The United States is now the biggest buyer of Indian exports (taking almost one fifth of the total), and it supplies close to 10 percent of imports into India. In the late 1990s, India's relations with Russia picked up as well, and trade between the two countries has increased somewhat.

But the India of the 1990s did not simply want the friendship of the United States or Russia. It was noted that the nuclear tests were a sign of its desire to be recognized as a major power. So, too, is heavy military expenditure: India had the third largest army in the world in the early 1990s, and defense now absorbs 15 percent of the budget (ten times the percentage it took in 1938). India is particularly interested in a permanent seat on the United Nations Security Council, which it sees as the badge of a great power. It has as much right to one as China had at the formation of the United Nations, and today may have a better claim than Britain or France.

Whatever its place on the world stage, India is unquestionably South Asia's dominant power. According to Inder Kumar Gujral, this meant that it could afford to make concessions to its neighbors, without demanding anything in return. One of the fruits of this was an agreement that ended a long-standing dispute with Bangladesh over the use of the waters of the Ganges. Vajpayee was particularly keen on improving relations with Pakistan. In February 1999, a bus service started between Delhi and Lahore, the largest city of northern Pakistan. Vajpayee traveled on the first run to meet the Pakistani prime minister Nawaz Sharif. The two leaders agreed to try to resolve their countries' disagreements and to reduce the risk of accidental or unauthorized use of their nuclear weapons.

In May 1999, however, India learned that armed bands had crossed the line between the Pakistani and Indian sectors of Kashmir and established control over territory on the Indian side. This was a significant change from hit-and-run attacks by militants, and it had apparently begun even before Vajpayee's bus trip. Nawaz Sharif claimed that the infiltrators were acting on their own initiative, but Vajpayee treated them as Pakistani invaders and ordered the Indian armed forces to drive them back across the line. India was victorious, and in July Nawaz Sharif promised to withdraw the remaining infiltrators. This confirmed that Pakistan had sent them: If they really had been independent guerrillas, Sharif would not have been able to control them.

The fighting produced a surge of patriotism in India, and this probably helped Vajpayee in the election. So did Sonia's Italian birth, which the National Democratic Alliance made a campaign issue. Some hard-core Hindu nationalist support may have drifted away from the BJP because of Vajpayee's sidelining of Hindutva issues, but the weaknesses of Congress (I) were far more serious. The longer Congress (I) is out of power at the Center, the longer it will be unable to dispense patronage. Without patronage, local bosses cannot bring out voters. Local notables with secure vote blocs can have themselves elected as independents, or get different parties to bid for their support. All this reduced support for Congress (I), as did Sonia's undynamic leadership.

In the end, the National Democratic Alliance took 54 percent of the Lok Sabha's 545 seats. The Congress (I) bloc fell to just 24 percent. Vajpayee's majority was secure, which ensured that it was he who would lead India into the twenty-first century. This century will bring many changes. The terrorist attacks in New York and Washington on September 11, 2001, and the resulting campaign in Afghanistan, will have major long-term effects on South Asia. The American military response to the attacks has led many Indians to demand that their country wage its own "war on terrorism" against the Pakistani supporters of militancy in Kashmir. The situation is complicated by the fact that since September 11, Washington has pursued close ties with both India and Pakistan. Just what will happen next is an open question.

For 130 years, a census has been held in India every ten years. The census of February 2001 found that the population has reached 1.03 billion. It is growing at a rate of 2 percent a year. The United Nations believes that between 2045 and 2050, India will overtake China as the world's most populous country, with 1.5 billion inhabitants. That is probably the safest prediction that can be made about India in this new millennium.

Notable People in the History of India

This biographical dictionary omits the Mughal emperors, British viceroys, and prime ministers of India, who are listed in the Appendix.

Advani, Lal Krishna (1927–   ). Leader of the Bharatiya Janata Party in the Lok Sabha 1986–1991, 1993–1998.

Ahmad, Mirza Ghulam (1835–1908). Muslim lawyer who claimed to be a prophet; founder of the Ahmadi movement.

Ala ud-Din Khalji (died 1316). Sultan of Delhi (1296–1316); subjugated much of India.

Ali Brothers. Mohamed Ali (1878–1931) and Shaukat Ali (1873–1938), two Muslim nationalist leaders prominent in the Khilafat movement.

Ambedkar, Bhimrao Ramji (1891–1956). Untouchable leader; one of the authors of the Indian constitution.

Ashoka (died c. 235 BCE). King of Magadha c. 272–235 BCE; one of the greatest rulers of ancient India.

Bajirav (1700–1740). Peshwa of the Maratha kingdom, 1720–1740; made the Marathas the most powerful force in India.

Bhindranwale, Sant Jarnail Singh (1947–1984). Sikh holy man; apparently instigated attacks on heterodox Sikhs, Hindus, and government institutions 1978–1984.

Bose, Subhas Chandra (1897–1945?). Nationalist leader; organized the Indian National Army to fight alongside the Japanese during World War II.

Buddha (Siddhartha Gautama) (c. 563–483 BCE? or died between 378 and 358 BCE?). Founder of Buddhism.

Chandra Gupta II (died c. 415 CE). The greatest king of the Gupta dynasty (c. 375–415 CE).

Chandragupta Maurya (died c. 297 BCE). King of Magadha c. 325 or 321–297 BCE; founder of the Mauryan dynasty.

Clive, Robert (1725–1774). Officer of the British East India Company; fought the French in South India, defeated Siraj ud-Daula 1757, and secured the appointment of his company as diwan of Bengal and Orissa 1765.

Gandhi, Mohandas Karamchand (Mahatma) (1869–1948). India's "Father of the Nation"; creator of the techniques of satyagraha.

Gandhi, Sonia (neé Maino) (1946–   ). Italian-born widow of Rajiv Gandhi (prime minister 1984–1989); president of Congress (I) since 1998.

Gobind Singh (formerly Gobind Das) (1666–1708). Guru of the Sikhs 1675–1708; created the Khalsa 1699.

Gokhale, Gopal Krishna (1866–1915). Nationalist leader.

Harshavardhana (died 647 CE). Last great king of ancient North India (606–647 CE).

Iltutmish, Shams ud-Din (died 1236). First sultan of Delhi (1210–1236).

Jinnah, Muhammad Ali (c. 1876–1948). Muslim nationalist leader; member of the Indian National Congress and later the All-India Muslim League; headed the demand for Pakistan in the 1940s.

Kautilya (also called Chanakya or Vishnugupta). Adviser of Chandra-gupta Maurya (died c. 297 BCE); said to have written the *Arthashastra*.

Mahavira (Vardhamana) (599–527 BCE?). Founder of Jainism.

Muizz ud-Din Muhammad Ghauri (c. 1150–1206). Muslim sultan of the Ghauri dynasty (1173–1206); ruled what are now Afghanistan and Pakistan; conquered North India 1192–1206.

Nanak (1469–1539). Founder of Sikhism.

Narayan, Jayaprakash (J.P.) (1902–1979). Nationalist leader and head of the socialists within Congress; joined the future prime minister Morarji Desai in leading the Janata Morcha in opposition to Indira Gandhi 1974.

Nehru, Motilal (1861–1931). Nationalist leader; father of the first prime minister Jawaharlal Nehru, and author of the Nehru report.

Patel, Sardar Vallabhbhai (1875–1950). Nationalist leader; deputy prime minister 1947–1950.

Ranjit Singh (1780–1839). Ruler of the Sikh empire 1799–1839.

Roy, Rammohun (c. 1774–1833). Hindu religious reformer and founder of the Brahmo Sabha (later Brahmo Samaj).

Saraswati, Swami Dayananda (1824–1883). Hindu religious reformer and founder of the Arya Samaj.

Shivaji (1630–1680). Leader of the Maratha rebellion against the sultans of Bijapur and the Mughal emperors; first ruler of the Maratha kingdom (1674–1680).

Singh, Manmohan (1932–). Finance minister 1991–1996; an architect of economic liberalization.

Siraj ud-Daula (1736/1737–1757). Nawab of Bengal (1756–1757); defeated at the Battle of Plassey, 1757.

Syed Ahmed Khan, Sir (1817–1898). Muslim religious reformer and founder of the Mohammedan Anglo-Oriental College (now Aligarh Muslim University).

Tagore, Rabindranath (1861–1941). Poet and philosopher; winner of the Nobel Prize in Literature 1913.

Tilak, Bal Gangadhar (1856–1920). Nationalist leader.

Tipu Sultan (1750–1799). Sultan of Mysore (1782–1799).

Tughluq, Ghiyas ud-Din (died 1324). Sultan of Delhi (1320–1324); subjugated almost all of India.

Vivekananda, Swami (1863–1902). Hindu religious leader and founder of the Ramakrishna mission.

Wellesley, Lord (1760–1842). Governor-general 1798–1805; brought much of India under British rule.

Appendix: Mughal Emperors, British Viceroys, Prime Ministers of India

MUGHAL EMPERORS

Babur (1483–1530), 1526–1530

Humayun (1508–1556), 1530–1540 and 1555–1556

Akbar I (1542–1605), 1556–1605

Jahangir (1569–1627), 1605–1627

Shah Jahan I (1592–1666), 1628–1658

Aurangzeb (Alamgir I) (1618–1707), 1658–1707

Bahadur Shah I (Shah Alam I) (1643–1712), 1707–1712

Jahandar Shah (1661–1713), 1712–1713

Farrukhsiyar (1683–1719), 1713–1719

Rafi ud-Darjat (died 1719), 1719

Rafi ud-Daula (Shah Jahan II) (died 1719), 1719

Muhammad Shah (1702–1748), 1719–1748

Ahmad Shah (1725–1774), 1748–1754

Alamgir II (1699–1759), 1754–1759

Shah Alam II (1728–1806), 1759–1806

Akbar II (1760–1837), 1806–1837

Bahadur Shah II (1775–1862), 1837–1857

BRITISH VICEROYS

Lord Canning (1812–1862), 1858–1862

Lord Elgin and Kincardine (1811–1863), 1862–1863

Lord Lawrence (1811–1879), 1863–1869

Lord Mayo (1822–1872), 1869–1872

Lord Northbrook (1826–1904), 1872–1876

Lord Lytton (1831–1891), 1876–1880

Lord Ripon (1827–1909), 1880–1884

Lord Dufferin (1826–1902), 1884–1888

Lord Lansdowne (1845–1927), 1888–1894

Lord Elgin and Kincardine (1849–1917), 1894–1899

Lord Curzon of Kedlestone (1859–1925), 1899–1905

Lord Minto (1845–1914), 1905–1910

Lord Hardinge of Penshurst (1858–1944), 1910–1916

Lord Chelmsford (1868–1933), 1916–1921

Lord Reading (1860–1935), 1921–1926

Lord Irwin (1881–1959), 1926–1931

Lord Willingdon (1866–1941), 1931–1936

Lord Linlithgow (1887–1952), 1936–1943

Lord Wavell (1883–1950), 1943–1947

Lord Mountbatten of Burma (1900–1979), 1947

PRIME MINISTERS OF INDIA

Jawaharlal Nehru (1889–1964), 1947–1964

Lal Bahadur Shastri (1904–1966), 1964–1966

Indira Gandhi (1917–1984), 1966–1977

Morarji Ranchhodji Desai (1896–1995), 1977–1979

Chaudhuri Charan Singh (1902–1987), 1979–1980

Indira Gandhi, 1980–1984

Rajiv Gandhi (1944–1991), 1984–1989

Vishwanath Pratap Singh (1931–   ), 1989–1990

Chandra Shekhar (1927–   ), 1990–1991

Pamulaparti Venkata Narasimha Rao (1921–   ), 1991–1996

Atal Bihari Vajpayee (1924–   ), 1996

Haradanahalli Doddegowda Deve Gowda (1933–   ), 1996–1997

Inder Kumar Gujral (1919–   ), 1997–1998

Atal Bihari Vajpayee, 1998–

Glossary

Agni: Brahminical god of fire.

Ahimsa: Nonviolence.

Ahmadi: Member of a Muslim sect founded by Mirza Ghulam Ahmad.

AIADMK. See All-India Anna Dravida Munnetra Kazhagam.

Akali Dal. See Shiromani Akali Dal.

All-India Anna Dravida Munnetra Kazhagam (AIADMK): Tamil regional political party, founded 1972.

All-India Muslim League: Political party, founded 1906; supported the creation of Pakistan from 1940.

Anandpur Sahib Resolution: Call for autonomy for Punjab, approved by the Shiromani Akali Dal in 1973.

Aranyakas: Brahminical and Hindu religious text; one of the Vedas.

Arthashastra: Ancient Indian political text, said to have been written by Chandragupta Maurya's adviser Kautilya.

Arya Samaj: Hindu reformist movement founded by Swami Dayananda Saraswati.

Aryan: "One to be respected," any ancient Indian who adopted certain social practices, the Brahminical religion, and the Vedic language.

Ashram: A refuge (modern pronunciation of Ashrama).

Ashrama: One of the four stages in the life of a Hindu man.

Atharva Veda: Brahminical and Hindu religious text; part of the Samhitas.

Babri Masjid: Sixteenth-century mosque at Ayodhya in Uttar Pradesh, built at what many Hindus believe was the birthplace of Rama; demolished 1992.

Bhagavad Gita: Section of the *Mahabharata*, in which Krishna explains the principles that should guide human actions; many Hindus regard it as the main message of their religion.

Bhakti: Devotional Hinduism, based on a loving relationship between God and humans.

Bharatiya Janata Party (BJP): Political party, founded 1980; supplied the prime minister 1996 and since 1998; part of the Sangh Parivar.

BJP. See Bharatiya Janata Party.

Bodhisattva: in Mahayana Buddhism, a being who in reward for living an exemplary life has the power to grant salvation.

Bollywood: The Bombay-based Indian film industry.

Brahma: In Hinduism, God in His form as creator.

Brahman: In Brahminical and Hindu philosophy, the substance from which all things in the universe emerged.

Brahmanas: Brahminical and Hindu religious text; one of the Vedas.

Brahmin: Aryan priest; member of one of the four Varnas; later, member of the highest-ranking Hindu Caste.

Brahminical: Having to do with Brahmins; applied here to the Aryan religion.

Brahmo Sabha: Hindu reformist movement founded by Rammohun Roy; later reorganized and renamed the Brahmo Samaj.

Caste: One of the traditional divisions of Hindu society, apparently formed through the merger of the Varna and Jati systems.

Center: The federal government of India.

Collector: The head of the administration of a district (subdivision of a state).

Congress, Congress (I), Congress (O), Congress (R). See Indian National Congress.

Dasa, Dasyu, Pani: Indian who did not adopt the Aryan ways; later forcibly incorporated into Aryan society (see Shudra).

Deccan: Peninsular India.

Deoband School: Seminary for Muslim theologians, founded in 1867.

Dhamma: The ethical policy of Ashoka (Prakrit form of Dharma).

Dharma: The Hindu religion; laws regarding human conduct.

Dhimmi: Follower of a non-Islamic religion (Judaism, Christianity, Zoroastrianism, Hinduism) that Muslims recognize as a legitimate faith, in return for payment of the Jizya.

Diwan: Head of the provincial taxation department in the Mughal empire.

DMK. See Dravida Munnetra Kazhagam.

Dravida Munnetra Kazhagam (DMK): Tamil regional political party, founded 1949.

Faraizis: Muslim reformist movement founded by Hajji Shariat Ullah.

Golden Temple: Spiritual center of Sikhism, at Amritsar in Punjab.

Granth Sahib or **Adi Granth**: The holy book of Sikhism.

Gurdwara: A Sikh temple.

Guru: A teacher; Nanak and his successors as spiritual leaders of Sikhism.

Hadith: Collection of stories about the Prophet Muhammad, which serve to guide the behavior of Muslims.

Hartal: A general strike, especially as a political protest.

Hinayana: The form of Buddhism that looks to ethical conduct and meditation for salvation (see also Mahayana and Vajrayana).

Hindutva: Hindu-ness, the principles on which Hindu nationalism is based.

IAS. See Indian Administrative Service.

ICS. See Indian Civil Service.

INC. See Indian National Congress.

Indian Administrative Service (IAS): Corps of elite bureaucrats in independent India; successor of the Indian Civil Service.

Indian Civil Service (ICS): Corps of elite bureaucrats in British-ruled India; renamed the Indian Administrative Service after independence.

Indian National Army (INA): Army recruited during World War II by Subhas Chandra Bose from Indian soldiers who had been captured by the Japanese; fought against the British.

Indian National Congress (INC, Congress): Political party, founded 1885; supplied prime ministers 1947–1977, 1980–1989, 1991–1996. Since 1969, Congress has split several times. Its offshoots include Congress (I) (for Indira Gandhi), Congress (O) (for Organization), and Congress (R) (for Requisitioned).

Indra: Brahminical god of war and weather.

Iqta: The right to keep the taxes from a specified region, used by Sultans to pay their officials (similar to a Jagir). A person who has an iqta is called a Muqta.

Jagir: The right to keep the taxes from a specified region, used by the Mughal emperors to pay their officials (similar to an Iqta).

Jan Sangh: Political party, founded 1951; merged into the Janata Party 1977.

Janata Dal: Political party, founded 1988; supplied prime ministers 1989–1991, 1996–1998.

Janata Morcha: Two antigovernment movements. The first was founded by J.P. Narayan and Morarji Desai in 1974, the second by V.P. Singh in 1987.

Janata Party: Political party, founded 1977; supplied prime ministers 1977–1980; broke up after 1980.

Jat: Hindu caste of North India.

Jati: In Aryan society, a group of related people; now means Caste.

Jizya: Tax paid by Dhimmis.

Karma: In Hinduism, deeds that determine the nature of our rebirth.

Khalifa: Successor of the prophet Muhammad as spiritual leader of Islam.

Khalistan: "Land of the Khalsa" or "pure land;" name of the proposed independent Sikh state.

Khalsa: "Pure ones," the body of Sikh men initiated according to the rituals devised by Gobind Singh.

Khilafat: The office of Khalifa.

Krishna: Character in the *Mahabharata*, regarded by Hindus as an earthly incarnation of Vishnu.

Kshatriya (originally called **Rajanya**): Aryan warrior and herdsman; member of one of the four Varnas.

Land Revenue: Tax on agricultural production.

Left Front: Political bloc in the Indian parliament, led by the Communist Party of India (Marxist); part of the United Front since 1996.

Liberation Tigers of Tamil Eelam (LTTE): Tamil rebel movement in Sri Lanka.

Lok Dal: Political party, founded 1974; merged into the Janata Party 1977 and the Janata Dal 1988.

Lok Sabha: The lower house of the Indian parliament.

LTTE. See Liberation Tigers of Tamil Eelam.

Mahabharata: Sanskrit epic poem, telling the story of the war between the Kauravas and the Pandavas and regarded as one of the Hindu scriptures; includes the Bhagavad Gita.

Maharaja: Title of many Hindu kings.

Mahayana: The form of Buddhism that looks to a Bodhisattva for salvation (see also Hinayana and Vajrayana).

Mandal Report: Report on the OBCs, completed 1980.

Mansab: Rank held by a Mughal noble (Mansabdar).

Mansabdar: Mughal noble, holding a Mansab.

Maratha: Hindu caste of Maharashtra.

Monsoon, Southwest: The winds that bring rain to India in June or July.

Muqta: The holder of an Iqta.

Muslim League. See All-India Muslim League.

National Democratic Alliance: Political bloc in the Indian parliament, led by the Bharatiya Janata Party; the ruling coalition at the Center since 1998.

National Front: Political bloc in the Indian parliament, led by the Janata Dal; the ruling coalition at the Center 1989–1990; part of the United Front since 1996.

Nawab: Title of most Muslim rulers who broke away from the Mughal empire in the eighteenth century.

Nirvana: A state of being attained by Buddhists.

Nizam: Title of the rulers of Hyderabad.

OBC. See Other Backward Classes.

Other Backward Classes (OBC): Disadvantaged Hindu communities that rank above Untouchables.

Panchayat: A council, forming the lowest elected level of government.

Permanent Settlement: Fixing the Land Revenue rate in perpetuity, carried out in Bengal and Bihar 1793.

Peshwa: Prime minister of the Maratha kingdom.

Prakrit: One of the spoken languages of the first millennium BCE.

President's Rule: Temporary administration of a state by the Center following the removal of the state government.

Quran: The holy book of Islam.

Rajput: Hindu caste of North India.

Rajya Sabha: The upper house of the Indian parliament.

Rama: King of Kosala and hero of the *Ramayana*, regarded by Hindus as an earthly incarnation of Vishnu.

Ramakrishna Mission: Hindu reformist movement founded by Swami Vivekananda.

Ramayana: Sanskrit epic poem, telling the story of Rama and his wife Sita and regarded as one of the Hindu scriptures.

Rashtriya Swayamsevak Sangh (RSS): Hindu paramilitary organization; part of the Sangh Parivar.

Rath Yatra: Chariot procession; journey undertaken in 1990 by Lal Krishna Advani, head of the Bharatiya Janata Party, to build support for replacing the Babri Masjid with a temple to Rama.

Rig Veda: Brahminical and Hindu religious text; part of the Samhitas.

Rita: In the Brahminical religion, the law that keeps order in the universe.

RSS. See Rashtriya Swayamsevak Sangh.

Rupee: The unit of Indian currency.

Sama Veda: Brahminical and Hindu religious text; part of the Samhitas.

Samhitas: The Rig Veda, Sama Veda, Yajur Veda, and Atharva Veda; one of the Vedas. (Sometimes, the term Vedas is applied specifically to the Samhitas.)

Sangh Parivar: Group of Hindu nationalist organizations, including the Bajrang Dal, the Bharatiya Janata Party, the Bharatiya Mazdoor Sangh, the Rashtriya Swayamsevak Sangh, and the Vishwa Hindu Parishad.

Sanskrit: The Vedic language as used for religious and literary purposes since the first millennium BCE.

Sant Nirankari: Member of a Sikh sect.

Sati: A custom by which a widow followed her husband onto the funeral pyre.

Satyagraha: Mahatma Gandhi's method of resolving conflict without violence.

SC. See Scheduled Castes.

Scheduled Castes: Hindu communities belonging to the Untouchable category.

Scheduled Tribes: Communities belonging to the Tribal category.

Shaikh: In India, typically refers to a Sufi holy man.

Shangam Literature: Ancient Tamil heroic poems.

Shiromani Akali Dal: Sikh political party, founded 1920.

Shiva: In Hinduism, one of the basic forms of God (see also Vishnu).

Shudras: Menial, originally a Dasa who had been forcibly incorporated into Aryan society; later an Aryan peasant and craftsman; member of one of the four Varnas.

Singh Sabhas: Sikh reformist associations established from 1873.

ST: See Scheduled Tribes.

Sufi: A Muslim who uses meditation, trances, and other similar techniques in worship.

Sultan: Title of many Muslim rulers.

Swadeshi: "Of one's own country"; the principle of buying Indian-made goods.

Swami Narayana Sampradaya: Hindu reformist movement founded by Sahajananda Swami.

Swaraj: Self-control, self-government.

Swatantra Party: Political party, founded 1959; merged into the Janata Party 1977.

Syndicate: Senior politicians who dominated the Indian National Congress 1964–1969.

Taalluqedar: Rural landowner, especially in Awadh.

Theosophical Society: Religious movement founded in New York in 1875; includes elements of Hinduism.

Tribal: Member of a community that traditionally lived in forested or hilly regions, typically by hunting and gathering or shifting cultivation.

Ulama: Interpreters of Islamic law.

United Front: Political bloc in the Indian parliament, formed by the Left Front and the National Front 1996; the ruling coalition at the Center 1996–1998.

Untouchable: Member of the lowest-ranking Hindu castes.

Upanishads: Brahminical and Hindu religious text; one of the Vedas.

Vaishya: Aryan peasant, later merchant; member of one of the four Varnas.

Vajrayana: The form of Buddhism that looks to magic for salvation (see also Hinayana and Mahayana).

Varnas: The four divisions of Aryan society (see Brahmin, Kshatriya, Vaishya, Shudra); sometimes confused with Caste.

Varnashramadharma: The law of caste and stage of life, by which Hindus should act.

Varuna: Brahminical father-god.

Vedas: Brahminical and Hindu religious texts, the Samhitas, Brahmanas, Aranyakas, and Upanishads; sometimes applied specifically to the Samhitas.

Vedic: Having to do with the Vedas; applied here to the Aryan language; later called Sanskrit.

Vishnu: In Hinduism, one of the basic forms of God (see also Shiva); Krishna and Rama are regarded as earthly incarnations of Vishnu.

Vishwa Hindu Parishad: Hindu nationalist organization; part of the Sangh Parivar.

Yajur Veda: Brahminical and Hindu religious text; part of the Samhitas.

Zamindar: Collector of the Land Revenue in Bengal and Bihar, made into a landlord under the Permanent Settlement.

Bibliographic Essay

Students of Indian history are fortunate to have Maureen L.P. Patterson's phenomenal *South Asian Civilizations: A Bibliographic Synthesis* (Chicago and London: University of Chicago Press, 1981), which lists over 28,000 books and articles in Western languages on all aspects of South Asia. This may be supplemented with the *Bibliography of Asian Studies*, published annually by the Association for Asian Studies—available in book form from 1941 to 1971, both in book form and on-line from 1971 to 1991, and on-line only since 1991. Most of the books named in this essay contain good bibliographies.

The two principal multivolume English-language histories of India are now dated: E.J. Rapson, Sir Wolesley Haig, Sir Richard Burn, Sir Theodore Morison, and H.H. Dodwell, editors, *The Cambridge History of India* (five of six planned volumes published, plus a supplementary volume by Sir Mortimer Wheeler; Cambridge: Cambridge University Press, 1922–1968); and R.C. Majumdar, general editor, *The History and Culture of the Indian People* (eleven volumes; Bombay: Bharatiya Vidya Bhavan, 1951–1977).

Good one-volume comprehensive histories are remarkably scarce, but see Hermann Kulke and Dietmar Rothermund, *A History of India* (3rd edition, New York: Routledge, 1998); R.C. Majumdar, H.C. Raychaudhuri, and Kalikinkar Datta, *An Advanced History of India* (4th edition, Delhi: Macmillan India, 1978); and Stanley Wolpert, *A New History of India* (6th edition, New York: Oxford University Press, 2000). A recent nonacademic history is John Keay, *India: A History* (New York: Grove Press, 2000).

For recent centuries, there are Sugata Bose and Ayesha Jalal, *Modern South Asia: History, Culture, and Political Economy* (New York: Routledge, 1998), which focuses on the last 300 years; Judith M. Brown, *Modern India: The Origins of an Asian Democracy* (2nd edition, Oxford: Oxford University Press, 1994), which is mainly concerned with the period from 1857 to 1947; and Sumit Sarkar, *Modern India 1885–1947* (2nd edition, New York: St. Martin's Press, 1989).

Useful surveys of pre-modern Indian cultural history are A.L. Basham, *The Wonder That Was India: A Survey of the History and Culture of the Indian Sub-Continent before the Coming of the Muslims* (3rd edition, London: Sidgwick & Jackson, 1982), and S.A.A. Rizvi, *The Wonder That Was India Volume II: A Survey of the History and Culture of the Indian Sub-Continent from the Coming of the Muslims to the British Conquest 1200–1700* (London: Sidgwick & Jackson, 1987). *Sources of Indian Tradition* (2nd edition, vol. 1, edited by Ainslie T. Embree, vol. 2, edited by Stephen Hay, New York: Columbia University Press, 1988) brings together 4,000 years' worth of writings by Indians about religion, philosophy, politics, economics, and society.

In recent years, there has been a veritable explosion of scholarship on ancient India. Notable works include Romila Thapar, editor, *Recent Perspectives of Early Indian History* (Bombay: Popular Prakashan, 1995), which brings together the research of some of the principal Indian historians of the period from the Harappans to the Muslim conquests; Gregory L. Possehl, editor, *Harappan Civilization: A Recent Perspective* (2nd edition, New Delhi: Oxford & IBH Publishing Co. Pvt. Ltd. and American Institute of Indian Studies, 1993); Edwin Bryant, *The Quest for the Origins of Vedic Culture: The Indo-Aryan Migration Debate* (New York: Oxford University Press, 2001); and F.R. Allchin, *The Archaeology of Early Historic South Asia, The Emergence of Cities and States* (Cambridge: Cambridge University Press, 1995).

Recent studies of the three great religions that emerged in ancient India are Peter Harvey, *An Introduction to Buddhism: Teachings, History, and Practices* (Cambridge: Cambridge University Press, 1990); Michael Carrithers and Caroline Humphrey, editors, *The Assembly of Listeners: Jains in Society* (Cambridge: Cambridge University Press, 1991); and A.L. Basham (edited and annotated by Kenneth G. Zysk), *The Origins and Development of Classical Hinduism* (Boston: Beacon Press, and New York: Oxford University Press, 1989).

The history of Islam and India from the earliest contacts to the thirteenth century is recounted in André Wink, *Al Hind: The Making of the Indo-Islamic World* (2 volumes, Leiden: E.J. Brill, 1991–1997). For the principal Muslim state of medieval India, see Peter Jackson, *The Delhi Sultanate: A Political and Military History* (Cambridge: Cambridge University Press, 1999). A provocative study of conversion to Islam is Richard M. Eaton, *The Rise of Islam and the Bengal Frontier, 1204–1760* (Berkeley: University of California Press, 1993).

The New Cambridge History of India (Cambridge: Cambridge University Press, 1987–   ) has little in common with its predecessor beyond the name: Rather than a connected narrative history of India, it is a collection of books on various aspects of Indian history since the fourteenth century, each by an authority on his or her subject. Among the volumes are: Milo Cleveland Beach, *Mughal and Rajput Painting* (vol. I.3); John F. Richards, *The Mughal Empire* (vol. I.5); C.A. Bayly, *Indian Society and the Making of the British Empire* (vol. II.1); J.S. Grewal, *The Sikhs of the Punjab* (vol. II.3); Om Prakash, *European Commercial Enterprise in Pre-Colonial India* (vol. II.5); B.R. Tomlinson, *The Economy of Modern India 1860–1970* (vol. III.3); Paul R. Brass, *The Politics of India since Independence* (vol. IV.1); Geraldine Forbes, *Women in Modern India* (vol. IV.2); and Susan Bayly, *Caste, Society and Politics in India from the Eighteenth Century to the Modern Age* (vol. IV.3).

The many books on colonial India include Mushirul Hasan and Narayani Gupta, editors, *India's Colonial Encounter: Essays in Memory of Eric Stokes* (Delhi: Manohar, 1993). The *Profiles in Power* series contains volumes on the two greatest figures in the struggle for independence: David Arnold, *Gandhi* (Harlow: Longman, 2001), and Judith M. Brown, *Nehru* (London and New York: Longman, 1999). For the formation of various South Asian identities since the nineteenth century, see Ian Talbot, *India and Pakistan* (London: Arnold, 2000). One of the most recent works in the growing field of studies of "Indian India" is Ian Copland, *The Princes of India in the Endgame of Empire, 1917–1947* (Cambridge: Cambridge University Press, 1997).

For a collection of assessments of India and Pakistan since independence, see Selig S. Harrison, Paul H. Kreisberg, and Dennis Kux, editors, *India and Pakistan: The First Fifty Years* (Cambridge: Woodrow Wilson Center Press and Cambridge University Press, 1999). Sarvepalli Gopal, editor, *Anatomy of a Confrontation: Ayodhya and the Rise of Communal Politics in India* (London: Zed Books, 1993), examines one of the principal issues in Indian politics in the 1990s.

Finally, readers interested in India should not miss the works of some of today's great Indian novelists. These include Rohinton Mistry, *A Fine Balance*; Arundhati Roy, *The God of Small Things*; and Salman Rushdie, *Midnight's Children*.

Index

Advani, Lal Krishna, 173–74, 185, 187
Afghans, 62
Agriculture. *See* Economy
Ahmad, Mirza Ghulam, 89
Ahmadis, 89, 110
Ahmadnagar sultanate, 46–47, 50, 53, 54
Akbar, 49–53, 56
Akbar, Muhammad, 58
Akbar II, 74
Alamgir. *See* Aurangzeb
Alamgir II, 65
Ali, Haidar, 67
Ali brothers (Mohamed Ali and Shaukat Ali), 102, 105–6
Aligarh Muslim University, 89, 170
All-India Anna Dravida Munnetra Kazhagam (AIADMK), 148, 191
All-India Hindu Mahasabha, 110
All-India Muslim League, 97–103, 110, 118–27
Ambar, Malik, 53

Ambedkar, Dr. Bhimrao Ramji, 115, 131
Amritsar Massacre, 106
Anandpur Sahib Resolution, 164–65
Andhras (Satavahanas), 22
Architecture. *See* Arts
Arjan, 56–57
Arts, 9–10; ancient and medieval, 12, 20, 21; Mughal, 51, 53, 55
Aryans, 14–16, 26–27
Arya Samaj, 91, 93, 110
Ashoka, 19–20
Assam, insurgency in, 134–35, 167, 172, 183
Attlee, Clement, 124
Aurangzeb (Alamgir), 55–60, 65
Awadh: British annexation of, 79–80, 81, 85; nawabs of, 62, 65, 69, 73
Aybeg, Qutb ud-Din, 35
Ayodhya. *See* Rama temple movement

Babri Masjid. *See* Rama temple movement
Babur, 39, 49, 51
Bahadur, Banda, 60–61, 62
Bahadur, Tegh, 57
Bahmanis, 45–46
Bajirav, 63
Bajirav II, 73, 80
Balaban, Baha ud-Din, 35–36, 40
Balvantrav (Nana Saheb), 63, 66
Banerjea, Surendranath, 96–97
Bengal, nawabs of, 61–62, 63, 65, 68–69
Bengal, Partition of, 96–101
Bengal sultanate, 38, 44–45
Bentinck, Lord William, 78
Besant, Annie, 92, 102, 105–7
Bhagavad Gita, 26
Bharatiya Janata Party (BJP), 5, 166, 170–93
Bharatiya, Kranti Dal. *See* Lok Dal
Bhat, Balaji Vishvanath, 63
Bhindranwale, Sant Jarnail Singh, 164–66
Bhonsle, Raghuji, 63
Bhonsle, Shahji, 54, 57
Bhonsle, Shivaji, 57–58, 94
Bijapur sultanate, 46–47, 50, 54, 57–58
Bikaner, maharaja Ganga Singh of, 103
Bindusara, 18–19
Birlas, 117
Bofors, 169
Bollywood, 10, 134
Bose, Subhas Chandra, 112, 118, 124
Brahminical religion, 15–17, 22, 24. *See also* Hinduism, Hindus, and Muslim rulers
Brahmo Sabha, later Brahmo Samaj, 88, 90
British India, 74, 85, 113–15, 117, 120
Bronze, 12
Buddha (Siddhartha Gautama), Buddhism, Buddhists, 17–18, 19, 21, 24, 33–34, 41–42

Cabinet Mission, 125, 126
Carnatic, nawabs of, 67–68, 73

Caste: Mandal Commission and report, 173, 185; in modern India, 8, 171, 185–86; origins, 26–27, 43; under British, 93
Chaitanya, 43
Chanakya (Kautilya, Vishnugupta), 18–20
Chandra Gupta II, 22–23
Charan Singh, Chaudhuri, 148, 156–58, 170
Chauhan, Prithviraj, 34–35
Chelmsford, Lord, 103–4
China War, 143–44
Cholas, 32–33
Christianity, Christians, 28, 82, 91, 115
Climate, 3
Clive, Robert, 67–69
Communalism (Hindu-Muslim tensions since 1947), 130–31, 170–71, 173–74, 183–85. *See also* Rama temple movement
Communications, 7, 9–10, 85
Communism, Communist Party of India, Communist Party of India (Marxist), Communists, 109, 136, 142, 148, 149–50, 152, 155, 187
Congress. *See* Indian National Congress, Indian National Congress (Indira), Indian National Congress (Organization), Indian National Congress (Requisitioned)
Constitution of 1950, 131–35, 150–51, 190
Cornwallis, Lord, 71–72
Cripps, Sir Stafford, 122–23, 125
Curzon, Lord, 96

Da Gama, Vasco, 46
Dal, Shiromani Akali, 111, 121, 126, 148–49, 164, 168, 170, 183
Dalhousie, Lord, 79–80
Defense of India Act, 102, 106
Delhi sultanate, 35–43
Deoband School, 89
Derozio, Henry Louis Vivian, 88
Desai, Morarji, 145–49, 155–58, 173
Deve Gowda, Haradanahalli Doddegowda, 188

Dharmapala, 31

Dhimmis, 33, 34, 42

Dhrangadhara, maharaja of, 150

Dravida Munnetra Kazhagam (DMK), 148–49, 170, 172, 188

Dravidian languages, 6, 22, 23, 94

Dupleix, Joseph, 67–68

Durrani, Ahmad Shah, 66

East India Company, English (later British), 59, 67–83

Economic liberalization. *See* Liberalization, economic

Economic planning. *See* Planned economic development

Economy: ancient and medieval, 11–13, 15–16, 20–23, 31–33, 37, 41, 46; colonial, 70–72, 75–78, 80, 83–87, 109, 112, 115–17, 122–23; Mughal, 52–53, 58–59; 1947–1991, 137–41, 147, 153–56, 166–67; since 1991, 6–8, 178–82

Education, 8–9, 79, 87, 109, 139–40

Elections, 4–5, 94–95, 96, 98–99; of 1920, 104, 107; of 1923, 108; of 1937, 117–19; of 1945–46, 125; of 1952, 1957, and 1962, 135–36; of 1967, 147–48; of 1971, 150–51; of 1977, 157; of 1980, 158–59; of 1984, 166; of 1989, 170–72; of 1991, 174–78; of 1996, 187–88; of 1998, 188–89; of 1999, 191–93

Emergency, 4, 156–58

Emigrants and emigration, 5

English language, 6, 79, 87, 109, 133–34

Faraizis, 87, 93

Farrukhsiyar, 61

Film, 10, 134

Five Year Plans. *See* Planned economic development

Foreign relations (since 1947), 129–30, 141, 143–44, 146, 149, 151–52, 158, 169, 184, 189–93

Gaharwars, 34

Gandhi, Indira, 4, 145–66

Gandhi, Mohandas Karamchand (Mahatma), 104–9, 112–31, 171

Gandhi, Rajiv, 161–75, 188

Gandhi, Sanjay, 156–57, 161

Gandhi, Sonia, 5, 174–75, 191–93

Ganga Singh, maharaja of Bikaner, 103

Ganges, 2, 15, 25

Geography, 1–3

Ghauri, Muizz ud-Din Muhammad, 34–35

Ghauris, 34–35

Ghaznawids, 34

Ghiyasids, 35

Gokhale, Gopal Krishna, 97–98, 102, 107, 118

Golkonda sultanate, 46–47, 50, 54, 58

Government: ancient and medieval, 14–16, 19–23, 30–32, 34, 39–43, 46–47; colonial, 69–71, 74–75, 83–85, 94–98; Montagu-Chelmsford reforms, 103–4; Morley-Minto reforms, 98–99; Mughal, 50–52. *See also* Constitution of 1950; Government of India Act (1935);

Government of India Act (1935), 112–20

Granth Sahib, 56

Great Revolt, 81–83

Green Revolution, 154–55, 163, 167–68

Gujral, Inder Kumar, 188, 192

Gulab Singh, Raja, 78, 129

Guptas, 22–23

Gurjara-Pratiharas, 31–32, 34

Harappans, 11–13

Harshavardhana, 23, 29

Hastings, Lord, 73–74

Health, 8–9, 109

Hindi, 6, 90, 119, 133–34

Hinduism, Hindus, and Muslim rulers, 33–34, 41–44, 46–47, 50; origins, 24–28; reform movements, 88–93; spread, 30–31. *See also* Brahminical religion

Hindu nationalism, 110. *See also* Bharatiya Janata Party; Communalism;

Jan Sangh; Rama temple movement; Rashtriya Swayamsevak Sangh
Home Charges, 83, 112, 123–24
Home Rule Leagues, 102, 106
Humayun, 49, 51
Hume, Allan Octavian, 96
Hyderabad, 62, 67–68, 72–73, 130. *See also* Ul-Mulk, Nizam

Ilbert Bill, 95
Iltutmish, 35
Indian Administrative Service (IAS), 142, 162. *See also* Indian Civil Service
Indian Civil Service (ICS), 71, 74, 95–96, 103, 141–42. *See also* Indian Administrative Service
"Indian India" and Princes: accession and merger, 126–30; under East India Company, 74–75, 79, 82; and Indira Gandhi, 150–51; and Great Revolt, 85; 1906–1947, 98–99, 103–4, 112–15, 119–20;
Indian National Army, 124
Indian National Congress, Indian National Congress (Indira), Indian National Congress (Organization), Indian National Congress (Requisitioned): and Indira Gandhi, 147–52, 158–63; and Nehru, Jawaharlal, 135–44; origins, 96–99; since 1991, 5, 177–78, 186–88, 191–93; and struggle for independence, 102–27
Indian states. *See* "Indian India" and Princes
Indo-European languages, 6, 14
Indo-Pakistani Wars (1947–1948), 130; (1965), 146; (1971), 151; (1999), 192
Indus, 2, 12–13
Industrialization, 7, 86–87, 101, 116–17, 137–39
Iqbal, Mohammad, 121
Iqta, 36–37, 40
Iron, 15, 22
Irwin, Lord, 112–14
Islam and Muslims: origins, 29–30; reform movements, 88–90, 92–93; since 1947, 136, 157, 158; spread in India, 33–35, 40, 41–47; under Mughals, 50–51, 54–55. *See also* All-India Muslim League; Communalism; Khalifa and khilafat; Pakistan movement

Jafar, Mir, 68–69
Jagir, 52
Jahan, Nur, 53
Jahangir (Salim), 53, 57
Jains, Jainism, 18, 28
Jammu and Kashmir. *See* Kashmir
Janata Dal, 170–88
Janata Morcha, 155–56, 169–70
Janata Party, 157–59, 170
Jang, Safdar, 62, 65
Jan Sangh, 136–37, 158, 170
Jats, 59, 62, 92
Jews, Judaism, 28
Jinnah, Muhammad Ali, 111, 118–27
Jizya, 33, 42, 50, 55, 61
Justice Party, 108

Kabir, 56
Kafur, Malik, 36
Kanishka, 21
Kashmir, 45, 78, 129–31, 146, 168, 172, 183–84, 192
Kautilya (Chanakya, Vishnugupta), 18–20
Khalifa and khilafat: in colonial India, 89, 106–8, 110; and medieval sultans, 34, 39–40, 45; origins, 30
Khalistan, 165–69, 183
Khalji, Ala ud-Din, 36, 40, 42
Khaljis, 36
Khalsa, 60, 62, 67, 77, 92, 164. *See also* Sikhism, Sikhs
Khan, Allahwardi, 62, 63
Khan, Murshid Quli, 61–62
Khan, Syed Ahmed, Sir, 89, 98
Khusrau, 53, 57
Kings, kingship. *See* Government
Kushanas, 21

Lahore Resolution, 121–22. *See also* Pakistan movement
Lakshmibai, 82

Land revenue (*lagaan*), 10, 20, 30–31, 36, 52–53, 71–72, 80, 103, 140
Language, 6, 14, 16, 90, 119,133–34. *See also* Dravidian languages; English language; Hindi; Prakrits; Sanskrit
Left Front, 187
Liberalization, economic, 178–82
Liberation Tigers of Tamil Eelam (LTTE), 169, 174
Linlithgow, Lord, 120–22
Literature, 6, 9, 14–15, 16–18, 23
Lodi, Ibrahim, 39, 49
Lodis, 39 49
Lok Dal (Bharatiya Lok Dal), 148, 156, 158, 170, 173, 186
Longowal, Harchand Singh, 164, 168
Lucknow Pact, 102–3, 110, 118

MacDonald, Ramsay, 113–15
Magadha, 16, 18–21
Mahabharata, 23, 26
Mahall, Mumtaz, 54–55
Mahavira (Vardhamana), 18
Mahmud the Ghaznawid, 34, 41, 174
Mandal Commission and report, 173, 185
Mansab, mansabdar, 51–52, 60
Manufacturing. *See* Economy; Industrialization
Marathas, 47, 54, 57–67, 72–74
Mathematics, 23
Maurya, Chandragupta, 18
Mauryas, 18–21
Mehta, Pherozeshah, 96, 102
Minto, Lord, 98–99
Mohammedan Anglo-Oriental College, 89, 170
Mongols, 35–38
Montagu-Chelmsford Reforms, 103–4
Morley-Minto Reforms, 98–99
Mountbatten, Lord, 126–27
Mughals, 39, 44, 47, 49–66, 74, 82–83
Muslim League. *See* All-India Muslim League
Muslims. *See* Islam and Muslims
Mysore, 67, 72–73

Nanak, 56
Naoroji, Dadabhai, 96
Narasimha Rao, Pamulaparti Venkata, 175–87
Narayan, Jayaprakash (J.P.), 155–58
National Conference, 168, 170
National Democratic Alliance, 189–93
National Front, 172–75, 187
Nationalism, Indian, 93–127
Nationalization, 138, 149–50, 153, 180–81. *See also* Planned economic development
Nawab, 65–66
Naxalites. *See* Communism, Communist Party of India, Communist Party of India (Marxist), Communists
Nehru, Jawaharlal, 112, 119–45
Nehru, Motilal, 111–12, 135
Nehru Report, 111–12, 118, 135
Nehruvian economic policy. *See* Planned economic development
Nobility, nobles, 36–37, 40, 51–52, 60. *See* Government; Land revenue; Zamindars
Nonalignment. *See* Foreign relations
Noncooperation campaign (1920–1922), 106–8, 118
Nuclear explosives and weapons, 155, 172, 189–90

Osman Ali Khan, Nizam of Hyderabad, 130
Other Backward Classes (OBCs), 8, 147–48, 173, 185–86, 188

Painting. *See* Arts
Pakistan movement, 121–27
Palas, 31
Pallavas, 23, 32
Panchayats, 143
Pandyas, 23, 32, 37
Panipat, 39, 66–67
Patel, Sardar Vallabhbhai, 126–35
Patna, maharaja of, 150
People, 5–9
Permanent Settlement. *See* Land revenue

Peshwa, 63, 66, 73, 80
Phadnis, Nana, 66
Planned economic development, 137–41, 147, 153–54, 158, 166–67, 178–82
Plassey, 68
Politics. *See* Elections; Government; *specific political parties*
Population, 5–6, 58, 109, 193
Portuguese, 46–47, 59, 141
Poverty, 7–8, 85–86
Prakrits, 16, 20, 22, 23
Princes. *See* "Indian India" and Princes
Privatization, 180–81

Quit India, 122–23
Quran, 29, 33, 40, 44, 88

Racial discrimination, racism, 71, 74, 84
Rajputs, 31, 47, 51, 54, 58, 62
Ram, Jagjivan, 157
Ramakrishna, Sri, 90
Rama temple movement, 171, 173–74, 184–85
Ramayana, 23, 171
Rashtrakutas, 32–33
Rashtriya Swayamsevak Sangh (RSS), 110, 137, 171, 185
Ray, Satyajit, 10
Raziyya, 35, 40
Reform movements, socioreligious, 87–93
Reincarnation, 17, 24, 26
Religion, 5. *See also under names of individual faiths*
Revolt of 1857, 81–83
Rig Veda, 14–15
Round Table Conference, 112–15
Rowlatt Acts, 106
Roy, Rammohun, 88

Saheb, Nana (Balvantrav), 63, 66
Salim (Jahangir), 53, 57
Salt Satyagraha (1930), 112–14
Sambhaji, 58
Sangh Parivar, 171
Sanskrit, 14, 16, 20, 22, 23
Sant Nirankaris, 164–65

Sarasvati (river), 12, 13
Saraswati, Swami Dayananda, 91
Satavahanas (Andhras), 22
Satyagraha, 104–8, 112–14, 121
Sayyid brothers (Sayyid Husain Ali and Sayyid Abdallah Khan), 61
Sayyids, 38
Scheduled Castes, 8, 133, 136, 142–43, 157, 158, 185–86. *See also* Untouchables
Scheduled Tribes, 8, 133, 136, 190. *See also* Tribals
Scindias, 65–66, 73–74
Sculpture. *See* Arts
Secularism, 131
Sen, Keshub Chunder, 90
Senas, 34
Shah, Ahmad, 65
Shah Alam II, 65–66, 69, 74
Shah, Bahadur, 60
Shah, Bahadur, II, 74, 82–83
Shah Jahan, 53–55
Shah, Jahandar, 60–61
Shah, Muhammad, 61–64
Shah, Nadir, 63–64, 66
Shahu, 60–63
Shah Wali Ullah, 88
Shamsids, 35
Shangam literature, 22, 23
Shastri, Lal Bahadur, 145–46
Shekhar, Chandra, 170, 174, 179
Shikoh, Dara, 55–56
Shir Shah (Shir Khan Sur), 49, 52
Siddhartha Gautama. *See* Buddha
Sikh Empire, 77–79, 83, 89
Sikhism, Sikhs: under colonial rule, 84, 92–93, 111, 115; since 1947, 134, 163–66, 168–69, 183; origins, 56–57; rise of the Khalsa, 59–61, 65–67. *See also* Khalistan; Khalsa; Sikh Empire
Simon Commission and report, 111–12
Singh, Bhagat, 109–10
Singh, Dalip, 78
Singh, Gobind (Gobind Das), 57, 59–60, 92
Singh, Hari, maharaja of Jammu and Kashmir, 129–30
Singh, Kalyan, 184–85

Singh, Manmohan, 179–82
Singh, Ranjit, 77–78
Singh, Vishwanath Pratap (V.P.), 169–77
Singh Sabhas, 92–93
Sinha, Satyendra Prasanna, 103
Socialism, socialists, 109, 118, 136, 155
Sports, 10
Subsidiary alliance, 68, 73–74
Sufis, Sufism, 40, 44, 50, 53
Sultan, Tipu, 67, 72–73
Sur, Shir Khan (Shir Shah), 49, 52
Swami Narayana Sampradaya, 87
Swatantra Party, 136–37, 150, 156
Syndicate, 144–49, 152

Tagore, Debendranath, 90
Tagore, Rabindranath, 94, 107–8
Tamerlane (Temür), 38
Tansen, 51
Tarabai, 59–63
Tatas, 87, 117
Temür (Tamerlane), 38
Theosophical Society, Theosophists, 91–92. *See also* Besant, Annie
Tilak, Bal Gangadhar, 97–98, 102, 107
Todar Mall, Raja, 52
Trade. *See* Economy
Transportation, 7
Tribals, 8, 11, 20, 26–27, 31, 41, 43–45, 63, 76, 133–35, 190. *See also* Scheduled Tribes
Tughluq, Firuz Shah, 38, 40, 42–43
Tughluq, Ghiyas ud-Din, 36–37
Tughluq, Muhammad, 37–38, 42

Ud-Daula, Siraj, 68
Ud-Din Aybeg, Qutb, 35

Ud-Din Iltutmish, Shams, 35
Ulama, 40, 50, 55, 89
Ul-Mulk, Imad, 65
Ul-Mulk, Nizam, 61–62, 67, 130
Unionist Party, 108, 110
United Front, 186–88
Untouchables, 8, 27, 42, 108–9, 114–15, 133. *See also* Scheduled Castes
Upanishads, 17, 24, 88, 90, 91
Urbanization, 7, 12, 16, 20, 41, 76
Urdu, 6, 90, 119

Vajpayee, Atal Bihari, 5, 16, 158, 187–93
Vardhamana (Mahavira), 18
Varna, 26
Vedas, 17, 27, 91
Vedic language, 14, 16. *See also* Sanskrit
Vijayanagara, 38, 45–47
Village settlements, 11–12, 15
Vishnugupta (Kautilya, Chanakya), 18–20
Vishwa Hindu Parishad, 171, 184–85
Vivekananda, Swami, 90

Wavell, Lord, 124–26
Wellesley, Lord, 72–73
Wildlife, 3–4
Women, status of, 8, 27–28, 45, 88, 131, 142–143, 170, 188, 190
World War I, 101–3
World War II, 120–24
Writing, 12–13, 14, 16, 19, 20

Zamindars, 68, 70, 71–72, 83, 85, 140
Zoroastrianism, 28
Zu'l-Fiqar Khan, 60–61

About the Author

JOHN MCLEOD is Associate Professor of History at the University of Louisville and is the author of *Sovereignty, Power, Control: Politics in the States of Western India, 1916–1947*.

Other Titles in the Greenwood Histories of the Modern Nations
Frank W. Thackeray and John E. Findling, Series Editors

The History of Argentina
Daniel K. Lewis

The History of Australia
Frank G. Clarke

The History of Brazil
Robert M. Levine

The History of Canada
Scott W. See

The History of China
David C. Wright

The History of France
W. Scott Haine

The History of Germany
Eleanor L. Turk

The History of Holland
Mark T. Hooker

The History of Iran
Elton L. Daniel

The History of Ireland
Daniel Webster Hollis III

The History of Israel
Arnold Blumberg

The History of Italy
Charles L. Killinger

The History of Japan
Louis G. Perez

The History of Mexico
Burton Kirkwood

The History of Nigeria
Toyin Falola

The History of Poland
M.B. Biskupski

The History of Portugal
James M. Anderson

The History of Russia
Charles E. Ziegler

The History of Serbia
John K. Cox

The History of South Africa
Roger B. Beck

The History of Spain
Peter Pierson

The History of Sweden
Byron J. Nordstrom

The History of Turkey
Douglas A. Howard